The Shari'a
History, Ethics and Law

The Institute of Ismaili Studies

MUSLIM HERITAGE SERIES, 5

General Editor: Amyn B. Sajoo

This series explores vital themes in the civilisations of Islam – including the nature of religious authority, ethics and law, social justice and civil society, the arts and sciences, and the interplay of spiritual and secular lifeworlds. In keeping with the Institute's mandate, the series is informed by the plurality of communities and interpretations of Islam, as well as their locus in modernity and tradition.

Previously published titles:
1. *A Companion to the Muslim World*, ed. Amyn B. Sajoo (2009)
2. *A Companion to Muslim Ethics*, ed. Amyn B. Sajoo (2010)
3. *A Companion to Muslim Cultures*, ed. Amyn B. Sajoo (2013)
4. *The Shi'i World: Pathways in Tradition and Modernity*, ed. Farhad Daftary, Amyn B. Sajoo and Shainool Jiwa (2015)

The Shariʿa
History, Ethics and Law

Edited by
Amyn B. Sajoo

I.B.Tauris *Publishers*
LONDON · NEW YORK
in association with
The Institute of Ismaili Studies
LONDON

Published in 2018 by
I.B.Tauris & Co. Ltd
London • New York
www.ibtauris.com

in association with The Institute of Ismaili Studies
210 Euston Road, London, NW1 2DA
www.iis.ac.uk

Copyright © Islamic Publications Ltd, 2018

All rights reserved. Except for brief quotations in a review, this book or any part thereof, may not be reproduced, stored in or introduced into a retrieval system, or transmitted, in any form or by any means, electronic, mechanical, photocopying, recording or otherwise, without the prior written permission of the publisher.

References to websites were correct at the time of writing.
Every attempt has been made to gain permission for the use of the images in this book. Any omissions will be rectified in future editions.

ISBN: 978 1 78831 316 2
eISBN: 978 1 78672 404 5
ePDF: 978 1 78673 404 4

A full CIP record for this book is available from the British Library
A full CIP record is available from the Library of Congress

Library of Congress Catalog Card Number: available

Typeset in Minion Tra for The Institute of Ismaili Studies
Printed and bound in Great Britain by T.J. International, Padstow, Cornwall

The Institute of Ismaili Studies

The Institute of Ismaili Studies was established in 1977 with the object of promoting scholarship and learning on Islam, in the historical as well as contemporary contexts, and a better understanding of its relationship with other societies and faiths.

The Institute's programmes encourage a perspective which is not confined to the theological and religious heritage of Islam, but seeks to explore the relationship of religious ideas to broader dimensions of society and culture. The programmes thus encourage an interdisciplinary approach to the materials of Islamic history and thought. Particular attention is also given to issues of modernity that arise as Muslims seek to relate their heritage to the contemporary situation.

Within the Islamic tradition, the Institute's programmes promote research on those areas which have, to date, received relatively little attention from scholars. These include the intellectual and literary expressions of Shi'ism in general, and Ismailism in particular.

In the context of Islamic societies, the Institute's programmes are informed by the full range and diversity of cultures in which Islam is practised today, from the Middle East, South and Central Asia, and Africa to the industrialised societies of the West, thus taking into consideration the variety of contexts which shape the ideals, beliefs and practices of the faith.

These objectives are realised through concrete programmes and activities organised and implemented by various departments of the Institute. The Institute also collaborates periodically, on a programme-specific basis, with other institutions of learning in the United Kingdom and abroad.

The Institute's academic publications fall into a number of inter-related categories:

1. Occasional papers or essays addressing broad themes of the relationship between religion and society, with special reference to Islam.
2. Monographs exploring specific aspects of Islamic faith and culture, or the contributions of individual Muslim thinkers or writers.

The Shariʻa

3. Editions or translations of significant primary or secondary texts.
4. Translations of poetic or literary texts which illustrate the rich heritage of spiritual, devotional and symbolic expressions in Muslim history.
5. Works on Ismaili history and thought, and the relationship of the Ismailis to other traditions, communities and schools of thought in Islam.
6. Proceedings of conferences and seminars sponsored by the Institute.
7. Bibliographical works and catalogues which document manuscripts, printed texts and other source materials.

This book falls into category two listed above.

In facilitating these and other publications, the Institute's sole aim is to encourage original research and analysis of relevant issues. While every effort is made to ensure that the publications are of a high academic standard, there is naturally bound to be a diversity of views, ideas and interpretations. As such, the opinions expressed in these publications must be understood as belonging to their authors alone.

Contents

List of Illustrations		ix
About the Contributors		xi
Standard Abbreviations		xv

1. Introduction: A Multifaceted Venture   1
   AMYN B. SAJOO

2. Foundations   19
   KHALED ABOU EL-FADL

3. Recovering the Ethical: Practices, Politics, Tradition   39
   EBRAHIM MOOSA

4. Sustaining and Enhancing Life   59
   KARIM H. KARIM

5. Spiritual Refinement   81
   SA'DIYYA SHAIKH

6. Women's Equality   101
   ZIBA MIR-HOSSEINI

7. Family Law to Finance   119
   MOHAMED M. KESHAVJEE AND RAFICQ ABDULLA

8. Bioethics   135
   AMYN B. SAJOO

9. Legitimising Authority: A Muslim Minority under Ottoman Rule   153
   AMAAN MERALI

viii   *The Shari'a*

10. Democratisation and the Shari'a: The Indonesian Experience   173
         CAROOL KERSTEN

11. The Shari'a in the Western Landscape   193
         REX AHDAR AND NICHOLAS ARONEY

12. Secularism and the Shari'a: Lessons from an Ontario Debate   215
         JENNIFER A. SELBY

Index   231

Illustrations

Chapter 11

11.1	Islam globally.	204
11.2	Muslims in Europe.	204
11.3	Muslims in North America.	205
11.4	Muslims in Oceania.	205

About the Contributors

Raficq Abdulla, MBE, is a barrister and visiting fellow at the University of Kingston (UK). He is a member of the Muslim Law (Shariah) Council (UK) and serves as a legal advisor to several charities and corporate bodies. He has contributed widely to literary journals and academic volumes, including *A Companion to the Muslim World* (London, 2009). He chaired the 2006–2007 Festival of Muslim Cultures in the UK. He has co-authored, with Mohamed M. Keshavjee, *Understanding Sharia: Islamic Law in a Globalised World* (London, forthcoming 2018).

Khaled Abou El-Fadl is the Omar and Azmeralda Alfi Distinguished Professor of Islamic Law at the University of California, Los Angeles (USA). He is the author of 14 books on various topics in Islam and Islamic law including *Speaking in God's Name: Islamic Law, Authority and Women* (Oxford, 2001) and *Rebellion and Violence in Islamic Law* (Cambridge, 2001). El-Fadl's most recent work is *Reasoning with God: Reclaiming Shari 'ah in the Modern Age* (Lanham, 2014), from which his contribution to this volume (Chapter 2) has been adapted with the kind permission of the publishers, Rowman & Littlefield.

Rex Ahdar is a Professor of Law at the University of Otago (New Zealand), and an adjunct professor of law at the University of Notre Dame in Sydney (Australia). He is the author/editor of several books, including *God and Government: The New Zealand Experience* (with John Stenhouse; Otago, 2000), *Law and Religion* (Farnham, 2000), *Worlds Colliding: Conservative Christians and the Law* (Farnham, 2001), *Religious Freedom in the Liberal State*, 2nd edn (Oxford, 2013) and *Sharia in the West* (with Nicholas Aroney; Oxford, 2010), from which his contribution to this volume (Chapter 11) is adapted.

Nicholas Aroney is a Professor of Constitutional Law and a Fellow of Emmanuel College at the University of Queensland (Australia). He has held visiting positions at Oxford, Paris, Edinburgh, Emory and Sydney universities and is the author of more than 100 books, articles and chapters. He is the author most recently of *The Constitution of the Commonwealth of Australia: History, Principle and Interpretation* (Cambridge, 2015) and co-editor with Rex Ahdar of *Shari'a in the West* (Oxford, 2010), from which his contribution to this volume (Chapter 11) is adapted. His writings on religion and law have also appeared in numerous journals.

Karim H. Karim is Director of the Centre for the Study of Islam and Professor of Communication Studies at Carleton University, Ottawa (Canada). He previously served as co-director of the Institute of Ismaili Studies, London (UK), and was a visiting scholar at Harvard University's Department of Near Eastern Languages & Civilizations (USA). His books include *Islamic Peril: Media and Global Violence* (Montreal, 2000), which received the 2001 Robinson Prize for Canadian studies in communication, *Re-imagining the Other: Culture, Media and Western-Muslim Intersections* (New York, 2014), *Engaging the Other: Public Policy and Western-Media Intersections* (New York, 2014) and *Diaspora and Media in Europe: Migration, Identity and Integration* (London, 2017). He has contributed widely to scholarly journals on themes relating to the cultural contexts of religion, transnationalism and technology.

Carool Kersten is Senior Lecturer in the Study of Islam and the Muslim World at King's College London (UK) and a research associate at the SOAS Centre of South East Asian Studies, University of London. He is the author of several books, including most recently *Islam in Indonesia: The Contest for Society, Ideas and Values* (London and New York, 2015) and *A History of Islam in Indonesia: Unity in Diversity* (Edinburgh, 2017). He is also the contributing co-editor of the three-volume anthology entitled *The Caliphate and Islamic Statehood* (Berlin, 2015) and of *Alternative Islamic Discourses and Religious Authority* (London and New York, 2013).

Mohamed M. Keshavjee is a London-based barrister and scholar-practioner in the field of alternative dispute resolution. He was the recipient of the Gandhi King Ikeda Peace Award for 2016 for his global work in the field of mediation. He is the author of two books: *Islam, Sharia and Alternative Dispute Resolution: Mechanisms for Legal Redress in the Muslim Community* (London, 2013) and *Into that Heaven Of Freedom* (Toronto, 2016), a memoir based on the experience of apartheid in South Africa. He has co-authored, with Raficq Abdulla, *Understanding Sharia: Islamic Law in a Globalised World* (London, forthcoming 2018).

About the Contributors xiii

Amaan Merali is a doctoral candidate in oriental studies at the University of Oxford's St Cross College (UK). His current work explores 19th- and 20th-century Ottoman intelligence-gathering in Greater Syria and India with reference to the Shi'a Nizari Ismailis. He previously worked in specialist Turkish and UK archives for his research on the mid-19th-century migration of the Ismailis from the Syrian mountains to a town on the edge of the desert.

Ziba Mir-Hosseini is an anthropologist and founding member of the Musawah Global Movement for Equality & Justice in the Muslim Family. She has held numerous research and visiting appointments and is currently Professorial Research Associate at the Centre for Islamic & Middle Eastern Law, University of London (UK). She was the 2015 recipient of the Martin E. Marty Award for the Public Understanding of Religion. Her books include *Gender and Equality in Muslim Family Law* (co-edited with L. Larsen, C. Moe and K. Vogt; London, 2013); and *Men in Charge? Rethinking Authority in Muslim Legal Tradition* (co-edited with M. Al-Sharmani and J. Rumminger; Oxford, 2015). Her contribution to this volume (Chapter 6) is adapted from an earlier version in *Retracing Footprints: Writing the History of Gulf Women* (Doha, 2012).

Ebrahim Moosa is Professor of Islamic Studies at the University of Notre Dame, Paris (France), where his research focuses on interpretive questions of tradition, ethics and law. He is co-director of the Contending Modernities project, a global educational and research initiative. His *Ghazali and the Poetics of Imagination* (Chapel Hill, 2005) was awarded the Best First Book in the History of Religions Prize by the American Academy of Religion. His other publications include *What is a Madrasa?* (Chapel Hill, 2015), *The African Renaissance and the Afro-Arab Spring* (co-edited with Charles Villa-Vicencio and Erik Doxtader; Washington, DC, 2015) and *Between Right and Wrong: Debating Muslim Ethics* (forthcoming). He is grateful to Nicholas Roberts for his research support and comments with regard to his contribution to this volume (Chapter 3).

Amyn B. Sajoo is Scholar-in-Residence at Simon Fraser University's Centre for Comparative Muslim Studies (Canada). He has held appointments at Cambridge and McGill universities (UK and Canada), the Institute of Southeast Asian Studies (Singapore) and The Institute of Ismaili Studies, London (UK). His books include *Muslim Ethics* (London, 2004), *Civil Society in the Muslim World* (London, 2002) and *Muslim Modernities* (London, 2008). His articles have appeared in *The Guardian*, *Christian Science Monitor*, *The Globe and Mail*, and *The Asian Wall Street Journal*. He was the Canada Department of Foreign Affairs 2010 Visiting

Academic in the Middle East. An earlier version of his contribution to this volume on bioethics (Chapter 8) appeared in *Studies in Religion*.

Jennifer A. Selby is Associate Professor of Religious Studies at Memorial University of Newfoundland (Canada). Her research considers Islam in contemporary France and in Canada, focusing on secularisation theory, Muslim studies, gender and religion, and public policy. She is the author of more than 20 articles and chapters, in addition to her book *Questioning French Secularism: Gender Politics and Islam in a Parisian Suburb* (New York, 2012). She is co-editor of *Debating Sharia: Islam, Gender Politics, and Family Law Arbitration* (with Anna C. Korteweg; Toronto, 2012), in which an earlier version of her contribution to this volume (Chapter 12) appeared. She is grateful for the assistance of Cory Funk in formatting parts of the text.

Sa'diyya Shaikh is Associate Professor of Religious Studies at the University of Cape Town (South Africa). Her research is situated at the intersection between Islamic and gender studies, with a special interest in Sufism. Her book *Sufi Narratives of Intimacy: Ibn Arabi, Gender and Sexuality* (Chapel Hill, 2012) won the UCT Book Prize in 2015 and was shortlisted for the American Association of Religion Constructive-Reflective Awards (2013). She co-edited *Violence Against Women in Contemporary World Religion* (with D. Maguire; Cleveland, 2007). As a 2016–2017 research fellow at the Wissenschaftskolleg zu Berlin: Institute for Advanced Study, she worked on 'Gender, Justice and Muslim Ethics'.

Standard Abbreviations

ADR = alternative dispute resolution
AKDN = Aga Khan Development Network
BOA = Başbakanlık Osmanlı Arşivi
CCMW = Canadian Council of Muslim Women
CEDR = Centre for Effective Dispute Resolution
EI2 = Encyclopaedia of Islam. Leiden, 1986.
EIs = Encylopaedia Islamica. Leiden, 2015.
EU = European Union
FBA = faith-based arbitration
FGM = female genital mutilation
HTI = Hizbut Tahrir Indonesia
IAIN al-Raniry = Islamic State Institute
ICMI = Indonesian Association of Muslim Intellectuals/Ikatan
Cendekiawan Muslim se-Indonesia
MUI = Indonesian Ulama Council
NGO = non-governmental organisation
NU = Nahdlatul Ulama
PBB = Crescent and Star Party/Partai Bulan Bintang
PKS = Justice and Prosperity Party/Partai Keadilan Sejahtera
UK = United Kingdom
US = United States

1

Introduction: A Multifaceted Venture

Amyn B. Sajoo

'Now we have set you on a clear religious path [shariʻa], so follow it.'

Qurʼan, 45:18[1]

'Ninety-nine per cent of shariʻa is about ethics, worship, the hereafter, and virtue. Only 1 per cent of it is about politics; the rulers are supposed to think about that part.'

Bediuzzaman Said Nursi (1877–1960),
Risale-i Nur Kulliyati (Istanbul, 1909)

A dance of ethics, law and spirituality – immersed in local cultures – is featured in all the world's faith traditions. Monotheisms offer a scriptural stage for this dance: the Old and New Testaments, the Qurʼan, as well as closely associated texts such as the Talmud and Hadith. And such a platform is not lacking in Buddhist, Hindu, Zoroastrian and other traditions: their body of canonical teachings likewise seeks to engage both the intellect and the spirit. Indeed, secular scriptures abound in the form of constitutions and human rights proclamations, where a constant rethinking of ethics, law and a deeper vein of truth is summoned up by citizens. A 'surplus of meaning' allows such texts to remain fresh and pivotal across the ages, as their readers engage in the remaking of a tradition.[2] So it is with the shariʻa.

In its unfolding since the 7th century, an array of social, philosophical and mystical resources have come into play. When the Qurʼan calls attention to this 'path' (45:18), it is manifestly the ethical

---

[1] *The Qurʼan*, trans. M.A.S. Abdel Haleem (Oxford, 2010), cited throughout this chapter. The verse addresses Muhammad ('you') and is dated to Mecca before his migration (*hijra*) in 622 CE to Medina.
[2] Paul Ricoeur, *Interpretation Theory: Discourse and the Surplus of Meaning* (Ft. Worth, TX, 1976).

2   *The Shariʿa*

teaching that defines it. This theme is revisited later in Muhammad's prophetic mandate, in the context of a shared Judeo-Christian-Muslim scripture:

> We have assigned a law and a path to each of you. If God had so willed, he would have made you one community, but he wanted to test you … and he will make clear to you what you differed about. (Qurʾan, 5:48)

The reference to a religious/spiritual path here stakes a claim to transcendence, beyond the particulars of rites and rituals. Muslims would come to develop a legal discourse (*fiqh*) around the ethical and spiritual teaching in the decades ahead, one that flourished over centuries into a full-blown juridical tradition. But the Qurʾan itself was minimally concerned in this regard, with few verses offering legal imperatives.[3] Indeed, when legal discourses were felt by some influential thinkers in the medieval period to have become too dominant an aspect of Islam, they pushed back to reclaim the ethical, notably through the idea of *maslaha*, the public good. For the shariʿa was felt to be more than mere rules that commanded how to be Muslim; on the contrary, regarding it as such would shortchange its *moral* scope.

This introductory chapter engages with the three broad avenues – history, ethics and law – through which the shariʿa is approached in this volume, the fifth in the Muslim Heritage Series. It will do so first through the lens of 'perception and reality,' with regard to diverse communities of Muslims, and indeed non-Muslims. How and why is the shariʿa understood in the ways that it is today? This is followed by an outline of our contributors' responses to the myriad issues of form and substance about the shariʿa – in effect, the dance of the moral and legal through history, down to modernity. Earlier volumes in the series addressed the shariʿa in diverse contexts, including a fulsome treatment of its locus between modernity and tradition by Abdullahi An-Naʾim in the preceding volume, *A Companion to Muslim Cultures*. Yet the subject has surely earned a claim to a distinct volume, given the evolving place of the shariʿa in the civilisational heritages of Islam. Moreover, it is difficult to conceive of a subject, and a term, that is today more charged with contentious meaning, among Muslims as

---

[3] According to the noted Egyptian judge and authority on the shariʿa, Muhammad al-Ashmawy, some 200 Qurʾanic verses offer substantial legal detail – a miniscule fraction of the scriptural text: *Maʿalim al-islam* (Milestones of Islam) (Cairo, 1989), p. 182.

Introduction 3

well as non-Muslims. In keeping with the mandate of this series, we seek to offer an *accessible* set of chapters, by scholars with considerable expertise in their particular areas of research, to sketch a rich portrait of the shari'a in its varied expressions.

What the Shari'a Is – and Is Not

As with the term *jihad*, the very mention of the shari'a conjures associations and images that speak to the climate of 'political religion'. For Muslims and non-Muslims alike, much is read *into* the understanding of the shari'a, with scant regard for its historical, cultural or theological underpinnings. The politics of identity, both secular and religious, that deeply inflects contemporary life has not spared the shari'a. During the 2010–11 Arab Spring, for example, many activists in Egypt, Libya, Syria, Tunisia and Yemen sought to appropriate the shari'a on behalf of their particular national project, on the premise of state custodianship and constitutional proclamation of this body of ethical and spiritual guidance. Many non-Muslim activists in the West have been equally certain about what the shari'a stands for: an austere code of law that is inherently hostile to liberal values. Women and men across the Muslim-majority societies of Central-South Asia, West Africa and the Middle East differ on whether, and how, the shari'a should shape legislation and public policy. In short, an abundance of heat and noise attends the idea, in striking contrast to the evidence of its locus in the lives of Islam's earliest communities. What would they make of these modern sentiments? It is time to address head-on the mythology around the shari'a today, with further elaboration in the following chapters.

Myth 1: The Shari'a Is a Framework of Divine Law

Muslims have from the outset regarded the Qur'an as the word of God revealed to the Prophet Muhammad, who duly conveyed every detail to individuals and to clusters of the faithful in Mecca and Medina between 610 and 632 CE. 'If divine guidance is needed, it is for the purpose of setting human life in good order', notes Wael Hallaq; Muslims took this to be about how to find peaceful accord with oneself, with society and with the world at large.[4] It was the quest to understand that guidance that gave birth to the shari'a: daily acts were categorised as 'required' (*wajib*), 'recommended' (*mandub*), 'disapproved' (*makruh*), 'forbidden'

---

[4]   W. Hallaq, *Shari'a: Theory, Practice, Transformations* (Cambridge, 2009), p. 84.

4 *The Shariʿa*

(*haram*) and 'neutral' (*mubah*). Inspired by the Qurʾan as well as the teachings and conduct of the Prophet (*Sunna*), the five categories are evidently both moral and legal in their tenor. They have remained authoritative for the faithful through the ages, applying far beyond the small stock of legal imperatives that are set forth in the text of the Qurʾan. But these distinctive categories are not part of 'revelation'; they appear neither in the Qurʾan nor the Sunna. Likewise, what are deemed to be the essential objectives (*maqasid*) of the shariʿa – the safeguarding of religion, life, intellect, lineage and property – emerged historically as interpretations. They underscore the fact that the shariʿa was a mortal endeavour to come to terms with divine guidance in particular social and historical settings; as such, the endeavour has not ceased since its founding age. To confuse the shariʿa with the Qurʾan is hardly a light matter for Muslims; nor should it be for non-Muslims. Further, since the Qurʾan, like any scripture, has always been subject to diverse readings, one expects the shariʿa, as a derivative framework of ethical-legal guidance and governance, to be highly pluralist in sensitivity to place and time.

Yet a significant number of Muslims regard the shariʿa as a divine legal code, one that is comparable to modern European ones.[5] This is borne out by a Pew Centre survey, in which majorities ranging from 75 to 81 per cent in the Middle East and South Asia (including Afghanistan) held this view, with smaller majorities of 44–69 per cent in Central and Southeast Asia.[6] The minority view was that the shariʿa was a human endeavour based on/inspired by the word of God. Opinion is more evenly divided as to whether the shariʿa is open to diverse interpretations, including in the Middle East and Southeast Asia, but a majority in South Asia hold to a single interpretation. Strong majorities in the latter, and more modest ones in the Middle East and Southeast Asia, as well as in much of West Africa, favour enacting the shariʿa as the law of the land.[7] The findings are consistent with a more specific survey by the Merdeka Centre in ethnoculturally diverse Malaysia, where there is a 'substantial disjuncture between popular consciousness and core epistemological commitments'

---

[5] A. Amanat and F. Griffel, ed., *Shariʿa: Islamic Law in the Contemporary Context* (Stanford, CA, 2007), Introduction, p. 13; A.A. An-Naim, *Toward and Islamic Reformation* (Syracuse, NY, 1990), pp. 11–12; J. Esposito and D. Mogahed, *Who Speaks for Islam: What a Billion Muslims Really Think* (New York, 2007), pp. 52–55.

[6] The Pew Research Centre, *The World's Muslims: Religion, Politics and Society* (Washington, DC, 2013), pp. 42–43: accessible at http://www.pewforum.org/2013/04/30/the-worlds-muslims-religion-politics-society-beliefs-about-sharia/.

[7] Ibid., pp. 44–46.

Introduction 5

in classical shari'a and Islamic law.[8] Ironically, such populist views are increasingly shared among non-Muslims in the western diaspora, with campaigns against 'shari'a law' and its supposed imposition on secular national codes.[9] Nearly one-third of Americans opined in a *Newsweek* survey that the imposition of Islamic law was viewed sympathetically by President Barack Obama.[10] Anxieties among Muslims and non-Muslims alike about identity and governance underpin these stances amid a host of isms: post-colonialism, secularism, orientalism, globalism, terrorism. Wherefore, then, the quest for a moral compass that impelled the shari'a in the first place?

Myth 2: The Shari'a Is Ritual and Social Regulation

The shari'a is commonly seen as a code of regulation for Muslims, governing matters that range from private devotion (affirming faith, modes of prayer, fasting, charity, pilgrimage) to communal conduct (family life, modes of dress, responsibility towards the poor/vulnerable, economic transactions, upholding the law, defending the faith). This relates to the oft-invoked Qur'anic injunction 'Be a community (*umma*) that calls for what is good, urges what is right and forbids what is wrong' (3:104). Typically, the shari'a is divided into the domains of *'ibadat* or ritual devotion (closely tied to revelation, hence unchanging) and *mu'amalat* or social relations (rooted in revelation but more amenable to adaptation). That both domains are pursuits of the 'good' surely underscores the scope of the shari'a as encompassing belief, intention and actual practice; one's relationship with God (*'ibadat*) and one's relationship with one's fellow humans (*mu'amalat*) were ethically intertwined. But the popular idea that the shari'a serves as a regulatory code means that *'ibadat* and *mu'amalat* are subject to the scrutiny of standards which are essentially juridical (and patriarchal). 'What is right' is thence reduced to what is lawful. And if this is tied to what is divine, then the shari'a is readily turned into a rigid code to be enforced by the powers that be, notably the modern state, on behalf of a transcendent

---

[8]   T. Moustafa, 'Islamic Law, Women's Rights, and Popular Consciousness in Malaysia', *Law & Social Inquiry* 38 (2013), pp. 168–188.

[9]   D. DeKok and T. James, 'Protesters Rally Against Islamic Law in Several US Cities', *Reuters*, 10 June 2017: accessible at http://www.reuters.com/article/us-usa-islam-protests-idUSKBN1910RC; M. Humphrys, 'Sharia Law in the West' (dedicated to anti-shari'a campaigns in Europe and North America): accessible at http://markhumphrys.com/sharia.west.html.

[10]   Accessible at http://nw-assets.s3.amazonaws.com/pdf/1004-ftop.pdf.

6 *The Shari'a*

authority.[11] This stands in stark contrast to the spirit of the historical shari'a, which sought to foster socioeconomic life in 'the interests of the communities of believers, not those of the ruler (or ruling class)'.[12]

Without its moral and spiritual vitality, the shari'a becomes nothing more than another corpus of law, albeit more 'intrusive' in its scope than a standard secular code. All the more so where its ethical authority, which necessarily relies on *voluntary* submission with regard to ritual and social matters alike, is treated instead as coercive regulation. Classical Islam was filled with communities, eminent teachers and whole traditions that thrived on this fuller appreciation of the shari'a; their legacy lives on in Shi'i and Sunni practice across the Muslim world and the diaspora today. Of the essence here is the 'esoteric and intuitive reading of the Qur'an,' which makes the shari'a part of the search for wisdom (*ma'rifa*) and, ultimately, the truth (*haqiqa*).[13] Consistent with the Qur'anic reminder of the pluralistic message of revelation itself (5:48), the shari'a is here conceived as one among many paths to God. But what of the argument that fiqh, as the vast legal 'expression' of the shari'a, is a fastidious regulatory corpus that commands compliance because of its link to the authority of the Qur'an and the Sunna? This still misses the mark: fiqh, like the shari'a, is not only the outcome of human interpretation in shifting contexts but is also a pursuit of understanding (the literal meaning of fiqh). In turn, this 'legal' pursuit yields particular rules or *ahkam* with regard to proper practice. The fallibility of this venture is brought out in Intisar Rabb's seminal account of the place of doubt (*shubha*) in Islamic legal reasoning from the outset; both the Prophet and Ali ibn Abi Talib (ca. 599–661), his closest companion as well as the fourth caliph, are reported to have adjudicated against scriptural punishment where there was ambiguity in the available evidence of criminality.[14] For Muslim jurists, 'the interpretive

---

[11] On the modernist appetite for codification, see Hallaq, *Shari'a*, pp. 367–370; A. Emon, 'Codification and Islamic Law: The Ideology Behind a Tragic Narrative', *Middle East Law & Governance* 8 (2016), pp. 275–309.

[12] Ibid., p. 366.

[13] For a succinct account, see S. Zubaida, *Law and Power in the Islamic World* (London, 2003), pp. 35–39.

[14] I. Rabb, *Doubt in Islamic Law: A History of Legal Maxims, Interpretation, and Islamic Criminal Law* (Cambridge, 2015), pp. 1–4, 25–27. See also Hallaq, *Shari'a*, pp. 308–312, noting that the handful of original shari'a punishments – for disruptions of social order around acts such as murder, theft and fornication – were tied to deterrence by an omniscient presence that 'knew each and every particular of human conduct', p. 309. Hence comparisons with the punitive apparatus of the secular state are deeply flawed.

Introduction   7

process used to deal (or duel) with doubt was a constant across all schools of Islamic law,' concludes Rabb.[15] Whether in social, ritual or juridical settings, reducing the shari'a to a rigid code of conduct simply will not do.

Myth 3: The Shari'a Is Incompatible with Modernity

What do Muslims want when they ask for the shari'a, and what do non-Muslims, particularly in the West, think that Muslims want in this regard? Taking the shari'a seriously is an intrinsic part of one's Islamic faith, and the relationship between faith and identity has become especially complex in modernity's secular age. There have been major initiatives to integrate the shari'a into secular systems of governance in the Muslim world, from the Ottoman civil code, the *Mecelle* (1869–1876), to civil codes drawn up across the Middle East by Abd al-Razzaq al-Sanhuri (1895–1971), to the more theocratic enterprises of Saudi Arabia and Iran, and various attempts in between, including 'constitutionalising' the shari'a during the Arab Spring.[16] Militant movements such as Ansar al-Shari'a, Boko Haram, Daesh, al-Qaeda, al-Shabab and the Taliban, which aimed to impose their radical version of fiqh in the guise of shari'a compliance, have all failed. Western liberal societies have also grappled with accommodating fiqh rules in family and commercial matters, along with less formal arbitration by Muslim-minority communities.[17] What these assorted initiatives have in common is the state-centred nature of modern discourse about the shari'a, regardless of location or political ideology. Perhaps not surprisingly, the shari'a is often seen as being in tension with the secular orientation of modernity, where the state is mandated to advance equal citizenship through law and public policy in separation from the institutions of faith. In this narrative, the shari'a is no less than the

---

[15] Ibid., pp. 317–318. In Shi'i and Sunni practice, Rabb notes, the jurisprudence of doubt was curtailed by the western advent of codification in the 19th century, a hallmark of legal modernity (pp. 320–321).

[16] See A. An-Na'im, *Islam and the Secular State: Negotiating the Future of Shari'a* (Cambridge, MA, 2008); R. Hefner, ed., *Shari'a: Law and Modern Muslim Ethics* (Bloomington, IN, 2016).

[17] See M. Rohe, 'Reasons for the Application of Shari'a in the West', pp. 25–46; A. Saeed, 'Reflections on the Development of the Discourse of *Fiqh* for Minorities and Some of the Challenges It Faces', pp. 241–255, in M.S. Berger, ed., *Applying Shari'a in the West* (Leiden, 2013).

Other of liberal society: what Muslims want is an alternative to the legal, political and social ethos of modernity. Within the western diaspora, this also puts the shari'a at odds with other faith traditions, more amenable to reasonable accommodation in pursuit of the 'overlapping consensus' which civic identity properly demands.[18] Among the pitfalls of this narrative is to assume an exclusive global brand of modernity, with its own trademark liberal secularism, of which all progressive individuals and societies must be willing consumers.

Surveys where Muslims broadly ask for the shari'a also show that they strongly favour democracy over authoritarian rule, oppose religious leaders having a large influence in politics, and support freedom of religion; most see no conflict between science and religion, or between piety and modern life.[19] Lately, amid the economic and social turmoil of the Arab Spring, a majority of Muslim youth in the Middle East have favoured stability over democracy, which surely reflects concern about the quality of governance.[20] A recent study of the shari'a in Nigeria offers potent insight into what Muslims want in practical terms when they ask for the shari'a: institutional accountability, equity and integrity.[21] That they expect this of the shari'a, rather than of secular forms of governance, is a measure of the level of corruption and inequity associated with their experience of the latter. It also recalls the strength of cultural and religious affinity for the authority of an ideal shari'a as pictured in the context not just of heritage but of everyday reality as well. Paul Kahn famously observed that the rule of law is about 'a way of being in the world,' which calls on 'our imagining its meanings.'[22] The conceit of modernity's dominant story is that liberal secular imaginings are blessed with a rationality that trumps the 'herd mentality' of other

---

[18] B. Turner and J.T. Richardson, 'Islam and the Problems of Liberal Democracy', in Berger, *Applying Shari'a in the West*, pp. 47–64; D. Gozdecka, *Rights, Religious Pluralism and the Recognition of Difference* (New York, 2016), pp. 144–146, 14–23. More generally, see S. Hamid, *Islamic Exceptionalism: How the Struggle Over Islam is Reshaping the World* (New York, 2016), pp. 238–268.

[19] See Pew, *The World's Muslims*; Esposito and Mogahed, *Who Speaks for Islam*, further noting that 'political freedom and liberty, and freedom of speech, is what they admire most about the West', p. 34.

[20] 'Arab Youth: Look Forward in Anger', *The Economist*, 6 August 2016: accessible at http://www.economist.com/news/briefing/21703362-treating-young-threat-arab-rulers-are-stoking-next-revolt-look-forward-anger.

[21] Sarah Eltantawi, *Shari'ah on Trial: Northern Nigeria's Islamic Revolution* (Oakland, CA, 2017).

[22] P. Kahn, *The Cultural Study of Law: Reconstructing Legal Scholarship* (Chicago, 1999), pp. 36, 84.

Introduction 9

ways of being. Yet populism and nativism, among other less than rational isms, have not spared liberal societies, past or present. Even as one challenges the historical and ethical rectitude of some claims about the shari'a (as a divine, purely regulatory, monolithic code), it bears acknowledging that this mythos is part of a wider tension around the plurality of secularisms/modernities in which religion and the citizen are engaged.[23]

History, Ethics and Law: This Volume

'While I may claim as a Muslim that moral rules emanate or originate from God, I cannot claim that any set of laws that attempt to implement or give effect to this moral commitment are divine,' observes Khaled Abou El-Fadl in setting forth the historical and philosophical arc of the shari'a (Chapter 2). This flows from a core aspect of the venture since the 7th century: the ideals of the Qur'an with regard to justice and the human condition can only be imperfectly understood and realised in practice. The shari'a 'is not a path in which believers submit their will, reason, and autonomy to God, and in return, are shepherded to the heavenly pastures' but rather a relationship of trust (*khilafat*) with the divine in which 'the autonomy of choice' is vital. This trust and autonomy are, for El-Fadl, fatally compromised where the modern state becomes the custodian and enforcer of the shari'a. Doing so is to make the moral into the political, and wilfully to forget the historical contingency of official interpretations of the shari'a as one endeavour among many. How then is the shari'a relevant to societies and communities today? The answer for El-Fadl is not fundamentally different from what the shari'a has been since its inception: 'reasoning with God' is what Muslims are enjoined to strive for through the shari'a, and the plurality of legal guilds across history is a reminder that none enjoyed a universal claim to truth.

How then do the particulars of 'reasoning with God' – as compared with plain reasoning – work out? Ebrahim Moosa (Chapter 3) upends the kind of legal-centric response that has become so dominant in the context of the modern shari'a. 'What is called Islamic law could effectively be described as a vibrant tradition of translating norms into lived societies,' he observes, which effectively makes it an exercise in ethics. Moosa illustrates this with 'Imrana's Case' from 2005, where

---

[23] See C. Taylor, 'How to Define Secularism', pp. 59–78; A. Stepan, 'Muslims and Toleration: Unexamined Contributions to the Multiple Secularisms of Modern Democracies', pp. 267–296, in A. Stepan and C. Taylor, ed., *Boundaries of Toleration* (New York, 2014).

a family rape sparked conflicting readings of Hanafi rules in India. If those rules were treated as 'law', the ensuing conflict with the most basic sense of human dignity would be impaired, in violation of the raison d'être of the shari'a. Those rules, he argues, are about 'discernment' (fiqh), without which the purposes of the shari'a plainly cannot be realised. Indeed, even when the shari'a historically conferred political legitimacy on the ruler, the underlying idea was to subject governance to the constraints of fiqh and its attendant values, not merely to empower caliphal (or de facto) rule.[24]

As for the continuing and ubiquitous relevance of the shari'a to Muslim societies and communities, Karim H. Karim pursues a pragmatic line of enquiry, anchored again in ethical purpose (Chapter 4). Governance in the broadest sense, from high politics to the effective working of social institutions, has long drawn inspiration from the principles of accountability, equity and compassion that are at the core of the shari'a. In this vein, the shari'a is effectively 'a guide to the entirety of life', notes Karim, finding sustained expression in charity and social welfare, medicine and learning, ecological stewardship and cultural renewal. In short, what the Aga Khan Development Network (AKDN) calls the 'social conscience of Islam through institutional development' is the flipside of the shari'a as moral commitment.[25] The roots of this claim go back to the earliest days, when the shari'a was about 'a communal ethos of mutual support' coupled with the 'public good' for Muhammad and his companions. Today, civil society is the vital space for that ethos, exemplified by the work of Shi'i and Sunni organisations as wide-ranging in scope as the Edhi Foundation in Pakistan, Hizmet in Turkey, the Canadian Council of Muslim Women and the global AKDN.

But what drives these commitments to ethical values and their expression in governance, law and civic culture? Why should Muslims take the moral framework of the shari'a seriously, beyond complying with the rules and practices that are associated with it? For Sa'diyya Shaikh it is nothing less than 'the spiritual landscape of the human condition' that serves as the rationale for having a shari'a at all (Chapter 5). Qur'anic fundamentals and their rich esoteric readings by Sufi traditions suggest a threefold struggle of the human spirit:

---

[24]   As Noah Feldman notes with regard to the reasoning of the key classical figure on constitutionalism, Abu al-Hasan al-Mawardi (972–1058): *The Rise and Fall of the Islamic State* (Princeton, 2008), pp. 36–40.

[25]   Aga Khan Development Network: accessible at http://www.akdn.org/about-us/akdns-approach-development.

Introduction 11

first, against its baser instincts (*nafs al-ammara*), then to a level of striving for the good (*al-nafs al-lawamma*), and finally the attainment of a state of tranquillity (*al-nafs al-mutma'inna*). In this progression towards what Ibn Arabi (1165–1240) described as *al-insan al-kamil*, the archetypal human in Sufi praxis, the shari'a plays a guiding role. There is also a vital practical aspect here, notes Shaikh, in that these teachings have 'subverted traditional patriarchal religious anthropology'. A transcendent spiritual landscape, after all, can hardly be captive to gender difference. In this regard, the legacy of the celebrated female Sufi master, Rabia al-Adawiyya (ca. 717–801), whose acolytes in Basra included eminent males, still inspires the spiritualist shari'a critiques of modern scholars such as Asma Barlas and Amina Wadud, as well as Shaikh.

The tension between ethical values and the practical sociocultural settings in which they unfold historically is a classic challenge for all great traditions, religious as well as secular. Ziba Mir-Hosseini (Chapter 6) draws on this inescapable reality in seeking to 'unveil the theological and rational arguments and legal theories' around gender in the shari'a.[26] Patriarchal assumptions, she argues, are embedded in the thinking of all the major schools of Islamic law, notably on marriage and divorce, and women's covering and seclusion. The encounter with colonial modernity and European legal systems brought fresh challenges to traditionalist fiqh approaches, but the former were hardly always liberal when it came to the status of women. In matters of inheritance and property ownership, for instance, Muslim women enjoyed superior rights. More broadly, however, the 19th century witnessed the rise of Islamic feminist critiques of shari'a-centred patriarchy, in law and public policy. Some 'neo-traditional' stances were and are defensive in their outlook, perceived as cultural assaults on Muslim identity; but others were and are more radical in their 'unveiling' of pre-modern assumptions. 'Rather than searching for an exclusively Islamic genealogy for gender equality, human rights and democracy (which was the concern of earlier reformers)', notes Mir-Hosseini, 'the new thinking emphasises how religion is understood and how religious knowledge is produced.' Yet these more trenchant critiques situate themselves within Islam: the shari'a, then, remains relevant in a thoroughly contemporary context where secular and sacred are fully entwined.[27]

---

[26]   See especially in this regard Leila Ahmed's landmark historical exposition in *Women and Gender in Islam* (New Haven and London, 1992), Chapter 3.

[27]   As shown, for example, in Marwa Sharfeldin's account of Egyptian feminist activism: 'Islamic Law Meets Human Rights', pp. 163–196, in Z. Mir-Hosseini, M. Al-Sharmani and J. Rumminger, ed., *Men in Charge?* (Oxford, 2015).

12   *The Shariʿa*

No less conspicuous in rethinking the shariʿa in everyday practice
is the burgeoning field of 'Islamic finance' – products and services
for commercial transactions small and large, now global in scope. In
their aspiration to be compliant with the shariʿa, a key concern is the
traditional norm regarding *riba* or usury. Should the norm be taken as
a blanket prohibition on charging interest, or is that a reductive reading
of a principle about exploitative conduct? In a parallel with the new
feminist critiques noted above, financial propriety is being rethought
to serve Islamic ethical objectives in the light of today's commercial
realities. 'That may require abandoning pietistic adherence to the
opinions of premodern jurists,' it is argued, 'but it may also be seen as
following their example more closely.'[28] Mohamed M. Keshavjee and
Raficq Abdulla (Chapter 7) extend this perspective to matters of family
law from divorce to child abduction. In Muslim-majority societies and
the western diaspora alike, family law issues must contend with the
demands for gender equity and also with contemporary standards in
administering justice, whether in courts, alternative dispute resolution
or public policy at large. The upshot: a bold retrieval of the role of
maslaha (the public good) in orienting the shariʿa as a 'purposive'
quest that serves the evolving needs of Muslims, beyond rigid rule
enforcement in the name of tradition.

The drive to rethink the shariʿa ultimately engages personhood:
the place of individual autonomy in the scheme of familial and social
existence. From choices about reproductive technologies (fertility,
surrogacy, abortion) to organ donation, stem-cell therapy and
euthanasia, the deepest human values are at stake. Indeed, bioethics has
been a central aspect of the negotiation of virtue from the earliest days
of the shariʿa, as Amyn B. Sajoo shows (Chapter 8). Aristotle's character-
centred stance on the virtues was keenly embraced in those early days,
as in Ibn Miskawayh's (932–1030) landmark *Tahdhib al-Akhlaq* (*The
Refinement of Character*), which laid the foundations of both Shiʿi and
Sunni ethical thought. Yet this had to compete, as already noted, with
a juristic mode of reasoning that deeply influenced the development
of the shariʿa, including in matters of public health. With personal
autonomy steadily emerging as the dominant facet of bioethics in the
modern period, the enabling framework of governance has been legal,

---

[28]   M.A. El-Gamal, 'Incoherence of Contract-Based Islamic Financial Jurisprudence in the Age of Financial Engineering', *Wisconsin International Law Journal*,
25:4 (2008), pp. 605–623. The tension between rule observance and equity is
especially evident in the expansion of 'Islamic banking' to poorer sectors in
Africa: 'Saharan Sharia', *The Economist*, 15 July 2017, pp. 63–64.

Introduction

and the mode of reasoning guided by rules or 'principlism'.[29] This latter
sits quite comfortably with traditionalism in the shari'a, which prizes
the *fatwa* as a tool of juristic decision-making.[30] But what of autonomy,
amid a traditional leaning in favour of communal (and patriarchal)
entitlements? Sajoo argues that *maslaha* can balance collective public
and individual entitlements, while resisting the logic of utilitarianism,
as part of its own heritage. At the same time, the evidence from a range
of biomedical and social practices discussed in the chapter suggests
that finding the balance will be a long struggle; for it is entangled with
perceptions of identity, particularly in an age of secular globalisation.

Identity in its various guises has never been far removed from the
shari'a, whether in adhering to or straying from its ideals. Affiliation
with a specific school of fiqh, gender, minority status (Muslim and non-
Muslim alike) and locus in the social hierarchy have all had implications
in this regard. There is also the overarching identity of rulers, local and
regional, where this is attached to custodianship of the shari'a. This was
certainly the case with the Ottoman Empire, which spanned large tracts
of the Middle East, North Africa and the Balkans over several centuries.
Amaan Merali (Chapter 9) shows how the political legitimacy of the
Ottoman sultanate in Istanbul drew on its stewardship of the legal,
social and ethical expressions of Sunni orthodoxy – a coupling of power
and identity that was sure to affect minorities, especially Shi'i ones.
The latter were also drawn into the imperial rivalry with Iran under
the Safavids (1501–1736), whose Shi'i identity of recent vintage gave
sectarian colour to Ottoman politics. The sultanate not only assigned
to itself the status of a caliphate in order to acquire religious authority,
but also merged secular and Islamic laws into an imperial system of
governance, engineered by the jurists Kemal Pashazade (1469–1535)
and Ebussu'ud (1490–1574). The institutionalisation of the judiciary,
and the subjection of government officials to the authority of *qadi*,
or judicial, courts (rather than extrajudicial *mazalim* tribunals that
commonly prevailed in the Muslim Middle East to which the public
could appeal against abuses of power by the ruler), certainly garnered
respect.[31] The Hanafi school of fiqh became that of the empire, though

---

[29] T. Beauchamp and J. Childress, *Principles of Biomedical Ethics*, 6th edn (New
York, 2009); A. Hinkley, 'Two Rival Understandings of Autonomy, Paternalism,
and Bioethical Principlism', pp. 85–95, in H.T. Engelhardt, ed., *Bioethics
Critically Reconsidered: Having Second Thoughts* (Dordrecht, 2012).
[30] Critiqued broadly in Tariq Ramadan, *Radical Reform: Islamic Ethics and
Liberation* (Oxford, 2009), pp. 113–155.
[31] Hallaq, *Shari'a*, pp. 208–209.

legal pluralism flourished in Ottoman domains, at least among Sunni, Christian and Jewish subjects. When it came to Shi'i communities such as the Ismailis and Nusayris in Syria, however, persecution was rife, both from Istanbul and by local governors. No matter how small, such communities 'were nonetheless integral to the development of an Ottoman identity, if only as a foil for defining orthodoxy', observes Merali.

In our time, the intersection of state and social identities in the life of the shari'a has a fresh twist. Nationalism, where 'imagined communities' strive for a shared identity, readily spills beyond its secular origins.[32] Its rise in Europe was fuelled by the Reformation's capitalist and literacy drives in the 16th century, which put nationalist sentiment in competition with traditional religion. And nationalism's success in the 19th and 20th centuries effectively put the secular state in control of religious institutions, including those of the minorities. Channelled into claims of statehood and sovereign power, or the aspirations of social movements and individual citizenship, nationalism can wash over and under religious sentiments. Turkey is exemplary on this score: republican identity was wary of ethnoreligious difference in the nationalism of Kemal Ataturk (1881–1938), and it has remained so under his less secular political successors today. Where does all this leave the shari'a, in the wake of its earlier custodianship under more diffused entities? Not surprisingly, given the contours of the modern state, public law is the site of sharp contestation between civic and religious identities, whether at the highest levels of the constitution or in local governance.

Is there a proper place for the shari'a in national constitutions, and, if so, on what terms?[33] Since the 2010–2011 Arab Spring the answers have varied drastically, even for Egypt's and Tunisia's respective Muslim Brotherhood movements, let alone for the Middle East at large.[34] Similar tensions prevail in the world's largest Muslim

---

[32] B. Anderson, *Imagined Communities: Reflections on the Origins and Spread of Nationalism* (London, 1983), especially pp. 48–58. For an illustration of this in sectarian contexts, see A. B. Sajoo, 'Modernity: The Ethics of Identity', pp. 349–370, in F. Daftary, A. B. Sajoo and S. Jiwa, ed., *The Shi'i World: Pathways in Tradition and Modernity* (London, 2015).

[33] See C. Lombardi, 'Constitutional Provisions Making Sharia "a" or "the" Chief Source of Legislation: Where Did They Come From? What Do They Mean? Do They Matter?', *American University International Law Review* 28 (2013), pp. 733–774.

[34] R. Owen, 'Egypt and Tunisia: From the Revolutionary Overthrow of Dictatorships to the Struggle to Establish A New Constitutional Order', pp. 257–272, in F. Gerges, *The New Middle East: Protest and Revolution in the Arab World* (New York, 2014); M. Zeghal, 'Constitutionalizing a Democratic Muslim State

Introduction   15

society, Indonesia. In the aftermath of a century of secularist Dutch colonial and post-colonial governance, Carool Kersten (Chapter 10) traces the ups and downs of public Islam, down to the conspicuous 'conservative turn' today. For decades, quietist movements such as the Muhammadiyah and Nahdlatul Ulama mobilised millions in the cause of an Islamic consciousness that also upheld *Pancasila*, the official doctrine of pluralist national consciousness. But this is now contested by a 'bottom-up' tendency of Islamisation, *perda syariah*, in which local legislation (especially in the restive Sumatran province of Aceh) proclaims adherence to shari'a principles. While designed to placate assorted quarters of the population that demand a more overt assertion of orthodox Islam, with robust influences from abroad, this trend is growing, Kersten finds. The most recent evidence of this comes from cosmopolitan Jakarta, where elections for the governor gave way to crude identity politics with judicial support, which in turn provoked an executive crackdown on 'extremism'.[35]

If the locus of the shari'a in public law and policy is in flux in diverse Muslim-majority domains, this has increasingly become the case in the Euro-North American diaspora as well. In the shadow of 9/11, the matter is readily linked to issues of national security and extremist violence. But what is at stake here runs deeper, as Rex Ahdar and Nicholas Aroney observe (Chapter 11):

> The existence of shari'a within the West is, for many, a confronting issue – perhaps a litmus test of the capacity of western liberal-democratic states to accommodate religious difference. This is because shari'a is much more than a matter of personal piety and private religious practice. It is, at its core, a vision of the good of life, expressed culturally and collectively, in private and in public. For many it regulates all manner of domains generally assumed in western societies to be differentiated and compartmentalised: marriage and family life, personal hygiene and etiquette, food and diet, trade and finance, taxation, crime and war.

---

without Shari'a: The Religious Establishment in the Tunisian 2014 Constitution', in Hefner, *Shari'a*, pp. 107–134.

[35] J. Cochrane, 'Christian Governor of Jakarta Is Found Guilty of Blasphemy', *The New York Times*, 10 May 2017, p. A11; J. Cochrane, 'Jakarta Protest, Tied to Faith, May Have Deeper Links to Secular Politics', *The New York Times*, 13 November 2016; J. Emont, 'Decree Frees Indonesia to Curb Islamist Group', *The New York Times*, 12 July 2017, p. A10. On external support and incitement of 'radicalism' in Indonesia, see S. Kinzer, 'Saudi Arabia is Destabilizing the World', *Boston Globe*, 11 June 2017.

16   *The Shariʿa*

Where public religion seeks exemption from law of general application, such as the wearing of Sikh turbans in place of motorcycle helmets required for safety, or the donning of headscarves in neutral spaces such as courts, accommodation is usually achieved within the ambit of liberal pluralist ideology. Anglo-American law and policy have inclined towards greater elasticity in this regard than the French and other European systems. Tensions run higher still when the accommodation sought is the 'enforcement of transactions governed by religious norms', Ahdar and Aroney argue, especially when it comes to marriage and family life where the larger vision of the shariʿa might be at stake.[36]

For Jennifer A. Selby (Chapter 12), this is ultimately about 'variances in the marking out of secularism': in the modern liberal context, after all, 'the secular consistently defines and manages religion'. In her comparison of recent episodes in Canada and France where Muslim family law and practice were particularly engaged, Selby finds that the public/private division of space, which is so central to traditional liberalism in its approach to religious accommodation, has consistently framed the shariʿa debate. Yet the core liberal claim of state neutrality in public space has been shifting in its meaning for some time; historically, it has been inconsistent when it comes to Christian claims of accommodation, as with regard to state funding of Catholic and Protestant schools in Canada. Furthermore, debates about family matters promptly shift into the politics of gender, where religion is typically seen as conflicting with the secular claims of human rights. 'Policing Muslim women in the name of gender equality is not a new phenomenon', notes Selby, with a long colonial history that today calls for a more reflective approach.[37] Why assume that a faith-based vision of the good life is necessarily incompatible with a robust commitment to equal citizenship?

The good life as a daily pursuit is captured in a multitude of ways in Muslim cultural expression. In the 16th-century Persian illustration

---

[36] See J. Waldron, 'Questions About the Reasonable Accommodation of Minorities', pp. 103–113; A. Shachar, 'State, Religion, and Family: The New Dilemmas of Multicultural Accommodation', pp. 115–133, in R. Ahdar and N. Aroney, ed., *Shariʿa in the West* (Oxford, 2013). More broadly on Muslim minority citizenship in western contexts, including perceived tensions arising from state custodianship of the shariʿa, see A. March, *Islam and Liberal Citizenship: The Search for an Overlapping Consensus* (Oxford, 2009).

[37] L. Ahmed, *Women and Gender in Islam: Historical Roots of a Modern Debate* (New Haven, 1992); L. Abu-Lughod, 'Do Muslim Women Really Need Saving? Anthropological Reflections on Cultural Relativism and its Others'. *American Anthropologist* 104 (September 2002), pp. 783–790.

Introduction 17

which graces this volume's jacket, the perennial locus of water in that pursuit is recalled: court activities and nature alike share a dynamic existence around its sustaining presence. From oases and wells to garden fountains and streams, a recurrent theme is the pathways that lead to and from such waters, a theme that can be found in Muslim architecture and design, sketches and paintings, poetry and colourful prose.[38] It is also the core metaphor of the shari'a as an ongoing human quest to grasp the substance of divine guidance in the conduct of devotional, social and economic life, including how one relates to the natural environment. Law and less formal norms of behaviour are necessarily vital to navigating the pathways at stake; rule-based frameworks offer the attractions of firmness in guidance and distinctiveness in identity. But they hardly define, much less exhaust, the shari'a. To return to our jacket image, there is only so much in the dense creative and natural activity that can fit into a universe of rules alone, or for that matter that can be subject only to an external (exoteric) measure of the good. The illustration is based on the poet Jami's work, *Haft Awrang* (The Seven Thrones), which contrasts the delights of the profane with those of the spiritual/mystical.[39] We are reminded, then, of the limits even of the refined sociopolitical order of the royal court.

Is the call of the shari'a beyond the legal and political still audible in our time? In *The Impossible State*, Wael Hallaq sees no tenable future for a state-centric shari'a in the 'moral quest' that is central to modernity; Saba Mahmood is sceptical that secularism as a 'statist project' can deliver on equality for faith communities.[40] Governance, institutions and the public sphere do matter, of course, as they always have for upholding the values of the shari'a. Yet the role of a pluralist civil society in this regard is critical in balancing the ever-growing claims which modern states can make on the lives of individuals and communities. The chapters in this volume offer much evidence, in diverse settings, of why treating the shari'a as part of the political enterprise of governments of any stripe is fraught. This is about not only the actual historical record

---

[38] S. Blair and J. Bloom, ed., *Rivers of Paradise: Water in Islamic Art and Culture* (New Haven, CT, 2009).
[39] R. Davis, 'Jami', in J. Meri, ed. *Medieval Islamic Civilisation: An Encyclopedia*, vol. 1 (New York, 2006), p. 412.
[40] W. Hallaq, *The Impossible State* (New York, 2014), pp. 167–170; S. Mahmood, *Religious Difference in a Secular Age* (Oakland, CA, 2016), pp. 208–213. See also A. El-Affendi's *Who Needs An Islamic State?* 2nd edn (London, 2008).

of governments and official actors but also the very idea of the shariʻa as an ethical enterprise – one that stakes its claim primarily on the conscience of Muslims, in private and public.

Further Reading

An-Naʻim, Abdullahi A. *Islam and the Secular State: Negotiating the Future of Shariʻa*. Cambridge, MA, 2009.

Banda, Fareda and Lisa Joffey, ed., *Women's Rights and Religious Law: Domestic and International Perspectives*. Abingdon, 2016.

Daniels, Timothy P., ed., *Sharia Dynamics: Islamic Law and Sociopolitical Processes*. New York, 2017.

Eltantawi, Sarah. *Shariʻah on Trial: Northern Nigeria's Islamic Revolution*. Oakland, CA, 2017.

Grote, Rainer and Tilmann Röder, ed., *Constitutionalism, Islam and Human Rights after the Arab Spring*. New York, 2016.

Hallaq, Wael. *The Impossible State: Islam, Politics, and Modernity's Moral Predicament*. New York, 2014.

Hefner, Robert, ed., *Shariʻa: Law and Modern Muslim Ethics*. Bloomington, IN, 2016.

Mahmood, Saba. *Religious Difference in a Secular Age: A Minority Report*. Princeton and Oxford, 2016.

Nielsen, Jørgen S. and Lisbet Christoffersen, ed., *Shariʻa As Discourse: Legal Traditions and the Encounter with Europe*. Abingdon, 2016.

Powell, Russell. *Shariʻa in the Secular State: Evolving Meanings of Islamic Jurisprudence in Turkey*. New York, 2017.

Rabb, Intisar. *Doubt in Islamic Law: A History of Legal Maxims, Interpretation, and Islamic Criminal Law*. New York, 2015.

Sajoo, Amyn B., ed., *Muslim Modernities: Expressions of the Civil Imagination*. London, 2008.

Shalakany, Amr. 'Islamic Legal Histories', *Berkeley Journal of Middle Eastern Islamic Law* 1 (2008), pp. 2–83.

SHARIA source at Harvard Law School (Islamic Legal Studies Program): https://shariasource.blog/about/.

2

Foundations

Khaled Abou El-Fadl

The shari'a is the way or path to goodness. While it is common to use the term interchangeably with Islamic law, the shari'a is in fact much broader. Traditionally, it invokes the idea of people bonded by a common set of beliefs or convictions. Sources such as the Qur'an often speak of 'the ways of previous generations' (*shar'* or *shari'at man sabaq* or *man qablana*), 'the Jewish way-of-life' (*shar'* or *shari'at al-yahud*) or even 'the methods of Greek logicians' (*shar'* al-falasifa or *tariqat al-falasifa*). *Shari'at Muhammad*, depending on the context, may refer to the Sunna or tradition of Muhammad or to Muhammad's way of life, but the expression is not used to refer to Islamic jurisprudence or law. Islamic law, or what is called *al-ahkam al-shari'a*, is the cumulative body and system of jurisprudential thought of numerous communities and schools with regard to the divine will, and its relation to the public good. Islamic law is thus the fallible and imperfect attempt by human beings over centuries to explore right and wrong, and to discern what is good for human beings.

If *shar'* *Allah* or the shari'a is about more than specific divine commands, and rather the ultimate good that God desires for human beings, then what is the relationship between that ideal and the lived experience of Muslims? How should we understand the historical quest to reconcile the two, and what should we make of modern demands to frame that quest in public law and constitutions? In responding to these questions, this chapter draws on Islam's fundamental texts and tenets, as well as its rich philosophical and legal discourses. Ultimately, shari'a comes down to 'reasoning with God', an endeavour that engages the full panoply of human intellectual, emotional and spiritual resources in seeking to live by the guidance of the divine, expressed and understood in diverse ways.

I

There is an obvious tension between the obligation to live by God's law, and the fact that this law is manifested only through subjective interpretations. Even if there is a unified realisation that a particular positive command does express the divine law, there is still a vast array of possible subjective executions and applications. The very notion of submission to the limitless God offers an equally limitless range of subjective engagements with the divine. Inevitably, human beings who submit to God, and through this submission reach for the sublime, will end up with a range of subjective experiences and various realisations of divinity or godliness. If God's beauty can manifest itself through a limitless range of subjective engagements, on what basis can there be a determinable law in the shari'a? If the shari'a does not have a determinable law, and if it does not offer a determinable path, then what is the point of having the shari'a?

This tension in legal Islamic discourses was resolved by distinguishing between the shari'a and fiqh. The shari'a, it was argued, is the divine ideal, immutable, immaculate and flawless. Fiqh is not. Fiqh was treated as the human attempt to understand and apply the divine ideal, and several schools of legal thought were considered equally orthodox and authoritative.[1] As part of the doctrinal foundations for this discourse, Muslim jurists focused on traditions attributed to the Prophet, stating: 'Every *mujtahid* (jurist who strives to find the correct answer) is correct', or 'Every *mujtahid* will be [justly] rewarded.'[2] This implied that there could be more than a single correct answer to the same exact question. For Muslim jurists, this raised the issue of the purpose or the motivation behind the search for the divine will. What is the divine purpose behind setting out indicators to the divine law and then requiring that human beings engage in a search? If the divine wants human beings to reach the correct understanding, how can every interpreter or jurist be correct?

The juristic discourse focused on whether or not the shari'a had a determinable result or demand in all cases, and, if there is such a determinable result or demand, are Muslims obligated to find it? Put differently, is there a correct legal response to all legal problems, and are Muslims charged with the legal obligation to find that response? The overwhelming majority of Muslim jurists agreed that good faith

---

[1] S. Mahmassani, *Falsafat al-Tashri' fi al-Islam*, 3rd edn (Beirut, 1961), pp. 21–24, 199–200; B.G. Weiss, *The Spirit of Islamic Law* (Athens, GA, 1998), pp. 119–121.

[2] The Arabic is *kull mujtahid musib* and *li kull mujtahid nasib*. Muslim jurists also debated a report attributed to the Prophet in which he says: 'Whoever performs *ijtihad* and is correct will be rewarded twice and whoever is wrong will be rewarded once.'

Foundations 21

and diligence in searching for the divine will are sufficient to protect a searcher from liability before God. Beyond this, jurists were divided into two main camps. The first, known as the *mukhatti'a*, argued that ultimately there is a correct answer to every legal problem, but that only God knows what the correct response is, and the truth will not be revealed until the Final Day. Humans, for the most part, cannot conclusively know whether they have found that correct response. In this sense, every *mujtahid* is correct in trying to find the answer. However, one seeker might reach the truth while the others might mistake it. Correctness here means that the *mujtahid* is to be commended for putting in the effort, but it does not mean that all responses are equally valid.

The second camp, the *musawwiba*, includes prominent jurists such as al-Juwayni (1028–1085), Jalal al-Din al-Suyuti (1445–1505), Abu Hamid al-Ghazali (1058–1111) and Fakhr al-Din al-Razi (1149–1210). It is reported that the Muʿtazila (the rationalist school of thought) were in this camp as well.[3] The *musawwiba* argued that there is no specific and correct answer (*hukm muʿayyan*) that God wants human beings to discover, in part because if there were a correct answer, God would have made the evidence conclusive and clear. God cannot charge human beings with the duty to find the correct answer when there is no objective means to discovering the correctness of a textual or legal problem. Legal truth, or correctness, in most circumstances depends on belief and evidence, and the validity of a legal rule or act is often contingent on the rules of recognition that provide for its existence. Humans are charged with the duty diligently to investigate a problem and then to follow the results of their own *ijtihad*, or intellectual investigation. Al-Juwayni explains this point by asserting: 'The most a *mujtahid* would claim is a preponderance of belief (*ghalabat al-zann*) and the balancing of the evidence. However, certainty was never claimed by any of them (the early jurists) … If we were charged with finding [the truth] we would not have been forgiven for failing to find it.'[4] In essence, human beings are expected to search, to live a life fully and thoroughly engaged with the divine.

Building on this intellectual heritage, I suggest that the shariʿa ought to stand in an Islamic polity as a symbolic construct for the divine perfection that is unreachable by human effort – a concept summed up in the Islamic tradition by the word *husn*, or beauty. It is the epitome

---
[3] For a discussion of the two schools, see W. al-Zuhayli, *al-Wasit fi Usul al-Fiqh al-Islami*, 2nd edn (Beirut, 1969), pp. 638–655.

[4] al-Juwayni, *Kitab al-Ijtihad* (Damascus, 1987), pp. 50–51.

of justice, goodness and beauty as conceived and retained by God. Its perfection is preserved, so to speak, in the mind of God, but anything that is channelled through human agency is necessarily marred by human imperfection. Put differently, the shari'a as conceived by God is flawless, but as understood by human beings is imperfect and contingent. Jurists ought to continue exploring the ideal of the shari'a, and expound on their imperfect attempts at understanding. As such, the shari'a is always a work in progress, a juristic argument about what God commands, and only potentially God's law.

This does not exclude the possibility of universal moral standards. It simply shifts the responsibility for moral commitments, and the outcome of such commitments to human beings. Morality could originate with God, or could be learned by reflecting on the state of nature that God has created, but the attempts to fulfil such a morality and give it actual effect are human. The paradigm proposed here would require certain moral commitments from human beings that ought to be adopted as the discharge of their agency on God's behalf.[5] While I may claim as a Muslim that moral rules emanate or originate from God, I cannot claim that any set of laws that attempt to implement or give effect to this moral commitment are divine.

Is the Qur'anic text locked into a specific set of meanings that cannot be reinterpreted or renegotiated by its readers? Do the *hudud* (fixed) criminal penalties remain an ultimate normative goal that can never be abandoned? To a great extent, the responses to these questions depend on our understanding of the nature and source of normative obligations in the shari'a, and the extent to which we expect the divinely inspired text to yield determinative results that transcend human contingencies. Alternatively, our responses are a function of how we understand the interpretive process to be guided by overriding evaluative principles such as compassion or reasonableness, which mediate and ultimately define the parameters of a legitimate negotiation between the human reader and the divine text.

II

Part of the predicament of shari'a discourses today is the ambiguity over the issue of the state and its obligation to implement a set of positive commandments that embody or represent the divine will.

---

[5] See R. Kane, *Through the Moral Maze: Searching for Absolute Values in a Pluralistic World* (New York, 1994).

Foundations   23

Puritanical Islamism has resolved this question by recognising the state's competence to claim that certain determinable laws are in fact divine and granting the state the power to implement these laws in God's name. Paradoxically, this ends up negating and undermining the very point of the shari'a. By ignoring the pressures of contemporary cosmopolitanism and the changing nature of the socialised being, this approach ends up defeating the pursuit of virtues such as justice, equity and fairness, as well as the imperative of reasonableness (*ta'aqqul wa al-'aqlaniyya*), in the mechanisms of the shari'a. The result of approaches that reduce the shari'a to a code enforced by the state in God's name is to degrade the shari'a's vital role as a normative agent for inspiration and moral guidance in Muslim lives.

My argument here is not about the separation of state and church, or whether religion should play a role in the public sphere. Indeed, my argument is that in Muslim societies, the state's position towards the shari'a should be akin to a modern state's duties towards the ethics of virtue. I do not believe that the modern state should remain neutral towards the existence or legitimacy of virtue ethics, or the obligation to search and pursue goodness and avoid harm. But this does not mean that the state should be granted the power or discretion to decide what constitutes the real meaning of virtue, to the exclusion of competing views or interpretations.

The issue of the state and its relationship to the shari'a depends, in large part, on how the shari'a is understood in the modern age. If it is seen as a basic value system equivalent to natural virtues, goodness and beauty, then it is far more feasible to reconcile a commitment to the shari'a with a commitment to non-authoritarian systems of governance. But if the state can exploit the shari'a to shelter itself from civic accountability and to immunise determinations made in the name of God, then it becomes difficult to maintain the requisite space for autonomy and self-development necessary for democratic governance. It is important at this juncture to recall the conceptual framework on which all definitions of the shari'a rely, and the relationship of the shari'a to objective values and to human subjectivities.

In classical paradigms of Islamic jurisprudence, the law of the state, as opposed to the law of God, was never recognised as objectively good or morally correct. The law of the state was always contingent and contextual. It was authoritative because it is the positive law of the land, and not because it is objectively correct or good. The legitimacy of the state's law was a function of the soundness or reasonableness of the state's interpretation of the rational and natural divine will. Therefore, the legitimacy of state law was invariably negotiable, contestable and, ultimately, accountable to objective shari'a values as argued and claimed by human beings. State law was thought to be based on political expedience, public interests and functionality. Hence the shari'a played a largely limiting, negative role in relation to the law of the state: it would only serve to censor or void state laws that were clearly in contravention of shari'a principles.

Classical jurists would underscore that what distinguishes and differentiates an Islamic legal system from other legal systems is that the sultan's or prince's legal authority is constrained and limited by the law of God; other non-Muslim legal systems were either limited by customary cultural practices without guiding principles or limitations, or gave absolute sovereignty to the crown that was fettered only by its own discretion. If a Muslim ruler violated his fiduciary duties towards the governed, he was liable for the grave sin of treachery and breach of trust before God. Some commentators contended that breach of trust could justify punishing the ruler, or removing him from office by force if necessary.[6]

What made jurists' law a presumptive part of the shari'a, executive rules of the state and rules based on customs and social practices not a part of the shari'a, was that executive and custom-based law were regarded as based on expedience rather than on principles of justice. There is a significant difference between the Islamic communal systems of law applied over many centuries in Muslim polities and the symbolic construct of the shari'a, which was employed as an archetypal signifier for the justice, dignity or mercy ordained by God. Hence it is not at all surprising to find throughout history both rebels and their opponents sincerely appealing to shari'a as an objective, and as the ultimate source of legitimacy for their respective positions. A substantial philosophical and jurisprudential discourse emerged that explored the relationship of the shari'a to ultimate moral values and virtues. Ibn Qayyim al-Jawziya (1292–1350) described the shari'a thus:

> The shari'a is God's justice among His servants, and His mercy among His creatures. It is God's shadow on this earth. It is His wisdom, which leads to Him in the most exact way and the most exact affirmation of the truthfulness of His Prophet. It is His light, which enlightens the seekers and His guidance for the rightly guided. It is the absolute cure for all ills and the

---

[6] A. al-Mawardi, *al-Ahkam al-Sultaniyya wa al-Wilayat al-Diniyya* (Cairo, 1983); K. Abou El-Fadl, 'The Centrality of Shari'ah to Government and Constitutionalism in Islam', in *Constitutionalism in Islamic Countries: Between Upheaval and Continuity*, in R. Grote and T. Roder, ed. (Oxford, 2011).

Foundations

straight path which if followed will lead to righteousness ...
Every good in this life is derived from it and achieved through
it, and every deficiency in existence results from its dissipation.
If it had not been for the fact that some of its rules remain
[in this world,] this world would become corrupted and the
universe would be dissipated ... For the shari'a which was
sent to His Prophet ... is the pillar of existence and the key to
success in this world and the Hereafter.[7]

Many such as al-Kindi (801–873) argued for a profound affinity
between the shari'a and *fadila*, or the virtue of achieving godliness
within oneself. Al-Ghazali argued that it is impossible for the shari'a
to diverge from civic value. Yet others saw the shari'a as an embodiment
of genuine and true philosophical wisdom (*hikma*). Of course, there
is also the very important orientation represented by Ibn Rushd (1126–
1198) that tended to see the shari'a as a blessed revealing light; he
believed the intellect to be the same, so 'the light of one cannot negate
the light of the other'. Still others emphasised the profound affinity
between the shari'a and *ihsan* or *husn* (the elevation of humans to a
beautified state of godliness).[8]

This did not mean that these approaches were willing to ignore the
literal command of the text when it conflicted with their theory of
reason, virtue, goodness or beauty. Muslims today often ask whether
jurists are willing to overlook the prescription of a legal text while
giving their own moral vision or sense of justice priority. This misses
the point: the real issue has always been the extent to which various
legal approaches are willing to devise methodological legal techniques
to navigate an explicit legal text, to achieve the higher objectives of the
legal system.

The shari'a was never simply a collection of positive prescriptions
or rules, nor was it only based on textual commands claiming to be
rooted in varying degrees in divine revelation. With the exception of
the most literalist and strict constructionist school, such as the followers
of Ahmad Ibn Hanbal (780–855), all legal schools understood that
claiming to read texts as if one is unpacking a mathematical equation
is a delusion. The irony is that even the Hanbali school produced some

---

[7] Ibn Qayyim al-Jawziyya, in 'Abd al-Rahman al-Wakil, ed., *I'lam al-Muwaqqi'in 'an Rabb al-'Alamin*, ed. (Cairo, n.d.), vol. 3, pp. 5–6.
[8] S. Murata and W. Chittick, *The Vision of Islam* (New York, 1994),
pp. 141–164; T. Izutsu, *Ethico-Religious Concepts in the Qur'an* (Montreal, 2002),
pp. 221–226.

of the most analytical and normatively dynamic legal scholars in the medieval period, such as Ibn Aqil, Najm al-Din al-Tufi and Ibn Qayyim al-Jawziyya. Whatever the approach of a school of thought or jurist, the innate relationship between the principles of natural justice and the shari'a has been a firm and unwavering part of Muslim consciousness from the earliest times. However, the ways in which this relationship is understood and expressed diverge greatly from one historical context to another, always deeply influenced by the prevailing ideas of the age. What remains constant is the association of the shari'a with natural justice, right or goodness, whether articulated in terms of the utopian city-state of philosopher kings or the modern making of civil societies and democratic polities.

It is naïve and misleading to believe that it is possible to avoid or ignore the specific social and intellectual context of each cultural age. And there is a serious problem with arguing that God intended to lock the context of the 7th century into the immutable text of the Qur'an, and hold Muslims hostage to this epistemology for all ages to come. As Muslim theologians would put it, since God has foreknowledge of coming changes and challenges, His mercy would enable adherents to have the tools to effectively deal with such shifts. To insist that the Qur'an is entirely bound by history may help to explain the contextual circumstances of the text and its discourses. Yet this approach would reduce the Qur'an to the historical particulars of the 7th century, with no larger meaning that is transcendent.

In my view, the issue is what the Qur'anic determination meant when it was revealed, and, assuming that the Qur'an is an active and dynamic ongoing revelation, what an historical determination means today. For instance, if we consider the *hudud* penalties in the Qur'an, these were well within the range of criminal penalties imposed at the time; they were not understood then as exceptional or unusual. I do not think that the prescribed penalties for specific acts of misconduct were intended to sanctify those forms of punishment over all others. Rather, there were reasons for these Qur'anic prescriptions – none of them having to do with the method of punishment – that were about the moral condemnation of certain acts of misconduct. The term '*hudud*' connotes the guarding of specific ethical boundaries.[9] Many Muslims today believe that the purpose behind the *hudud* penalties is effective deterrence. Yet criminal deterrence, as opposed to moral denunciation and censure, was not part of the relevant

---

[9]   *Hadd* (pl. *hudud*) means boundary, borderline or limit.

Foundations 27

epistemological dynamic of the *hudud* Qur'anic verses.[10] It would be quite unreasonable to leap from the logic of deterrence in ancient Mosaic laws, or the laws of Medina in the 7th century, to a claim about deterrence in the very different social and economic realities of the 21st century.

There is a further consideration here with regard to the coercive powers that the modern state may claim to punish offenders in the name of God. When Qur'anic prescriptions addressed the Prophet and his community of early Muslims, law was governed by communal standards that adhered to very different rules of inclusion and exclusion from our own. This is powerfully demonstrated in the Qur'anic discourse in which a rhetorical but potent question is put to people who were oppressed and subjugated: 'Was not God's earth spacious enough for you to move away?'[11] Today, this might imply something different from what was originally intended. It could refer to the spiritual, moral and intellectual space that needs to be reclaimed by the oppressed to resist subjugation and maintain a reasonable autonomy of conscience. Physical migration, autonomy and communal self-determination are far more complex in the age of nation-states, monitored boundaries and passports. And the state's ability to obtain coercive compliance to its laws through the use of force is diametrically enhanced by the current advances in communication, surveillance and the processing of information. Part of the modern state's arsenal of power and control is the practice of codifying laws, so that ultimately it is the state that retains the power to define legal causes, material interests and the procedural rules of the very mechanics by which grievances are raised and resolved.

Traditional Islamic law worked through semiautonomous legal guilds that resembled the common law system in its most salient features. The Islamic legal system was communal in the sense that the processes for resolving conflicts and disputes relied heavily on localised customs and practices, and on the mitigating and negotiating functions played by community elders, tribal chiefs and semiofficial neighbourhood patriarchs (e.g. the *shaykh al-hara*, the *mukhtar* and the *'umda* respectively, among many others in the cultures of the Muslim world). This network of community leaders provided an invaluable resource for the judiciary in assessing the credibility

---

[10] See I. Rabb, 'Islamic Legal Maxims as Substantive Canons of Construction: *Ḥudūd*-Avoidance in Cases of Doubt', *Journal of Islamic Law & Society*, 17 (2010), pp. 63–125.

[11] Qur'an, 4:97.

of witnesses, and in reaching reasonable judgments within the matrix of dominant social and cultural practices. These community elders usually gained respect and credibility not so much for their wise decisions or probative judgments but for their ability to act as consensus-builders, to consult with influential notables, and to settle or resolve conflicts without involving the state. Therefore when inspecting certain genres of text in the classical jurisprudential tradition, such those on *ahkam al-qada* (judicial processes) and *al-mukhasamat wa'l munaza'at* (litigation), one notices that judges often sought to have litigants work with community leaders to resolve or arbitrate conflicts amicably. Communal arbitration or conflict resolution was deemed more conducive to the preservation of social harmony than formal litigation or official judicial determinations.

Muslim jurists resisted codification and also the co-optation of the legal system by the state well into the Ottoman and Safavid periods. The real challenge is that the communal model of judicial administration that developed in the Islamic legal system, which relied on legal pluralism and the differentiation between the law of the state and the common or communal law, required strong social institutions with a balance of power between the state, judiciary, tradesmen and mercantile classes, landed nobility and, most importantly, professional guilds such as the Islamic law guilds. Amid the rise and fall of various ruling dynasties, it was the social institutions and guilds, especially the vast network of Islamic *awqaf* (endowments), that gave the Islamic civilisation its intellectual and cultural continuity.

Colonialism, with its system of economic and legal capitulations and the creation of mixed courts, started a systematic movement towards legal codification that eventually led to the dismantling of the traditional Islamic system. The formidable challenge is that sociologically communal legal systems take many centuries to construct but that the movement towards codification, like other drifts towards centralisation and consolidation of power, is swift. In the modern age, even countries with a solid common law tradition have found themselves drawn towards statutory restatements of legal doctrines. This underscores the predicament of the shari'a today. All modern attempts at grafting some form of Islamic law upon existing modern political systems in Afghanistan, Nigeria, Pakistan or Saudi Arabia, for example, have only produced grotesque mutations that cannot be identified as being part of any recognisable legal tradition.

But my point here is even more basic. In contemporary democratic systems of governance, the law belongs to the people and their representatives. Modern political theories presume that sovereignty belongs to the citizenry of the state, and thus the citizenry is the

Foundations   29

source of legitimacy which includes the legitimacy of power and law. Indeed, all states whether democratic or despotic claim to govern in the name of their citizenry, and base their claim of authority over law on their purported status as the people's representatives. This implies that controlling, navigating and changing the law is regarded as a critical function of the modern state. It is practically inevitable that any attempt to apply Islamic law in the contemporary system of nation-states will place the state in the position of the custodian and guardian of that law. In other words, what Muslim jurists resisted for more than a millennium has now become the inescapable reality. To say the least, this constitutes a radical reconstructing of the whole epistemological framework of Islamic jurisprudence.

At this point it is useful to return to a theme mentioned earlier, one that a contemporary scholar has aptly called 'the fatigue' of the shari'a.[12] The classical debate flagged the ominous prospect of a time when the shari'a would cease to be relevant among Muslims, when divine guidance would elude humanity because people, and Muslims in particular, would have turned away from His grace. Interestingly, in the writings of the classical scholars, the most often imagined circumstance for this occurrence was a time when all the gifted and truly qualified scholars of the shari'a became either irrelevant or extinct. There are a number of ways of understanding this debate. It is possible that Muslim jurists imagined that, because of the lack of piety or proper spirituality, it would become increasingly difficult for students of the shari'a to comprehend fully or appreciate its purposes and commands. But it is also possible that Muslim jurists imagined that believers themselves would become so alienated from their religion that they would no longer be willing to defer to the guidance provided by the shari'a specialists. In other words, it is possible to see this perceived danger as either a supply or demand problem, one in which the supply or production of competent jurists would become scarce, or alternatively one in which the demand for competent jurists would dry out or become minimal.

Importantly, the imagined predicament was not thought to be in the vanishing of the instruments of shari'a application or enforcement. The classical scholars did not conceive of the problem as one in which the rulers would no longer implement Islamic law. Yet in the minds of most modern Islamists, it is supposedly the failure of the state to enforce and implement Islamic law that is the very definition of failure and lack of commitment to the shari'a. However, I think the problem is

---

[12]   A. Ahmad, *The Fatigue of Shari'a* (New York, 2012).

more complex. If the state adopts a single determinative interpretation of the law of God, and implements it without regard to competing interpretations and constructions, the state has in fact caused the extinction of the shari'a: it has in effect usurped the shari'a and equated the state's interpretations to the will and truth of God.

Alternatively, if the state keeps all shari'a values out of the public sphere and insists that all demands and all articulations of normative values be made in strictly non-religious and non-shari'a terms, this also means effectively the extinction of the shari'a. The exclusion of the shari'a from the public sphere extinguishes the possibility of furthering godliness in society. If religion is excluded from the public sphere, this only means that the shared space occupied by civic institutions favours non-religious rationales, arguments and values. If in the public arena non-religious justifications are favoured over religious justifications, it is disingenuous to pretend that the space dedicated to the functioning of civil society is neutral towards what may be called godliness. According to the logic of the shari'a, Muslims are obligated to investigate what God wants from and for them, and to pursue divine goodness, not just within the realm of their own private consciences but also by to striving to advocate and promote godliness in the norms that guide society as far as possible. The theological demand to bear witness on God's behalf, and to enjoin the good and resist what is not good (*al-amr bi'l ma'ruf wa'l-nahy 'an al-munkar*), is core to the imperative of furthering godly social norms. For the sake of brevity, I shall refer to the obligation of striving to promote guiding social norms that reflect divine values as 'the imperative of godliness'.

The imperative of godliness is emphasised repeatedly in the Qur'an, in a narrative that calls on Muslims to be a nation of people who enjoin goodness and resist wrongfulness as a necessary function of bearing witness for the divine.[13] On the one hand, it is reasonable to believe that the imperative of godliness mandates that the state be involved in upholding, or rather protecting, the divine boundaries in some way or fashion. But to presume that the state has an exclusive claim to knowing what is good or bad, or that it is especially qualified to understand or pursue godliness, is highly problematic. In fact, as noted above, because of its exceptional ability to leverage power, the modern state is especially positioned to exploit the label of godliness for very ungodly reasons. Moreover, very often the imperative of godliness and the obligation to bear witness mandate that just people testify against power, and not for it. More often than

---

[13]   Qur'an, 3:104, 110, 114; 4:114; 7:157; 9:71, 112; 22:41; 31:17.

Foundations   31

not, the very possession of power, especially the kind of power that is backed by the exclusive right to use force, is fundamentally at odds with godliness.

It is somewhat of a paradox, then, that the imperative of godliness requires the modern state to respect and safeguard certain values and virtues, such as human dignity and the sanctity of life, as God-given objective truths. For the same imperative makes it critical that people bear witness against the state's mishandling or abuse of these objective truths. From an Islamic perspective, while it is important that the respect and honour of the principle of godliness be upheld, it is exceedingly dangerous that the state be permitted the pretence of being godly. Because power is inherently corrupting, one must be cognisant of the fact that the truly just or pious will stand at a distance from power. It is reasonable to expect that the state should respect the principle of godliness, and it is reasonable for just people to demand that the state act in ways that are consistent with this principle. It is also critical that it be understood that the modern state is inherently corrupted by power and that, ultimately, godliness cannot be achieved through the power of the state.

Even more, in the modern age, fields of knowledge such as political science and the sociology and psychology of power demand that there be a new epistemological paradigm shift in the way we think about the state, the shari'a and power. In this paradigm shift, we need to recall that once the jurists, the traditional defenders of the shari'a, were co-opted by power, they lost all legitimacy and credibility, and for the most part became corrupted themselves. Once co-opted, the juristic class lost its influence over the hearts and minds of Muslims. Hence the required paradigm shift is not for the shari'a to become part of the oppressive apparatus of the modern state but rather for the shari'a, as the symbol of God's normative order, to become the vehicle by which testimony is rendered for God and against power.

The modern state cannot and should not pretend to be the representative of God's law. The state is not a consecrated church that has been empowered to discover God's will, and in all cases the coercive power of the state makes its enforcement of some version of God's law inherently oppressive and tyrannical. Yet there is no question that Islam obligates its followers to search for and act on divine guidance. There is an inevitable tension in the idea of an objective or determinative shari'a that ought to be asserted in opposition to state power, but not by the state in furtherance of its power. If the shari'a were an objective and determinative set of divine commands then it would follow that the state, civil society and individuals would be able to comprehend and assert it. In other words, if the shari'a is a known set of laws – of dos and don'ts, or rights and wrongs – it ought to follow that these known laws could be validly asserted. Indeed, it is common among many Muslims to claim either that the shari'a is a quantifiable and known sum that should be faithfully applied by the state, or that Muslims can never quantify a well-defined and known shari'a and, therefore, it ought not be applied at all. I find both approaches to be unsatisfying. When I encounter revelation that commands Muslims to rule by God's law or to act as a nation that pursues goodness and resists evil, I do not believe that the Qur'an is commanding what is impossible or non-existent.[14] The life of the Prophet Muhammad is a testimonial and exemplar, to Muslims not just as individuals but also as social communities. However, social and communal obligations do not necessarily have to be state duties; in fact, they must not be so.

Reason and revelation are both engaged in the search for guidance which Islamic jurisprudence calls textual and rational indicators. All believers are deputised to represent godliness on earth, a key doctrinal principle for Muslims (*khilafat Allah* or vicegerency). However, it is unrealistic to expect that the citizenry at large of a modern state will base its social demands and desires on a sagacious and diligent study of the rational and textual indicators of the divine will. So one may reasonably enquire as to who, then, speaks for the divine will in our modern age, and how God's law is to play any meaningful role. These questions are not about the institutions or instrumentalities of the political system in modernity but about the very nature of divine guidance. We must differentiate between the nature of guidance and what makes the norms of guidance obligatory. It might be that whether a norm is obligatory or not depends on my subjective belief as to whether such a belief is mandatory. Yet my subjective belief about whether I am bound by such a norm tells us nothing about the nature of the norm itself. In other words, whether I consider myself bound by the norm or not does not affect the nature of that norm, which could truly be from God or be a product of my personal delusions. At the same time, the understanding, articulation and assertion of divine norms can hardly be free from subjective contingencies. Since God's law is discoverable through reason and revelation, which involves the deployment of rational indicators as well as textual indicators in reflecting on particular issues, subjectivities are deeply engaged. The very meaning of rationality is epistemologically contingent: our understanding of logic, relativity, proportionality, and time and space is constantly developing. Likewise, our understanding of the texts of

---

[14] Qur'an, 2:213; 3:79, 81; 4:58, 105; 5:44–45, 47, 49; 6:114; 8:46; 24:51.

Foundations   33

revelation is not fixed but epistemologically contingent and developing. Our grasp of the nature of texts and their symbolic functions, and more broadly of philology, hermeneutics, narrative, social memory, communities of meaning, and historical transmissions and transfusions, is in constant flux. The search for divine reason is, critically, a process of reasoning with God.

III

The Qur'anic mandate to enjoin the good and resist evil is addressed to the umma as a whole. Numerous Qur'anic prescriptions call on societies to establish justice or conduct all affairs through consultation, all of which likewise impose collective obligations towards the making of societies that bear witness for God. The shari'a's concern with social acts is again evident in the central idea of *maqasid al-shari'a al-kulliyya*, or the overarching objectives of the shari'a. According to this doctrine, the shari'a aims to protect five essential social values: life, lineage, reputation, mind or reason, and property, though many jurists add religion as a sixth.[15] In other words, a vital component of what makes the shari'a a path to goodness, or godliness, is that it is acutely engaged with social values or the norms that ought to prevail in society. Although not all jurists historically added religion as one of the core values of the shari'a, there can be little doubt that Muslim theorists at large held religion to be a foundational value for a healthy society. Most jurists further divided the basic shari'a values into two types: protection through affirmative and positive acts (*al-hifz min janib al-wujud wa al-ijad*) and protection through prevention of negative or counter-acts (*al-hifz min janib al-'adam aw al-man'*). In effect, this juristic distinction is between establishing a virtuous society affirmatively and preventing the corruption of society defensively. This duality is repeated in the Qur'anic norm of enjoining good and resisting evil as a primary or first-order obligation.

Returning to the initial question, do modern Muslims need the shari'a? Do not logic and reason potentially offer a sufficient basis for all of our mores and morals, as well as for the pursuit of social virtues? I believe that reason and rationality can interrogate social values. Reason can decipher good from its opposite, and can establish and defend first

---

[15] M. Kamali, *Principles of Islamic Jurisprudence*, 3rd edn (Cambridge, 2005); A. al-Raysuni, *Imam Al-Shatibi's Theory of the Higher Objectives and Intents of Islamic Law* (London, 2005), pp. 317–323.

34   *The Shariʿa*

principles of ethics, such as reciprocity or treating people as you would like to be treated. But the shariʿa provides a metanarrative of admirable or praiseworthy attributes, which acknowledge the qualities of character necessary for virtuous personhood. Modern Muslims often repeat the dogma that the shariʿa is a way of life. On its face, this statement is true, but not because of the oft-held view that the shariʿa has hard-and-fast rules which apply to every action a person might take. The shariʿa is a way of life because it is a path of salvation and redemption from the moral failures of egoism and idolatry.

The shariʿa is not a path on which believers submit their will, reason and autonomy to God, and in return are shepherded to the heavenly pastures. It is a path that necessarily begins with human beings becoming the trustees and viceroys of God on earth. By virtue of this trust, human beings are dignified and honoured with the autonomy of choice.[16] The instrument of choice and attribute of our own divinity is rationality – the capacity to think, reflect, ponder and decide. By rationality, I do not mean the philosophical power of reasoning but the ability to acknowledge the attributes of goodness and the obligation to be good. Most importantly, human beings have been honoured and dignified by God in being endowed with the capacity to grow morally and elevate towards higher states of being. However, this is not a simple mechanical, pedantic process during which a person attains a moment, or multiple moments, of absolution.

According to the Islamic tradition, the possibilities and the potentialities for growth exist not only because of God's compassion and mercy but also through engagements with the divine in moments of doubt and certitude, trial and error, disappointment and triumph. In other words, through the process of reasoning with the divine, a reciprocated love of God is sought in which a state of peace and tranquillity is achieved. Self-knowledge becomes possible through the dialectics of self-engagement, through compliance and rebellion. A tradition attributed to the Prophet holds: 'Whoever comes to know oneself, will come to know his Lord.'[17] Reasoning with God is a process in which the quest is godliness. This quest uses all the indicators of God, rational and revelatory, to reflect and achieve the balance necessary for a just and good character.

---

[16]   Qur'an, 7:69, 74; 27:62. See F. Rahman, *Major Themes of the Qur'an* (Chicago, 1980), pp. 54–60.

[17]   See A. ibn ʿUmar Abu Zayd al-Dabusi, *Taqwim al-Adilla fi Usul al-Fiqh* (Beirut, 2001), vol. 2, p. 452. See also Ibn ʿArabi, *Divine Governance of the Human Kingdom*, trans. T. Bayrak al-Jerrahi al-Halveti (Louisville, KY, 1997), pp. 231–254.

Foundations 35

How does the quest for godliness inform our discussion about social acts, and about the role of the shari'a in modern polities? At the individual level, embracing the shari'a in an effort to grow into godliness is a duty on any person desiring to be a Muslim. But beyond this personal commitment, any community of Muslims has an obligation of unity, cooperation, mutuality and support. This is powerfully expressed in the Qur'anic exhortations: 'Let there be arising from you a nation inviting to all that is good, enjoining what is right and forbidding what is wrong' and 'Cooperate in righteousness and piety, but do not cooperate in sin and aggression.'[18] Further, the Prophet Muhammad is reported to have said: 'Help your brother whether he is an oppressor or is oppressed ... You can keep him from committing oppression. That will be your help to him.'[19] Muslims are reminded of their obligation, not only individually but also collectively, to search for and promote attributes that recognise and reinforce the qualities of character necessary for a virtuous society.

In reason-based arguments, one is forced to find a rational justification, not just for the construction of social units, such as civil society, but also to overcome the theoretical challenge of explaining why such social units ought to serve a normative moral good, such as justice or equality. The shari'a, however, situates the source of obligation for purposeful social growth within the narrative of revelation. Secular social theories can provide a rational defence as to why it would be in the best interests of every member of society if individuals were guaranteed basic civil rights. These basic rights could be premised on the promotion of happiness, the potential for intellectual growth and the preservation of human dignity inter alia.

The shari'a, on the other hand, is an ongoing discourse about how to be a good Muslim within a communal system and a metanarrative on being a good human being within human society. As the history of Islamic legal guilds demonstrates, it is not important that Muslims agree on the same determinations or laws. What matters is that they recognise shared common standards of virtue and godliness. At a minimum, the ultimate objective is peace, repose and tranquillity (i.e. *salam*). But this *salam* cannot exist without justice (*qist*), balance and proportionality (*mizan* and *tawazun*), compassion, love and care for one another (*tarahum*, *tahabub* and *takaful*). There is an interdependent relationship between these elements and the essential values of the shari'a (life, intellect

---

[18] Qur'an, 3:104; 5:2.
[19] Imam al-Nawawi, in M. 'Abd al-'Aziz and A. 'Ali, ed., *Riyad al-Salihin* (Cairo, 1994), 103.

or mind, reputation, lineage or family and property). I find it highly doubtful that the constituent elements of a virtuous or godly society are possible unless the essential values and their necessary derivatives are guaranteed and protected. Again, this is not about the shariʻa as a set of laws (*ahkam*) or adjudications (*qada*). Rather, it is about the shariʻa as normative discourse on what is good and bad, and about what ought or ought not to be.

Mindful of its larger historical context, cultural roots and communal engagement, the shariʻa becomes a metanarrative about the foundational and defining norms of a people, at once transcendent and contingent in its outlook. It is a never-ending discourse about what ought to be eternal and what ought to be contingent, about who we are and what we could become. A shariʻa-oriented society is not about God as political sovereign – an idea that is fundamentally flawed and has been thoroughly taken apart in the course of Muslim history. A shariʻa-oriented society reasons with God. It consistently visits and revisits the rational and textual indicators to stay on the *sirat al-mustaqim*, the straight path, knowing full well that anyone who claims to have an exclusive claim over the *sirat* has by definition deviated from it. As the Qurʼan points out, the blessing of the *sirat* comes as an act of grace that can never be taken for granted.[20] Reasoning with God means endlessly searching and engaging the divine with hope and belief in God's continued guidance and grace.

Further Reading

Abou El-Fadl, Khaled. *The Great Theft: Wrestling Islam from the Extremists*. New York, 2007.

Abou El-Fadl, Khaled. *Reasoning with God: Reclaiming Shariʻah in the Modern Age*. London and New York, 2014.

Ahmad, Ahmad Atif. *The Fatigue of Shariʻa*. New York, 2012.

Al-Raysuni, Ahmed. *Imam Al-Shatibi's Theory of the Higher Objectives and Intents of Islamic Law*. Herndon, VA, 2005.

Auda, Jasser. *Maqasid al-Shariah as Philosophy of Islamic Law: A Systems Approach*. Herndon, VA, 2008.

Hefner, Robert. *Shariʻa Law and Modern Muslim Ethics*. Bloomington, IN, 2016.

Kamali, Mohamed Hashim. *Shariʻah Law: An Introduction*. Oxford, 2008.

---

[20] Qurʼan, 1:6–7; 2:142–143; 3:101; 20:133–135; 23:73–74; 37:118–128. On 'the straight path', see Rahman, *Major Themes of the Qurʼan*, pp. 3–20, 60.

Masud, Muhammad Khalid. *Shatibi's Philosophy of Islamic Law*. Islamabad, 1995.

Raab, Intisar. *Doubt in Islamic Law: A History of Legal Maxims, Interpretation, and Islamic Criminal Law*. New York, 2014.

Shihadeh, Ayman. *The Teleological Ethics of Fakhr al-Din al-Razi*. Leiden, 2006.

3

Recovering the Ethical:
Practices, Politics, Tradition

Ebrahim Moosa

'I asked Shaykh Abd-Rabbih al-Ta'ih: "How will the ordeal we are suffering end?"
He answered: "If we come out safe, that's a mercy: and if we come out doomed, that is justice."'

Naguib Mahfouz,
Echoes of an Autobiography (New York, 1997)

In this chapter I explore the relationship between religion and morality. Mindful that the idea of the shari'a is essential to Muslim tradition, and that this tradition is a guiding factor in Muslim life, I begin with an overview of how the shari'a has been thought about in innovative ways. A contemporary case study illustrates how interpreting the shari'a through a juridical lens can often belie the Qur'anic mandate to respect human dignity. I argue that the shari'a must be properly understood as an ethical paradigm, as it once was.

Muslim jurists in the past were aware of at least two aspects in the pursuit of the ethical. First, they coupled religion with morality. Second, they voiced the need to pursue intellectual creativity and innovation. Contemporary Muslim scholarship in ethics could profit from a deepened conversation around each aspect. Granted, ethics and morals are closely associated with the idea of religion (*din*) in the history of Muslim thought, but the debate about morality in Islam today demands finer distillation, elaboration and application of a comprehensive ethical approach. Explorations in ethical debates would profit from embracing an interdisciplinary stance, with a readiness for fresh thinking.

This approach is evident in the work of many classical philosophers. Contemporary experts in Islamic ethics, especially those who draw on the juristic tradition (fiqh), have been inattentive to subtle elements of the medieval canon and thus have also been negligent about innovation. Abu al-Hasan al-Mawardi (974–1058), the understudied Basra-born

40   *The Shariʻa*

jurist and judge (qadi), was a leading voice of the Shafiʻi school and a part-time diplomat for the Shiʻi Buyid dynasty. In his treatise *Ethics of the World and Religion* (*Adab al-dunya wa al-din*), he shows how morals are tied to the idea of salvation practices, known as *din*.[1] In contemporary times, *din* is often defined as religion, in line with the western understanding of the concept, with its bearing towards beliefs that operate in the private sphere. But *din* in al-Mawardi's understanding could mean a general way of life focusing on participation in the public sphere towards the common good.

Innovative Foundations

In the pre-modern Muslim lexicon, *din* referred to a normative order, the desire to conform to the principles of the community. Norms that inhabited the framework of *din* were derived from existing customs and conventions. Adherence to such principles signalled belonging to a norm-based community: performing these norms meant a commitment to that order. In its primary sense, *din* included those devotional and moral practices that were required for salvation. Similarly, it signified a public discourse of moral behaviour. Further, in 8th-century Arabia, *din* enabled one to think of salvation in a way that had both this-worldly effects and after-worldly consequences. Thus 'religion' here includes the performance of moral practices that serve salvation, and the performance of acts of good in this world.

In addition to al-Mawardi, many classical Muslim philosophers wrote mystical treatises and piety manuals framed as discussions about ethics. They found ways to link mysticism with the category of *din*. In much of the classical literature, the ethical and religious dimensions are viewed as almost inseparable. Many authors who studied Qurʼanic and prophetic traditions felt that acting on an ethical and a moral imperative was equal to meeting the requirements of religion itself. Many scholars wrote about how the possession of character and moral habits, known as *khuluq* (pl. *akhlaq*), meant being fully engaged in performing the acts of religion. In other words, the ethical underpins the very idea of religion, and religion sees its primary role as a host for ethical proclamations. A popular aphorism used by Muslims throughout history states that one cannot claim to perform acts of salvation (*din*) if one does not possess ethics (*la din li man la akhlaq lahu*). The

---

[1]   C. Brockelmann, 'al-Mawardi', *EI2*, vol. 6, p. 869.

Recovering the Ethical   41

renowned Hanbali authority Ibn al-Qayyim al-Jawziyya (1292–1350)[2] concluded: 'All of *din* (salvation practices/religion) was about morals.'[3]

In some ways, debates about religion and morals in medieval Islam are similar to the equally spirited debate in modern times. For Michael Oakeshott, a 20th-century British political theorist, the 'connection between religion and the moral life' is an obvious one, provided 'we could discover it.'[4] Drawing on the work of John Wood Oman, an early 20th-century philosopher and theologian, Oakeshott notes that religion may be viewed as identical with morality itself, or it may serve as a sanction for morality. He criticises both views as inadequate because they impede the development of moral personality in the ethical subject. Oakeshott sees religion as the completion of morality.[5] I agree with him and others who argue that moral responsibility requires a relatively high degree of autonomy. Further, it is acquired through the cultivation of personal insight or moral personality. Oakeshott's argument coincides with that of al-Mawardi, who also argued that religion served the role of completing morals. All of the preceding conversation can be summed up in the words of the famous prophetic tradition, where Muhammad described his mission thus: 'I was sent to perfect [literally "to complete", *li utammima*] excellence in morals.'[6] Furthermore, the Prophet often declared that the best among Muslims were the ones with the purest character/morals.

Al-Mawardi's creative ethical thinking has an abundance of wisdom for the modern person. In a bold insight, he described his method as one that will 'weld the verities of the jurists to the subtleties of the litterateurs.'[7] Certainly, he drew inspiration from the Qur'an and the Sunna, but he did not restrict his enquiry to these sources. He also drew on the parables found in the writings of philosophers and the literary insights found in the work of the rhetoricians and poets. This 11th-century scholar adopted a flamboyant approach as he felt confident addressing ethical concerns that affected salvation both in the present and in the afterlife.

---

[2] H. Laoust, 'Ibn Ḳayyim al-Ḏjawziyya', *EI2*, vol. 3, pp. 821–822.

[3] Muhammad ibn Abi Bakr Ibn Qayyim al-Jawziyya and Muhammad Hamid Faqīi, *Madarij al-salikin* (Beirut, 1973), vol. 2, p. 307.

[4] M.J. Oakeshott, *Religion, Politics, and the Moral Life*, ed. Timothy Fuller (New Haven, CT, 1993), p. 39.

[5] Ibid., 42.

[6] *Al-Muwatta of Imam Malik Ibn Anas, The First Formulation of Islamic Law*, rev. and trans. Aisha Abdurrahman Bewley (Inverness, 2004), Book 47 'Good Character', Hadith no. 8, p. 382.

[7] 'Ali ibn Muhammad al-Mawardi, *Adab al-dunya wa-al-din* (Beirut, 1987), p. 3.

42   *The Shari'a*

But why and how did al-Mawardi forge such a unique, interdisciplinary approach to knowledge? Perhaps he felt that the existing methods and sources used by the jurists were limiting. And, in order to move beyond what he deemed unsatisfactory outcomes, he needed to risk proposing a change in the method of how ethics were conceptualised. Risk, it is said, is the price paid for progress. Restricting oneself to limited sources of learning was unproductive. In al-Mawardi's words, 'The hearts take comfort in multiple disciplines (*funun*), and become bored with a single discipline.'[8] Literally, *funun* means art forms, but al-Mawardi used it to mean 'multiple disciplines [of art]'. Al-Mawardi extolled the benefits of finding solutions by drawing on multiple intellectual and disciplinary traditions. While others might have viewed the multiplicity of methods and insights as a stain on scholarship, al-Mawardi insisted that it was actually a blessing.

After all, words and their meanings (philology) shape and reveal our understanding of reality. In their multiplicity, words expose a complex pattern of existence. The polymath Ibn Arabi (1165–1240) wrote that spoken words and all other things that exist ('existents' or *mawjudat*) 'are the words of God (*kalimat Allah*)'.[9] How do existents come to be the words of God? In Ibn Arabi's view, existents become words as a result of 'aural signification' (*al-dalala al-sam'iyya*). Commonly known words, he explains, are composed as a result of a coherent organisation of letters. An external being, God or Providence inspires the coherence of letters that in turn are articulated by a living being. These utterances denote and connote a range of meanings in the form of what we call 'words'.

In asserting the importance of an interdisciplinary stance, al-Mawardi cited the Prophet's cousin, Ali b. Abi Talib, who declared: 'One's feelings [lit. hearts] become wearied, just as bodies become tired. Therefore, enliven the hearts with the most exquisite of wisdom.'[10] Ali's advice encouraged al-Mawardi to adopt a nomadic approach in the pursuit of knowledge. To bolster his approach, al-Mawardi recalled the habit of the Abbasid caliph al-Ma'mun (r. 813–833) who apparently paced about incessantly when thinking about a problem. When asked why he paced, al-Ma'mun was fond of reciting the noted poet Abu al-Atahiyya (748–ca. 825/6): 'One cannot make progress in planning, unless one constantly moves from one position to another.'[11]

---

[8] Ibid.

[9] Abu Bakr Muhyi al-Din Ibn 'Arabi, in Ahmad Shams al-Din, ed., *al-Futuhat al-Makkiya* (Beirut, 1999), vol. 4, p. 30, Bab 198.

[10] al-Mawardi, *Adab*, pp. 3–4.

[11] Ibid.

Recovering the Ethical   43

History, Tradition and Change

Given the authority of the canonical tradition in shaping fiqh, commonly translated as Islamic law or the shari'a, the very idea of change tends to be seen by 'traditionalists' as unwelcome. This is especially true in view of the power invested in Muslim clerics as the guardians of tradition. Yet the canonical tradition also provides sources in favour of change. Ibn Khaldun (1332–1406) noted that change is inherent to all societies. 'The condition of the world and of nations, their customs and sects, does not persist in the same form or in a constant manner,' he declared. 'There are differences ... and changes from one condition to another. "This is the custom of God already in effect among His servants or among mortals" [Qur'an, 40:85].'[12] Still, lamented Ibn Khaldun, 'Rarely do more than a few individuals become aware of it [change].'[13]

Other Muslim scholars viewed change less positively, fearing it would impinge on the ascetic ideals of Islam's origins. Piety-minded scholars often associated change with the end-times, when good and bad become inverted. The renowned polymath Abu Hamid al-Ghazali (1058–1111) used these tropes to show how degraded society had become in his time, citing remarks made by the Prophet's companions to support his claims. What was once approved or disapproved could, and frequently did, become reversed at other times, leaving society adrift.[14]

Ibn Khaldun, or any other sociologist, would agree that change may result in conventions and practices that were once deemed unfavourable becoming transmuted, and thus approved. For al-Ghazali, ethical shifts from the approved to the disapproved (and vice versa) were signs of the end-times. But a different hermeneutic can be applied to the apprehension voiced in this regard by some of the Prophet's companions. The litmus test for change rests on the vigilance of the learned in every era: as long as they were attentive to the truth (*haqq*) and the big picture of what was right, ethical change would not be catastrophic.

The examples which al-Ghazali provided make it clear that these were highly subjective matters, and his choices reflected his later ascetic

---

[12] 'Abd al-Rahman Ibn Khaldun, Darwish al-Juwaydi, ed., *Muqaddimat Ibn Khaldun* (Beirut, 2000), p. 35; Ibn Khaldun, *The Muqaddimah: An Introduction to History*, trans. Franz Rosenthal (New York and Princeton, 1980), vol. 1, pp. 56–57.

[13] Ibn Khaldun, *The Muqaddimah*, pp. 56–57.

[14] Abu Hamid Muhammad b. Muhammad al-Ghazali, *Ihya 'ulum al-din* (Beirut, 2001), vol. 1, p. 79.

44 *The Shariʿa*

orientation. Al-Ghazali objected to mosques being constructed of stone and marble, which he said were different from the construction of more modest mosques built during the Prophet's lifetime. Yet he could also have mentioned that, while in the early Muslim community taking a salary for teaching the Qur'an was frowned on, Muslim jurists nevertheless settled on the practice as permissible. Al-Ghazali guarded against introducing heretical beliefs and practices (*bidʿa*). He allowed, however, for new and constructive ones: one perpetrated 'heresy (*bidʿa*) only in defiance of a transmitted prophetic tradition'.[15] Al-Ghazali argued for understanding the totality of the shariʿa in a formula demarcated by the preservation of five things: religion, life, intellect, property and family.[16] This formulaic presentation was new at the time; today it is widely accepted as articulating the ethical aims of Islam.

The Shariʿa as Ethical Truth

Since al-Ghazali, other scholars have provided ethical definitions of the essentials of the shariʿa. 'The Shariʿa is designed in order to internalise the most exemplary character,' wrote Jamal al-Din al-Qasimi, an influential early 20th-century orthodox Muslim thinker.[17] Al-Qasimi's claim resonates with the words of al-Raghib al-Isfahani, a leading 11th-century scholar who wrote: 'The attractions of the shariʿa are wisdom, upholding justice among people, self-control, beauty, virtue and to adopt these excellences until you reach paradise in proximity to God the powerful and high.'[18]

In the 14th century, scholars in Baghdad debated the place of policy or politics in shariʿa governance. In *Paths of Governance*, Ibn Qayyim al-Jawziyya responded to this debate with a nod towards earlier scholars:

> The foundation of the shariʿa is wisdom and the safeguarding of people's interests in this world and the next. In its entirety it is justice, mercy and wisdom. Every rule that transcends from

---

[15] Ibid., vol. 2. p. 272.

[16] Abu Hamid Muhammad b. Muhammad al-Ghazali, Muhammad Sulayman al-Ashqar, ed., *al-Mustasfa min ʿilm al-usul*, 2 vols (Beirut, 1997).

[17] Jamal al-Din al-Qasimi, *Tafsir al-Qasimi al-musamma mahasin al-taʾwil*, 20 vols (Cairo, 1957).

[18] Abu al-Qasim al-Husayn ibn Muhammad al-Raghib al-Isfahani, *Kitab al-dhariʿa ila makarim al-Shariʿa*, ed. Abu al-Yazid Abu Zayd al-ʿAjami (Cairo, n.d.), p. 83.

justice to tyranny, mercy to its opposite, the good to evil, and wisdom to triviality does not belong to the shariʻa, although it might have been introduced into it by implication. The shariʻa is God's justice and mercy amongst His people. Life, nutrition, medicine, light, recuperation and virtue are made possible by it. Every good that exists is derived from it [the shariʻa], and every deficiency in being results from its loss and dissipation. For the shariʻa, which God entrusted His prophet to transmit, is the pillar of the world and the key to success and happiness in this world and the next.[19]

Similarly, Ibn Qayyim wrote in *Iʻlam*:

God sent His Prophets and revealed His books so that people could establish justice … When the indices of truth are established, when the proofs of reason are decided and become clear by whatever means, then surely that is the Law of God, His religion, His consent and His command. And God the sublime has not restricted the path [methods and sources] of justice and its indices, its signposts in one genus [of methods] to one thing, only to invalidate it in other methods, which are more clear, more explicit and self-evident. In fact, God clarified in terms of the paths that he had ordained that His purpose was to establish truth and justice and to ground people in equity. So by whatever means truth is established and justice is discovered then governance has to follow its obligation and demands. And paths [methods] are causes and means that are not intended on their own, rather the goal are the ends, namely the purposes…[20]

In this statement, Ibn Qayyim demonstrates his solidarity with fellow Hanbali scholar Abu al-Wafa Ibn Aqil (1040–1119), while being aware that it could be a treacherous path, filled with risks. Ibn Aqil equated shariʻa governance with justice and equity in matters of public policy and politics. He was interested in what made a government's authority legitimate. He questioned whether political authority must always be grounded in the Qur'an and Sunna. Ibn Aqil was a cosmopolitan Hanbali, and a deeply learned man. In making

---

[19] Ibn Qayyim al-Jawziyya, *al-Turuq al-hukmiyya* (Beirut, 1995).
[20] Al-Jazwiyya, *Iʻlam al-muwaqqiʻin ʻan rabb al-ʻalamin* (Beirut, 1998), vol. 4, p. 349.

46 *The Shari'a*

his case, he had to correct jurists who argued that his opinions were directed at the famous al-Shafi'i (767–820).[21] Al-Shafi'i was alleged to have claimed: 'There are no rules of governance (*siyasa*) except those which correspond or comply with the revelation (*shar'*).'[22] Ibn Aqil's response to this was: 'Look, governance is what actions people do in order to bring them closer to the good (*salah*), and to put themselves at a distance from corruption and harm (*fasad*). Even if it means those ways [of governance] are ones that the Prophet did not prescribe nor did revelation provide directives.'[23] Then, speaking rhetorically, he addressed al-Shafi'i and his other detractors: 'If you mean by *"there is no governance except that which corresponds to the revelation"* that governance is that which does not oppose what the revelation had uttered, then you are indeed right. But if you mean governance has to comply with what the revelation had uttered, then you are wrong.'[24]

In other words, Ibn Aqil said that he agreed with those jurists who concurred that there was broad agreement between the purposes of revelation and the practice of governance. He disagreed with their claim if they meant that every action of governance had to line up with a specific instruction from revelation. Ibn Aqil did not believe that revelation gave tutorials in advance of every future human contingency. In his view, it certainly did not apply in the realm of governance. By pushing against what sounded like rhetorical excess on the part of some jurists, he provided an interpretative resolution.

Like al-Mawardi, Ibn Aqil thought in terms of the big picture view of the shari'a. He did not allow practices developed in the cultural milieus of 7th-century Arabia, strikingly different from his own Iraq in the 11th century, to undo the big picture. Jurists such as Ibn Aqil and Ibn al-Jawzi were attentive to what scholars today call the anthropology and sociology of Islamic law – the social construction of shari'a practices. They attended to the logic of values and purposes behind the rules rather than being bogged down by the specifics of the law. Hence they did not support a divine command theory of the law.

The Shari'a as Ethical Norms

There is a conundrum in framing Muslim norms in the language of law, and in describing the shari'a as a legal system. The very idea of 'Islamic

---

[21] Al-Jawziyya, *al-Turuq al-hukmiyya* (Beirut, 1995), pp. 10–11.
[22] Al-Jazwiyya, *I'lam*, vol. 4, pp. 348–349.
[23] Ibid., vol. 4, p. 349.
[24] Ibid. Emphasis added by this author.

law' is, in many ways, a misnomer. While classical jurists (*fuqaha'*) adjudicated everything from prayers and fasting to war and trade, it is uncertain whether they were engaged in law-making as we understand law today. It would be more accurate to say they were engaged in identifying norms derived from teachings inspired by revelation as well as the experiences of the early Muslim communities, and in describing how these practices translated into the realities of their own societies. What is called 'Islamic law' could effectively be described as a vibrant tradition of translating norms into lived societies. Classical jurists linked revelation with lived reality. It is the absence of this sensibility that results in deeply troubling interpretations and applications of norms today.

One way forward in Muslim norm-making today is to think of Islamic law as an enterprise in ethics. In ethical thinking there are values that can be harnessed from the legal tradition which are often framed in a utilitarian idiom of interests (*masalih*). However, the legal and moral, as well as spiritual and philosophical, traditions of Islam also deliberate about the ethical as the essential imperatives that underpin the good life. Ultimately, this is about human flourishing and living a virtuous life.

The jurist and philosopher Ibn Rushd (1126–1198), also known as Averroes, wrote a well-known book called *The Jurist's Primer*. He explained that his writing on the shari'a might sound like duties and rules (*ahkam*) but, in reality, they were ethical and moral values. This might surprise those who think that the shari'a or Islamic law is a compendium of rigorous and uncompromising rules. Ibn Rushd asserted that the purpose of the shari'a, especially those tenets that are unenforceable via judicial authority, is to cultivate the virtues of the soul (*al-fada'il al-nafsaniyya*). Rituals and devotions (*'ibadat*), as well as the virtues that arise from observing these rituals, stem from what he called 'the norms of dignity (*al-sunan al-karamiyya*)'.[25]

Ibn Rushd also explained how the shari'a reinforces virtues such as decency, justice, courage and generosity. Practices regulating marriage and food cultivate decency, while those regulating war, criminal offences, torts and personal dignity all seek to cultivate justice. Similarly, practices regulating wealth and charity seek to cultivate generosity, while practices regulating governance and leadership enforce social equity. He pushed us to contemplate what he called the norms of dignity and brought the conversation about Islamic law back to ethics and morality.

---

[25] Abu al-Walid Ibn Rushd, *Bidayat al-mujtahid wa nihayat al-muqtasid* (Beirut, 1998), p. 389.

Negotiating the Ethical in Contemporary Muslim Ethics

Is the application of the shari'a a matter of complying with rules, or is it about purposes? The rule-based approach has a long history, one that lays claim to being the epitome of Muslim tradition. In Muslim-majority countries today, community groups, legislators and governments fervently seek to adopt the shari'a or Islamic laws. Often, these are attempts to burnish the credentials of politicians and legislators, making them out to be shari'a-compliant, pious Muslims. Although many Muslims do not agree with the application of harsh shari'a rules, they succumb to an orthodoxy that tells them to abide by 'God's laws' or face rebuke. An absence of literacy in matters of religion only complicates matters for ordinary people.

The shari'a, norms provided by God for humans to follow on the path to water/to live the ethical, is meant to provide Muslims with the tools for judging between right and wrong. But how do we know what is right? This question has engaged humanity for millennia. While we have found reasonable answers to what is moral and ethical, we are challenged on a daily basis to improve our ethical thinking and practice. For some, this is about an acquired sensibility derived from philosophy, religion or some other authority. Others claim we have an intuitive sense of right and wrong. Is it conceivable or even desirable to make an absolute distinction between what is right and wrong? If we are unable to do so, some would argue, then we lose all sight of the ethical. I provide here a case study that explores how tradition and ethics are, and can be, understood.

Rape and Nullification of Marriage: The Imrana Case

In 2005, Imrana, a mother of five living near the city of Muzaffarnagar in the state of Uttar Pradesh in India, claimed to have been raped. She alleged that the rapist was her father-in-law. He was tried and convicted for the crime under Indian criminal law. A *mufti* (jurist-consult) affiliated with the Darul Uloom Deoband, a leading Islamic seminary near Delhi, issued a fatwa (juridical opinion) on the case. He declared that Imrana, as the victim of rape by her father-in-law, was no longer married to her lawful husband. Why?

For the prevailing Hanafi school of fiqh (or version of shari'a reasoning), intercourse with relatives automatically created certain permanent prohibitions. A son cannot marry a woman with whom his biological father has had intercourse, just as a daughter cannot marry

Recovering the Ethical 49

a man with whom her biological mother had intercourse. This stance is not shared by the other Sunni schools, which hold that a licit marriage creates a permanent boundary; sex outside wedlock cannot create such barriers. But the Hanafi law school holds that such boundaries are also created by sex out of wedlock, including rape. By raping Imrana, her father-in-law rendered her permanently forbidden to her husband, the rapist's son.[26]

The reasoning behind this Hanafi position stems from a verse in the Qur'an, which states: 'Do not marry (*tankihu*) those whom your fathers [by implication parents] have married (*ma nakaha*) [Qur'an, 4:22].' Most commentators believe this verse was intended to stop the repugnant marriages (*ziwaj al-maqt*) of the pre-Islamic period, where a son would marry his father's previous wives, except for his biological mother. But the more general rendering of the verse could also mean: 'Do not contract marriages with those whom your parents have *married by acts of consummation*' (emphasis added by this author).

The disagreement turns on the meaning of the verb *nakaha*. Nakaha can mean contracting or consummating a marriage. While most schools of interpretation understand that contracting valid marriages constructs the barriers of consanguinity, the Hanafi school takes the implied meaning to say that any sexual act, even those conducted outside wedlock, serves as a trigger for this commandment. And rape can be viewed as adultery by coercion.[27]

This debate generated a counter-argument from the strict scripturalist Ahl-i Hadith school, an Indian incarnation of salafism. This school holds that the commandment applied only to sex *within* a marriage. Barriers of consanguinity, they argued, were not created by an unlawful act such as rape or adultery.[28] Much to the chagrin of the Deoband school, in the Ahl-i Hadith school's view, Imrana was perfectly lawful to her husband and the marriage was not voided.

Deobandi ulama fiercely defended their position. They drew on classical authorities to demonstrate that their argument was supported by tradition and backed by authorities of the Hanafi school.[29] Her unfortunate status as a rape victim was ignored by both sides of the

---

[26] See H. Azam, *Sexual Violation in Islamic Law: Substance, Evidence, and Procedure* (New York, 2015).

[27] Ibid., p. 177.

[28] Personal communication, Abu 'Abd al-Haqq 'Abd al-Salam bin Abi Aslam al-Madani, 2006.

[29] Habib al-Rahman A'zami, *Tahqiq-i mas'ala-i hurmat-i mu aharat* (Deoband, 2005); Mufti Muhammad Yusuf Taaulvi, *Hurmat-i musaharat Qur'an o hadith kiroshni main* (Deoband, 2005).

50   *The Shariʿa*

debate but especially by the traditional authorities at Deoband, for
whom rape was just another form of adultery by coercion.

The Deobandis upbraided the critics of their ruling, dismissing them
as *faux* reformers, unqualified to opine on religious matters. They also
lambasted critics for possessing the temerity to challenge the authority
of the ulama. Muslim critics who challenged their ruling, they claimed,
were driven by malice and ignorance, and the goal of earning cheap
publicity.[30] However, a small minority of Deobandis conceded that some
classical Hanafi authorities had, in fact, questioned whether unlawful
sex could create the barriers of consanguinity as a moral offence. But in
public the majority dutifully skulked behind the façade of centuries-old
legal prose and interpretations, with a solemnity that their critics alleged
bordered on idolatry.

Making Sense of Norms

To dissent from the rules on blasphemy, or to ignore the complicated
rules of sexual violation involving relatives, means going against
established religious tradition. Scholars who question the ulama are
interpreted as also challenging the consecrated paradigm of Muslim
knowledge. Those who dissent from a legal school, such as the Hanafi,
risk their reputation and livelihood. One could even be accused of
disrespecting the Prophet if one did not demonstrate zeal for the
retention of Pakistan's controversial blasphemy laws. The power to
interpret is part of a complicated network of authorisation adopted by
the ulama that runs deep into the knowledge and power configurations
of Muslim orthodoxy's political-theological DNA.

It appears from the Imrana case that the ethical and legal paradigms
used by each contender attempted to secure specific interests that are
not neutral or value free. The Deobandis felt accountable to a moral
tradition that viewed sexual relations with relatives to be morally offensive; their loyalty was to their moral tradition. For the Deobandis, their
perceived moral responsibility to revoke Imrana's legal marriage was
more important than reporting the rape as a crime to public authorities.

The Ahl-i Hadith critics, in turn, valorised the authority of scripture
and a plain reading of it. But their argument with the Deobandis was
also part of a centuries-long theological dispute. The Hanafis, as
protagonists of a canonical law school, view their authority to be that
of an uninterrupted hierarchy of a tradition that requires mandatory
adherence. Their Ahl-i Hadith rivals view such loyalty to human

---

[30]   Aʿzami, *Tahqiq-i masʾala*, pp. 52–56.

Recovering the Ethical 51

authority to be a mortal sin. For the secular critics of the Deoband fatwa, the violation of Imrana as a crime enjoyed priority, and they petitioned for the writ of the secular state to be enforced. They were outraged by the double jeopardy that Imrana suffered: a violation of her dignity and the end of her marriage.

There is another aspect of this controversy that has received little attention. The various understandings of the shari'a represent different moral anthropologies of the self, especially in relation to sexual mores. This might be what Bernard Williams calls 'cultural relativism at a distance'. He also cautions against projecting an ethical fantasy onto societies we do not understand.[31] So it is not surprising that these notions of self are highly contested categories in modern times. A modern, secular ethos valorises an autonomous self; however, the Hanafi Deobandis advocate a notion of the self that is in some instances interdependent, not independent. Certain acts committed by the self, or acts committed to the self, have consequences on both the person and others. So for Imrana the violation means that her relationship with her husband is also impacted. The son of the rapist, Imrana's husband, cannot nullify his biological affinity to his father. Even though Imrana was violated against her will, the facts or realities independent of her own volition as a result of the rape have altered her social and marital status.

One can imagine how the shame she suffered from the rape by her father-in-law disrupted her relationship with her husband. Furthermore, if she remained married to her spouse, she would likely be forced to interact with her father-in-law after he served his prison sentence. Such subsequent interactions could have negative consequences for Imrana's well-being and could trigger memories of her trauma. Against this backdrop, the Hanafi-Deobandi ruling of separation, when contextually considered among a certain class of families in India, is possibly a more humane solution. Of course, if Imrana has no social support outside her marriage, her separation could have dire physical and material consequences for her. While allowing her to remain in her marriage could turn out to be a form of psychological cruelty, a divorce without an adequate social welfare net could destine her to a life of poverty. Perhaps the better option would be to give Imrana the requisite psychological and social counselling in order to enable and empower her to make an informed decision. After all, she was the victim of a rape, but also the victim of authorities nullifying her marriage. If she received counselling,

---

[31] Bernard Williams, *Ethics and the Limits of Philosophy* (Cambridge, MA, 1985), p. 162.

52   *The Shariʿa*

she might be better positioned to evaluate whether life after marriage is economically feasible or whether the marriage is indispensable to her dignity and the well-being of her five children.

The Deobandi mufti activated the Hanafi law ruling in a mechanical manner without considering the dignity of the people involved. Nor was the Hanafi mufti courageous enough to look outside Hanafi tradition for guidance. Had he drawn on the Shafiʿi tradition, for example, Imranaʾs marriage would not be nullified as a result of rape. At the same time, it would be untenable for her to live in a community where everyone knew that religious authorities had deemed her marriage illicit. Nor could she and her spouse, for convenience, claim to follow the Ahl-i Hadith, which did not void her marriage.

So Imrana and her spouse might pose themselves the question that Veena Das asks about herself in her study of Muslim practices in India:

> How do I cultivate morality as a dimension of everyday life, when certain forms of knowing … contradict my feelings that there are forms of being together that I can come to experience as part of my ordinary mode of life, that I wish to acknowledge but for which I should not be required to give justifications?[32]

Yet Imrana and her spouse are not the sole arbiters of their moral destiny. Marriage is not only a practice deliberated in the domestic sphere. In India, Muslim marriages are linked to the state via personal law statutes. Multiple informal moral authorities (the ulama) also shape the couple's moral sphere, as do secular discourses about crimes such as rape and folk perceptions of morality. While the juridical discourse of the ulama looms large, there are also alternative narratives of ethics.

In India, freedom is often conceived differently from how it is in the West. Notions of respect, dignity and honour do not have a singular narrative, nor can they be sustained without proper consideration. 'Cultures, subcultures, [and] fragments of cultures', as Williams observes, 'constantly meet one another and exchange and modify practices and attitudes.'[33] The ways one thinks about tradition in changing moral contexts should acknowledge the power of tradition for Muslims, as well as the tradition's cultural and political contexts.

---

[32] Veena Das, 'Moral and Spiritual Striving in the Everyday: To Be a Muslim in Contemporary India', in Anand Pandian and Daud Ali, ed., *Ethical Life in South Asia* (Bloomington, IN, 2010), p. 233.

[33] Williams, *Ethics and the Limits of Philosophy*, p. 158. See also P. Rabinow, *Essays on the Anthropology of Reason* (Princeton, NJ, 1996), on the 'particularities' of culture, p. 56.

Recovering the Ethical　　53

Tradition in Moral Contexts

Imrana's story provides a window to the heart of the debate about Muslim ethics. Male ulama are committed to implementing the canonical tradition of fiqh, claiming to do so with integrity, and as acts of piety and religiosity. However, many Muslims question whether the ulama can remain faithful to tradition without violating contemporary moral norms. Indeed, this challenge is shared across cultures: a 'language of universality' in tension with the repeated 'translation' of incommensurable levels of living and meaning'.[34] In this in-between space, which I have called the *dihliz* elsewhere, the gap between universality and translation comes with risks. It requires that we foster a certain future and goal, or what Bernard Williams calls a 'teleologically significant world'.[35]

If such a world is out of reach, then it can bring about an epistemology of despair that the truth is out of reach. Humans have sought to avoid this despair by placing faith in an omnipresent, all-knowing God who embodies the truth (*tawhid*). But in a tawhid-centred truth world, the goal should not be certainties of right versus wrong. Ethics is the realm of the undecided, where we find ourselves between the contending norms and multiple realities of life. Ethical space is also an aesthetic space, where beauty manifests itself in life and all its forms, including the violent and the tragic. So the obligation is to cultivate an ethos, a space or a dwelling for habitation. Equality, compassion, justice, freedom and other moral virtues take place within this space. Action is always framed by ethos, which prevents action from becoming oppressive. When action and ethos combine, new possibilities of the ethical emerge. Tradition, truth-seeking and optimism are critical parts of ensuring that the truth is discoverable. But for this to be possible, an ethos must be situated in a space in between 'what is' and 'what ought to be' – the *dihliz*.

In Islam, truth-seeking in ethics begins with discernment. The term fiqh, often used to describe the body of knowledge consisting of the applied rules of the shari'a, actually signifies knowledge and discernment.[36] Over time, this tradition of discernment ceased to be a process of active thinking about ethical knowledge and became an

---

[34]　H.K. Bhabha, *The Location of Culture* (London, 1994), p. 124.

[35]　Williams, *Ethics and the Limits of Philosophy*, p. 128.

[36]　Abu al-Baqa Ayyub b. Musa al-Husayni al-Kafawi, ed. 'Adnan Darwish and Muhammad al-Masri, *al-Kulliyat: Mu'jam fi al-Mustalahat wa al-Furuq al-Lughawiyya*, 2nd edn (Beirut, 1998), pp. 690–691.

54   *The Shariʻa*

exercise in learning the opinions of one's predecessors.[37] The need to
follow tradition under the imprimatur of obeying canonical authority
(*taqlid*) became a priority. Following tradition became a sign of fealty
to a law school. The dynamic act of discerning (fiqh) the discourse of
revelation – the shariʻa – and its intentions faded. In its place rose an
impressive tradition of scholarship that canonised the authority of the
ulama but was less creative. Fiqh became displaced from its ethical centre.

As early as the 11th century it took someone like al-Ghazali to
castigate jurists (*fuqaha*) for being obsessed with the mechanics of
rules. The applied rules governed the worldly needs of the moral subject
or of public life (*fiqh al-zahir*). But al-Ghazali agonised and struggled
to make sense of how such formal rules might govern and deepen the
discernment of one's soul (*fiqh al-batin*). Al-Ghazali reoriented the fiqh
tradition – whether social conduct (*muʻamalat*) or devotional and ritual
conduct (*ʻibadat*) – in narratives about the ethics of each practice. He
did so by finding concordance between the external practice of rules
applicable to the body and social conduct, and the governance of the
self by repairing the soul. His work, *The Revivification of the Sciences of
Religion* (*Ihyaʼ ʻulum al-din*), demonstrates his efforts to make this point.
Among the ways believers expressed their love for God, according to
him, was showing deference to God's commandments and abstaining
from libertinism.[38]

The norms and commandments that al-Ghazali cherished were
rooted in Muslim tradition. They included elements of both continuity
and change since the first generations of Muslims. Al-Ghazali's predecessors repeatedly renarrated the tradition to give it coherence. The
norms that influenced al-Ghazali made sense in his medieval society,
but they did pose challenges – and he pushed back against some of the
cosmologies of his predecessors. He renarrated certain aspects of Ashʻari
theology and provided space for rival interpretations of that theology.
In the sphere of the moral and ethical, he took pains to provide a new
account of how the ethical tradition of his time related to its past. While
his interpretations garnered much appeal, he also encountered opposition. After all, such arguments are a feature of conflicts within traditions
across different societies and religions.[39]

---

[37]   F. Rahman, *Islam* (Chicago, 1979), p. 101.

[38]   al-Ghazali, *Ihyaʼ ʻulum al-din*, vol. 4, p. 288. Obedience to God, for al-
Ghazali, is a sign of a servant's love for God. See R. Brague, *The Law of God:
The Philosophical History of an Idea* (Chicago, 2007), p. 184, n. 41.

[39]   A. MacIntyre, 'Epistemological Crises, Dramatic Narrative and the
Philosophy of Science', *The Monist* 60(4) (1977), p. 461.

We now live in a world shaped by the Enlightenment, which altered cosmologies of science, politics and religion. Hence important aspects of the narratives of tradition that made sense to al-Ghazali and other intellectuals no longer really apply. Today, renarration of tradition is not happening fast enough, nor is it generating meaningful moral consensus among Muslims. The rupture from the pre-modern to the modern has caused deep fissures in the Muslim self, and in Muslim political orders. As a result, apologetics have become more dominant, giving a superficial account of tradition in a bid to displace the facts of the world in which we are living. But the modern Muslim is not struggling simply with an epistemological crisis where the 'schema of interpretation which he has trusted so far has broken down irremediably in certain highly specific ways'.[40] Rather, a chronic condition is at play.

The builders of Muslim orthodoxy do not recognise this state of affairs, much less that a renarration of tradition is urgently called for. Even if the Muslim community came to recognise this crisis, another fear would immediately present itself. Many worry that any path out of this crisis will rely on resources derived from the non-Muslim West, which a significant number of Muslims regard as hostile to Islam. What this foreshadows, then, is a clash-of-civilisations narrative.[41]

Conclusion

Muslim thought uses different vocabularies to reflect traditions on which it is based. Only a greater sense of today's shared human web of interaction can effectively counter the-clash-of-civilisations narrative and its violent implications. For more than a century, Muslim religious scholars who were sensitive to the crisis at hand sought to address it by invoking *ijtihad* (independent, new thinking) and abandoning *taqlid* (imitation of the past). However, not enough work has been done to re-establish conceptions of the shari'a as a set of ethical and moral norms rather than a set of rigid rules or laws.

Some years ago, in a private exchange with Rached Ghannouchi, the spiritual leader of Tunisia's Renaissance Party (Ennahda), we debated the need for radical rethinking (*ijtihad*) in a time of western

---

[40] Ibid., p. 458.
[41] To cite MacIntyre (ibid., p. 451), 'It is yet another mark of a degenerate tradition that it has contrived a set of epistemological defenses which enable it to avoid being put in question or at least to avoid recognizing that it is being put in question by rival traditions.'

hegemony.[42] Ghannouchi asserted that *ijtihad* during a time of the political and cultural decline of Muslims could result in the colonisation of Muslim religious thought. I fervently argued the opposite, stating that such rethinking was especially needed to pull Muslim culture and religious thought out of its intellectual and moral quagmire. We did not manage to persuade each other 22 years ago. However, when his party won elections in 2011, Ghannouchi demonstrated visionary leadership in moving Tunisia towards democracy. In 2016, Ennahda abandoned political Islam, resolving to function strictly as a political party. Ghannouchi's party intellectuals sought to provide a fresh interpretation of Muslim political realities, using *ijtihad* to abandon one version of politics and embrace another. In this ethical pivot, Ennahda lent credence to Muslim tradition while enlivening it with the context of new realities.

The upshot here is the imperative for thinking anew. A potent reminder in this regard comes from the work of the émigré German Jewish political philosopher Hannah Arendt. Her use of the phrase the 'banality of evil' aimed to capture the facile, superficial defence of the Nazis and their sympathisers: 'We were just performing our patriotic duty.' As she strove to make sense of the evil committed by her compatriots that resulted in the near extermination of European Jews, she made an even more insightful remark. What startled her most in the accounts of such prominent Nazis as Adolf Eichmann, whom she observed on trial in Jerusalem, was the 'total absence of thinking'.[43]

Arendt's introspection is both haunting and edifying. She quarrelled with the question of whether 'thinking as such, the habit of examining and reflecting', could alone prevent evil.[44] Yes, thinking can disrupt our existing habits of thought, she conceded, and it can lead us to discover new ways of questioning. But the 'wind of thought', Arendt's way of describing the harvest of thinking, was not knowledge as such. Thinking should result in moral reasoning that equips us with the 'ability to tell right from wrong, beautiful from ugly'. The conviction to declare 'This is wrong' or 'This is beautiful' involves a certain way of thinking.

For contemporary Muslim traditions, the need for ethical coherence calls for nothing less than 'a revolutionary reconstitution'.[45] This begins

---

[42] Rached Ghannouchi during an extended visit to South Africa in March–April 1994 had several exchanges with me during which we discussed many of these ideas. He has also over time rethought some of his previous positions.

[43] Hannah Arendt, *Responsibility and Judgment* (New York, 2003), p. 160.

[44] Ibid.

[45] MacIntyre, 'Epistemological Crises, Dramatic Narrative and the Philosophy of Science', p. 461.

Recovering the Ethical   57

with thinking, which requires the freedom to state unequivocally that some things are right and others are wrong. Imrana's story should stand as testimony that violating human dignity and ignoring the ethical is nothing short of a moral and theological offence – a failure of thinking. We ignore the larger lessons at our collective peril.

Further Reading

Ahmed, Shahab. *What is Islam? The Importance of Being Islamic.* Princeton, NJ, 2015.

Ali, Kecia. *Sexual Ethics and Islam: Feminist Reflections on Qur'an, Hadith, and Jurisprudence.* London, 2006.

Hallaq, Wael. *Sharī'a: Theory, Practice, Transformations.* New York, 2009.

Hefner, Robert, ed. *Shari'a Law and Modern Muslim Ethics.* Bloomington, IN, 2016.

Masud, Muhammad Khalid. *Shari'a Today: Essays on Contemporary Issues and Debates in Muslim Societies.* Islamabad, 2013.

Mir-Hosseini, Ziba, Mulki Al-Sharmani and Jana Rumminger, ed. *Men in Charge? Rethinking Authority in Muslim Legal Tradition.* London, 2015.

Moosa, Ebrahim. *Ghazālī and the Poetics of Imagination.* Chapel Hill, NC and London, 2005.

Rahman, Fazlur. *Major Themes of the Qur'an.* 2nd edn. Chicago, IL, 2009.

Ramadan, Tariq. *Radical Reform: Islamic Ethics and Liberation.* London, 2009.

Safi, Omid, ed., *Progressive Muslims: On Justice, Gender, and Pluralism.* Oxford, 2003.

Sajoo, Amyn B. *Muslim Ethics: Emerging Vistas.* London, 2009.

Vogt, Kari, Lena Larsen and Christian Moe, ed., *New Directions in Islamic Thought: Exploring Reform and Muslim Tradition.* London, 2011.

4

Sustaining and Enhancing Life

Karim H. Karim

This chapter discusses the shariʿa as a means of societal governance with regard to the quality of life, an idea that is embedded in the word's etymology. The foundations of the shariʿa as an ethical and intellectual construct were laid in the centuries after the Prophet Muhammad. The shariʿa's orientation towards the public good allows for continual evolution to respond to the changing conditions in which Muslims find themselves. What has this meant for aspiration to a 'good life', as promulgated by the Qur'an and the example of the Prophet? Historically, a dynamic, problem-solving methodology emerged in diverse Muslim locales. However, the limitations that were eventually placed on individual reasoning (*ijtihad*) generally gave rise to a view of the shariʿa as a rigid set of prohibitions and punishments.

Whereas there have been frequent calls over the last century for the restoration of *ijtihad* as a way to assist in the contemporary development of Muslim-majority societies, few governments demonstrate a sound understanding of the broad nature of the shariʿa. Nevertheless, there are some encouraging signs, as in the recent drafting of the Tunisian constitution, which does not explicitly mention the shariʿa but resonates with its ethos. Similarly, civil society organisations have also demonstrated ways in which the quality of life can be improved by working within Islamically inspired frameworks. I draw on several examples in this chapter – both local and transnational – to illustrate features of the 'purposive' landscape of the ethical shariʿa today.

Material and Spiritual Enhancement

The word 'shariʿa' has come to be associated primarily with Islamic law. However, the Arabic term existed before Islam; its incorporation into Islamic vocabulary derives from the Qur'anic verse 'We have set thee on a clear path (shariʿa) of commandment' (45:18). The word's original meaning as the path (route, way) to a watering place holds considerable significance in understanding its relation to social governance, particularly with respect to bettering quality of life. There is in this meaning a much more elemental aspect of life, beyond law. Water's value in the arid landscape of Arabia, the site of the Islamic revelation, is obvious, but this resource is universally necessary for sustaining human existence. Examining the original sense of the word is important in understanding the larger objective of the shari'a. Despite its identification with religious law, its underlying idea reflects a more fundamental purpose: to support and to enrich life. Viewed through the prism of the Qur'anic verse, the word gains the meaning of travelling the path that leads to essential nourishment at the well of spiritual and material fulfilment. The symbolic significance of the Islamic shari'a in relation to its original meaning as a path to the life-giving resource of water points to the indispensability of spirituality and the ethics that derive from it for the individual and community. In this sense, it is much more profound than merely a set of rules and regulations; it is the support for governing the development of both the person and society.

The shari'a relates to spiritual well-being and to material life because matters of *din* (religion, faith, spirit) and *dunya* (world, life, matter) are intertwined in Islamic perspectives. Morality and ethics derived from spiritual sources enable the believer to pursue a life characterised by goodness. The shari'a is not only important for sustaining a good life but also for its enhancement. Since human beings are dependent on each other and live in communities, the shari'a has to relate to the endeavour of sustaining an entire society and improving the quality of life. It encompasses not only a system of law but also other aspects governing society. Moving beyond slaking an individual's immediate thirst, the principle behind the shari'a as the metaphorical path to enhance the conditions of life was historically actualised in early Muslim history. An example was the fourth Rashidun caliph and first Shi'i imam Ali ibn Abi Talib's (599–661) funding of a scheme that was voluntarily proposed by a group of people to improve an area's irrigation potential.[1] Muslim rulers of later centuries sponsored large watering networks to support the agricultural systems that fed substantial populations.[2] This

---

[1] The Institute of Ismaili Studies, 'Aga Khan Development Network (AKDN): An Ethical Framework': accessible at http://www.iis.ac.uk/aga-khan-development-network-akdn-ethical-framework.

[2] I.M. Lapidus, *A History of Islamic Societies*, 3rd edn (Cambridge, 2014), pp. 54–55. Lapidus notes that imperial considerations often drove such sponsorship, but that it was nevertheless in contrast to the neglect that Muslim rulers inherited in places such as Iraq.

Sustaining and Enhancing Life   61

broad sense of the shari'a underwrites the establishment of social
organisation and its governance to meet the essentials of human
sustenance and, in a larger way, the shaping of civilisation. In the 21st
century it bears the potential to contribute substantially to developing
the modes of governance that respond effectively to the large-
scale poverty, rampant corruption, cultural disorientation, political
instability and internecine and international conflict experienced by
many Muslim-majority countries.

A caveat is in order here. Despite the significant place of the shari'a
in Islam, Abdullahi An-Naim, a leading scholar of the shari'a, writes
that, 'in keeping with the spirit of each individual seeking out the truth
without compulsion ([Qur'an,] 2:256), it is of the essence for Muslims to
live by the ethics of the sharia as a matter of *voluntary* choice' [original
emphasis].[3] This is a statement of particular significance in the context
where many Muslim societies are debating the place of the shari'a in the
contemporary world. 'There is certainly more to Islam than the sharia,
which is only part of the rich experience of being a Muslim,' An-Naim
notes.[4] He appears to be saying that it is possible to be a Muslim without
following the institution of the shari'a. The latter is interlinked with, but
remains distinct from, Islamic theology, matters of belief, creed and
various forms of spiritual search. Among Sufis and other mystically
oriented Muslim groups, the shari'a is an important aspect of Islamic
piety but it is only the first step in the seeker's spiritual ascent: it leads
to, and may be superseded by, what they see as the higher levels of the
tariqa (the way), the *haqiqa* (truth) and the *ma'rifa* (gnosis).[5] According
to these views, there is more than one path to the watering place – that
is, to attain spiritual enlightenment and apprehend truth. Adherence to
the shari'a as a historically and socio-culturally constructed institution,
therefore, remains as a voluntary choice; whether or not one chooses
to follow this path among other paths does not essentially affect one's
status as a Muslim and as a participant in Islamic spirituality. Indeed,
revered Muslims who lived before the shari'a was historically formulated
(e.g. the 8th-century sage Hasan al-Basri) did not necessarily abide by
what came to be its formal prescriptions.

The shari'a did not exist as an institution in the time of the Prophet
Muhammad. He interpreted the Qur'an as it related to the practice
of everyday Muslim life in his own lifetime. It was the quest of later

---

[3]   A. An-Naim, 'Modernity: Secular and Sacred,' in A. B. Sajoo, ed., *A
Companion to Muslim Cultures* (London, 2012), p. 37.
[4]   Ibid., p. 38.
[5]   S.H. Nasr, *Ideals and Realities of Islam* (London, 1975), pp. 121–144.

62 *The Shariʿa*

generations to adhere to Islamic principles and values that led to the scholarly endeavour to develop 'an amalgam of law, ethics and methodology' that came to be known as the shariʿa.[6] The shariʿa although it is sometimes referred to as 'divine' or 'holy' law, is not divine in the sense that Muslims consider the Qurʾan to be; it is a construct produced by the engagement of the human intellect with divine/holy revelation and other sources in specific temporal and sociocultural contexts. The methods of consensus (*ijma*), analogy (*qiyas*), individual reasoning (*ijtihad*), exceptional deviation from a rule (*istishsan*), unprecedented judgment motivated by public interest (*istislah*) and custom (*urf*) have produced a rich, dynamic and enabling resource that has provided Muslims with a socio-cultural and legal framework that has 'unchanging bearings as well as ... major means of adjusting to change'.[7] Whereas the primary structure of the shariʿa emerged in the centuries following the Prophet's death, its evolution is a process that continues to this day.

The British Muslim polymath Ziauddin Sardar remarks that, 'For a Muslim civilisation, the Shariʿah represents that infinite spiritual and worldly thirst that is never satisfied: a Muslim people always seeks better and better implementation of the Shariʿah on its present and future affairs.'[8] It is not a fixed entity but a fluid, organic, changing and pluralistic body of knowledge, being shaped by the ways in which Muslims seek to respond to shifting circumstances. Notwithstanding the widely held notion of the closing of the gates of *ijtihad* in the late medieval period, the shariʿa develops over time in response to new conditions and growing human knowledge. Whereas precedence and consensus are important in its formulation, culture and custom play vital roles in keeping it relevant to the vast diversity of regions in which Muslims live. And as custom changes in a particular location, so do aspects of the shariʿa which relate to it. The latter has also incorporated elements of other cultures that reflect values that are compatible with those of Islam. For example, the formulation of the system of *waqf* endowments, which has long been an integral part of Islamic charity and is used to fund institutions such as schools, hospitals, hostels and social welfare bodies, drew from Byzantine and Sasanian precedents.

The Qurʾanic revelation and the practice of the Prophet (Sunna) are the primary sources for the shariʿa. The Sunna reflects a clear attention

---

[6] Z. Sardar, 'The Shariʿah as a Problem-Solving Methodology', in S. Inayatullah and G. Boxwell, ed., *Islam, Postmodernism and Other Futures: A Ziauddin Sardar Reader* (London, 2003), p. 66.

[7] Ibid., p. 64.

[8] Ibid.

Sustaining and Enhancing Life 63

to improving the well-being of society. Muhammad demonstrated deep concern for the elderly, the poor, the weak and the sick, as is apparent from his traditions (Hadith). He was not only charitable towards widows, orphans, slaves and others who were at a disadvantage, but actively worked to develop societal solutions to improve their respective positions. This was often manifested in the innovation of processes and institutions that came to characterise a more just society. Muhammad's reforms included the establishment of social systems and rights in society and within families (especially those of wives and children). Upon the Prophet's move to Medina with his followers, the 'Constitution of Medina' was instituted, specifying the duties and status of the Muslims of Mecca and Yathrib (Medina), as well as of the Jews of Yathrib.[9] Rights and protection were also accorded to Christians through the Treaty of Najran. Muhammad fostered the growth in social mobility supported by a primary Islamic tenet of egalitarianism. These reforms were supported by Qur'anic revelations regarding matters dealing with issues of inheritance, alimony, support for the poor and other means of social welfare. The systems he established were underpinned by a moral order that valued kindness, forgiveness and mercy. A communal ethos of mutual support came to characterise Muslim society. Whereas Muhammad's reforms did not eradicate social inequality and injustice, the Sunna became the ideal of Islamic life and civilisation, and the model for the development of the shari'a.

The Prophet's biography (*sira*) gave the examples of the modes in which he tackled problems. These ranged from issues of everyday life to those of governing the early Islamic state. Both the development of institutions and the processes by which they were produced became instructive for the formation of the shari'a. The Prophet's social, political and economic reforms were informed by an inherent spirituality. Given the symbiotic relationship between faith and the material world in Islamic perspectives, deeds in the physical world were seen as affecting one's spiritual existence. Therefore the shari'a's framework identifies two separate but linked categories of actions: *'ibadat* (acts of worship) and *mu'amalat* (which include acts within commercial and civil arenas). The distinction between them is not that between the religious and the secular in dominant western worldviews. Morality derived from the Islamic revelation has a strong bearing on the conduct of everyday life. This extends also to the work of governments and other institutions.

The shari'a includes a body of law (fiqh) that was developed through reasoned reflection on the Qur'an and the Sunna by a number of major scholars in the two centuries following the Prophet's death. Several Sunni

---

[9]   W. Montgomery Watt, *Muhammad at Medina* (Oxford, 1956), pp. 221–260.

schools of law (*madhahib*), including the Shafi'i, Hanafi, Maliki, Hanbali and Zahiri, flourished in this early period. The latter, which was popular in al-Andalus, eventually lost prominence. The Jafari *madhhab* is the major Shi'i school of law. It gives greater significance than Sunni schools to the traditions and teachings of Shi'i imams. This also applies to the shari'a as a whole, as understood and applied by adherents of Shi'i Islam. Religious law has an important but circumspect role in Muslim societies. All the aspects of fiqh are not adjudicated by courts, and mediation is strongly encouraged. This is not a rigid system: judgments are not singular but are modulated by counter-judgments. Another important characteristic is the even more fluid and localised operation of religious law in rural areas of Muslim-majority countries, where a vast majority of the adherents of Islam live but where law courts are scarce. Here, the larger context of the shari'a, of which law is only a part, comes to the fore. In any case, the place of custom, culture and the local community's understanding of the Sunna are all relevant in the general practice of justice in Muslim milieus.

Whereas the processes of colonialism, westernisation and secularisation weakened the relationship between Islamic mores and governance, several Muslim-majority countries are now increasingly exploring how to re-establish the link between a culturally resonant body of ethics embedded in the shari'a and the work of governing. However, the shari'a is often cast by many politicians as a strict legal code, and is sometimes reduced to the harshest of criminal laws, the *hudud*, a term that refers to injunctions touching on the extreme limits of the law. In the context of governance, the shari'a is much broader than merely the means to preserve public order. It seeks to gives integrity to the person and society, and to enable broad-based improvement in quality of life. Unfortunately, often acting under pressure from religious extremists and without proper consideration of the broader nature and overall objectives of the shari'a, the tendency of some governments has been to institute extreme punishments in order to proclaim that Islam has been re-established. Apart from causing substantial social instability, this approach has been morally and ethically errant in relation to the framework of the shari'a, whose long-established methodology requires significant intellectual effort and wide consultation, as well as consideration of the cultural and religious pluralism of populations.

It is not uncommon for societies to lose sense of the original purpose of institutions that were established hundreds of years ago. The shari'a is a human construct whose fundamental aim is to foster spiritual and material existence in an ethical manner. However, it is often reduced in popular discourse to the formulaic binarism of what is permissible (*halal*) and what is not (*haram*), rather than being a sophisticated means of engaging with one's intellect and spirituality to address issues as a religious aspirant and as a citizen of a society. Instead of viewing the shari'a as a resource that enables improvement of the quality of life, it has often become a means of control that stunts social development. Such tendencies fail to see that the shari'a is in itself a means of implementing change to carry out corrective processes to conditions that cause disorder – that is, it is a 'problem-solving methodology'.[10]

Governance and the Public Good

Contemporary Muslim-majority societies are facing significant difficulties in matters of governance. The latter is not viewed here as dealing only with the functioning of the state but as also including the leadership and management of a range of institutions, such as those in the private sector and civil society. Constitutions, policy frameworks, legislative structures, rules and regulations, codes of conduct, and custom and tradition support governance processes in various sectors of life. Direct engagement with the concept of governance has emerged as a relatively new endeavour in Muslim-majority societies: the term *hukm*[11] and the derivative neologism *hakama*[12] (both from the same Arabic root) are used to refer to 'governance'.

The shari'a has been a basis for Islamic governance. It promotes the kind of moral economy that provides for policies, structures and rules designed to enable favourable conditions for human sustenance, dignity, peace, order, health, education, economic success and spiritual well-being. The objectives of the juridical aspects of the shari'a, including the laws that address criminality, also pertain to the overall goal of promoting individual and societal welfare. Whereas the juridical shari'a has a set of general principles, most of its prescriptions respond to local conditions. Over the last few decades, the focus of many scholars has been primarily on criminal punishments and 'Islamic finance'. These matters are part of the concerns of the shari'a but they are not central to it. Their prominence in contemporary Muslim discourse has tended to narrow the understanding of the shari'a among both Muslims and

---

[10]   Sardar, 'The Shari'ah', p. 74.
[11]   M.S. Ellis et al., *Islamic Law and International Human Rights Law* (Oxford, 2012), pp. 109–110.
[12]   The World Bank, 'Putting the Citizen at the Heart of "Hakama"': accessible at http://www.worldbank.org/en/news/feature/2013/10/30/putting-the-citizen-at-the-heart-of-hakama.

non-Muslims, leading to the reduction of its much broader purpose that enables the believer to pursue the path to salvation, promote the public good, live in a just society, enjoy personal and communal security, and improve quality of life.

Individual conscience and obligation are linked with the public good in the shari'a. Whereas the concept of the public good has become a key aspect of secular systems of governance, it originally arose in the contexts of faith and natural justice. Most religions promote ideas of communal welfare. The Islamic concept of *fard al-'ayn* ('everyone's obligation') encourages selfless individual service in the interests of the larger society. Faith-driven, ethical underpinnings of law and governance can revitalise modes of thought and behaviour that serve common purposes in a time when the individual's freedom of choice contends with communal values. These ideas relate to the concept of *maslaha*, used by various scholars of Islamic jurisprudence to refer to the principles of the common good and public welfare.

Maslaha is integrally interrelated with the shari'a's methodology, as discussed elsewhere in this volume, particularly with respect to the method of *istislah* (the two words are derived from the same Arabic root). The latter permits scholars to use their intellect to take into consideration conditions that did not exist in the Prophet's time in order to address the contemporary welfare of individuals and communities. This makes the shari'a a dynamic and living resource that is able to address the constantly evolving circumstances in which Muslims live. When faced with situations to which the Qur'an and the Sunna refer neither directly nor indirectly, *istislah* enables the development of judgments based on matters of public interest. Scholars have produced a range of *maslaha* categories on the basis of this form of reasoning. Abu Ishaq al-Shatibi, a prominent 14th-century CE Andalusian jurist, viewed *maslaha* as concerning, among other things, 'the subsistence of human life ... [and] the completion of man's livelihood'.[13] This speaks to the original meaning of the word *shari'a*, which relates to the sustenance and enhancement of life. The end purposes of the Islamic shari'a are therefore pursued by valorising the common good of society.

However, the widespread notion of the closing of the gate of *ijtihad* limited the use of *istislah* along with other means of scholarly reasoning. This caused a narrowing of the understanding of the shari'a and the decline of Muslim civilisation, as well as quality of life. Reform

---

[13]   M.K. Masud, *Islamic Legal Philosophy: A Study of Abu Ishaq al-Shatibi's Life and Thought* (Islamabad, 1984), p. 173.

Sustaining and Enhancing Life   67

movements have been seeking to turn back centuries of neglect caused by this limitation on the use of reason. *Maslaha* has gained renewed attention among scholars since the second half of the 19th century, when the scholar and jurist Muhammad Abduh stressed its use in the reforms of the court systems of Egypt and Sudan. It has become a vital consideration in developing approaches in the shari'a that address those matters of public good that have not been encountered before in the domain of governance. This is particularly pertinent under the circumstances of modernity. It is the nation-state, shaped by western political ideas, that has become the primary locus of governance in Muslim-majority countries over the last two centuries. The nation-state is also the primary frame within which issues of societal development are conceptualised and operationalised.

The Shari'a and Development

What relation does the shari'a have to development as understood today? The two overlap in several ways. At its emergence in the mid-20th century, the concept of development was thought of primarily in terms of building the economic structures of non-industrialised countries, including Muslim-majority states. Over time, the idea has incorporated social and cultural dimensions within its ambit. Programmes to deal with issues such as communications, cultural revival, education, employment, the environment, food cultures, health, human rights, security, social welfare and sport have been placed under the rubric of development. Even though dominant discourses apply the concept mostly to non-industrialised societies, all countries – even those in the western world – are in the process of developing or 'modernising' as new technologies and increasingly sophisticated ways of organising society emerge. Additionally, not all parts of a country are at the same level of advancement: some sections of a poor country may be comparable to rich ones in terms of their level of industrialisation and social organisation. On the other hand, many highly industrialised states have people, especially in the countryside who are deprived of some of the basic necessities of life, such as clean water.

Development and modernisation are frequently thought to be the same as westernisation, which means that an Asian or African society would have to imitate western ways of organising itself in order to become developed. Those who promote this outlook view the idea of 'progress' moving in a way that does not allow for non-western cultures to be modern. They see the coexistence of modernity with a non-western society's traditions as contradictory. This view has been challenged by the

68   *The Shari'a*

ideas of 'alternative modernities' and 'multiple modernities', which hold
that there can be different ways to develop a society that are just as valid
as western models. Therefore, in addition to western modernities, there
are Muslim modernities, Asian modernities, African modernities and
so forth.

In dominant discourses, development operates primarily as a secular
concept that rarely touches on matters of the spirit.[14] From Muslim
standpoints, development is understood as relating not only to economic
betterment but also as a means to assist in the endeavour to improve all
aspects of the human condition. The Qur'an encourages believers to
have a strong social conscience, to uphold the dignity of human beings
and to show compassion for all creatures. Islamic ethics are therefore
a vital element in indigenous approaches to development in Muslim-
majority societies. From Islamic perspectives, actions in the material
world (*dunya*) cannot be separated from the context of faith (*din*), and
therefore building a world that is spiritually empty leads to the lack of
fulfilment for its inhabitants. This view sees as imperative the fostering
of societies where people are able to engage with complex challenges of
material life and also to explore the profound mysteries of the spiritual
world. The goal is to promote harmony and balance in all aspects of
people's existence, striving to ensure that the diversity of human
aspirations is respected and the dignity of all individuals is upheld.

The endeavour of developing a society is often beset with
problems of corruption, cronyism and other social ills. In Muslim-
majority societies, religious exhortations are used in the endeavour
to prevent these misdemeanours. Remaining ethical in an effort to
make a better life for everyone is central to the shari'a. Individuals
in a society have a duty to prevent corruption in order to ensure
justice and fairness. Religious obligations behove Muslims to work
towards building an ethical society in which trust, accountability
and equity are upheld. Sharing one's time, knowledge, skill and
material resources with others is also part of Islamic values. Service
to humanity and the voluntary actions for the betterment of the
weak and marginalised were common characteristics among
Muhammad and his Companions (*Sahaba*). They strongly believed
in the importance of promoting social justice in order to ensure that
people were not treated unfairly. Charity (*sadaqa*) is a key part of
Islamic practice, reflecting the social responsibility promoted by the
Qur'an. But whereas Muslims are expected to share some of their

---

[14]   See Amartya Sen, *Development as Freedom* (New York, 1999); Charles
Taylor, *The Malaise of Modernity* (Toronto, 1991).

Sustaining and Enhancing Life 69

wealth, the Prophet also emphasised that, where possible, the needy should work to become self-reliant and others should assist them in achieving this.

The Sunna provided a body of exemplary behaviours and policies that were upheld by Muslim authorities in the centuries after the Prophet. Notwithstanding some serious lapses in judgment and abuses by some rulers, a general ethos promoting the common good was fostered in societies under Muslim rule. The shari'a was a guide to a form of governance that nurtured the material as well as the spiritual enhancement of the lives of individuals and communities. It led to the growth of the most advanced social systems and economies of their time, as well as a good quality of life. A pluralistic culture of intellectual engagement among elites of Muslim and other backgrounds produced an erudite body of philosophy, scientific discoveries, technical innovations, and artistic, architectural and literary creativity. Agriculture, craftsmanship and commerce flourished. Governments developed the means to engage with other states in diplomatic and military manners to ensure the security of domains and trade routes. It was a period during which the classic works of theological debate and writings describing profound forms of spiritual engagement were composed. Muslims of the time confidently interacted with other cultures and religions, learning from and contributing to them. Movements such as the Renaissance and the Enlightenment in Europe were beneficiaries of such interactions. The shari'a was treated as an organic, enabling and dynamic resource rather than a rigid set of restrictions and punishments as it generally came to be viewed later. This was the apogee of medieval Muslim civilisation. It was enabled by a mode of governance supported by the shari'a as a problem-solving methodology.

In the 13th and 14th centuries there began to emerge a discourse on the closing of the gate of *ijtihad* (reasoning). This was rationalised by the belief that the Qur'an and the Sunna had been sufficiently interpreted for all time and there was no need for further intellectual examination of these sources using the methods that had been applied to formulate the shari'a. This discourse had widely taken hold by the 16th century, and the signs of decline were becoming clear in various Muslim-majority societies, particularly in Arab lands. Other regions such as the Safawid, Mughal and Ottoman empires maintained their vibrancy for a longer period, but they too began to wane by the 18th century. The evidence of decline was visible in the narrowing of scholarship, the drop in the sophistication of architecture and other arts, the decay in diplomatic and military prowess, and a deteriorating quality of life. Muslim-majority societies turned inwards and became reluctant to engage with other cultures. They were largely unaware

70   *The Shariʿa*

of the growth of science, technology and culture in Europe, and Napoleon Bonaparte's routing of Egyptian and Syrian forces in 1798–1801 came as a shock. The crushing defeat of the Mughal army by the British East India Company and the characterisation of the Ottoman Empire as the 'sick man of Europe' in the mid-19th century finally brought home the realisation that the golden age of the Muslim civilisation was long over.

The Ottomans engaged in a reform period, the Tanzimat, lasting from 1839 to 1876. They sought to ward off internal challenges as well as external pressures on the empire as a result of increasing nationalism in its various provinces. Certain features of European law and practices were adopted in the process. Westernisation increased after the collapse of the Ottoman Empire in the aftermath of World War I. The Balkan provinces became independent states (with mostly Christian majorities), and Muslim-majority regions in the Levant and North Africa came under colonial control. Muslims in Africa, Central Asia, South Asia and Southeast Asia found themselves under the rule of various European powers, but (Saudi) Arabia, Iran and Afghanistan were among the few that escaped colonisation. However, westernisation began to take hold in almost all Muslim-majority countries. Turkey, the sole remnant of the Ottoman Empire, itself embarked on a vigorous process of Europeanisation under the leadership of Ataturk; Iran adopted a similar policy under Reza Shah. These developments in both countries were strongly tinged with secularisation. Some European powers sought to incorporate Islamic laws into the legal systems of some of their Muslim-majority colonies. 'Droit Musulman' operated in Algeria under the French, and the British in India formulated 'Anglo-Mohammedan law', which was an amalgam of English and Islamic laws, concepts, institutions and jurisprudence used to administer a range of legal matters pertaining to Muslims. However, these hybrid legal systems did not reflect the broader purposes of the shariʿa as a means to enhance life. The education, social welfare and general quality of life of Indian Muslims under British rule declined in relation to those of Hindus. This had a lasting impact that continues to affect the overall socio-economic status of Muslims in contemporary India.[15]

There have been many calls over the last century to reinstitute *ijtihad* and to bring about reforms responding to the circumstances of the modern age. Jamal al-Din al-Afghani, Muhammad Abduh,

---

[15]   Government of India, *Social, Economic and Educational Status of the Muslim Community of India* (New Delhi, 2006).

Rashid Rida and Muhammad Iqbal were among the reformists in the late 19th and early 20th centuries. They influenced Islamic thought in the later decades. However, as Muslim-majority states began to gain independence, they were led largely by secular-minded governments, which sought to modernise their countries according to western ideas of socialism or capitalism. Religious opposition movements have grown steadily over many decades. Many of them have demanded the re-institution of the shari'a as 'the law of the land'. Whereas some of them have asked for a process of *ijtihad*, many have a poor understanding of the broad nature of the shari'a. Muslim-majority countries such as Morocco, Iran and Indonesia have engaged in forms of *ijtihad* to formulate legislation on matters such as human rights and family.[16] However, few states have promulgated a comprehensive approach to development that aligns with indigenous Muslim perspectives.

State Constitutions

The drafting of the 2014 constitution of Tunisia was a Muslim interaction with modernity in an apparent spirit of integrity. There is a tradition of constitutionalism in this state going back to the mid-19th century. Its constitution of 1860, the first to be written in an Arab country, incorporated *maslaha* as a key principle. It listed three of its primary components as 'liberty, security and equality'.[17] There was a clear intent in the document to engage with modernity from Islamic approaches. However, later developments made the Tunisian state's outlook, even after independence in 1957, more secular. The Ennahda Movement arose in the 1980s as a Muslim opposition group. Yet, unlike similar organisations in neighbouring countries, it has tended to support a democratic approach to governance.

The uprisings that came to be known as the Arab Spring began in Tunisia and resulted in the overthrow of the government of Zine El Abidine Ben Ali in 2011. Elections were held to form the Tunisian Constituent Assembly, and Ennahda won the largest number of seats under the leadership of its founder, Rached Ghannouchi. However, the party stepped down in the run-up to the final drafting of the 2014 constitution, which was conducted by a neutral interim

---

[16] Anicée Van-Engeland, 'Bridging Civilisations: The New Hermeneutics of Islamic Law', in K.H. Karim and M. Eid, ed., *Engaging the Other: Public Policy and Western-Muslim Intersections* (New York, 2014), pp. 111–132.

[17] Masud, *Islamic Legal Philosophy*, p. 70.

government. The result was a constitution that does not mention the shariʻa formally but is resonant with its ethos. This was in marked contrast to the constitutional process in Egypt, where the Muslim Brotherhood-related Freedom and Justice Party, led by Mohamed Morsi, came to power in 2012 and drafted a constitution that officially gave the 'principles of the shariʻa' a place of primacy as a source of legislation. The document stated that these principles 'include general evidence, foundational rules, rules of jurisprudence, and credible sources accepted in Sunni doctrines and by the larger community'.[18] This indicated a focus mainly on the rule-based and jurisprudential aspects of the shariʻa rather than reflecting its core concept of sustaining and enhancing life. Whereas it has some progressive provisions, it was heavily biased towards Muslims whom it gave a hegemonic status. Morsi was overthrown in a military coup in 2013 and his government's constitution was abrogated.

The present Tunisian constitution upholds the 'Arab-Islamic identity' of the country but balances it with an acceptance of other cultures and religions.[19] It grants a broad-based freedom of conscience and belief. Unlike the Freedom and Justice Party's document in Egypt, it does not mention the shariʻa. However, the Tunisian constitution is consonant with the values of the latter regarding the endeavour to enable people to sustain and enhance their spiritual and material lives. Beyond guaranteeing the freedom of conscience and belief, as well as the free exercise of religious practice, this basic law explicitly mentions the state's duty to protect places of worship from 'partisan instrumentalisation', to disseminate the values of moderation, tolerance and the protection of the sacred, and the prohibition of all violations thereof. It undertakes equally to prohibit and fight against calls for *takfir* (accusing a person of apostasy) and the incitement of violence and hatred. The constitution's intent is to value the sacred while at the same time countering religious extremism and political exploitation; it upholds the shariʻa view of Islam as 'a middle way' that eschews extremes.[20]

---

[18] Government of Egypt, *The New Constitution of the Arab Republic of Egypt*, trans. by International IDEA: accessible at http://constitutionaltransitions.org/wp-content/uploads/2013/05/Egypt-Constitution-26-December-2012.pdf.

[19] Government of Tunisia, *Tunisia's Constitution of 2014*, trans. by United Nations Development Programme: accessible at https://www.constituteproject.org/constitution/Tunisia_2014.pdf?lang=en.

[20] Ennhada has formally distanced itself from 'political Islam'. See K. Piser, 'Why Ennahda, Tunisia's Islamist Party, Shed Its "Political Islam" Label', *World Politics Review*, 20 May 20 2016: accessible at http://www.worldpoliticsreview.com/trend-lines/18850/why-ennahda-tunisia-s-islamist-party-shed-its-political-islam-label.

Sustaining and Enhancing Life 73

There are firm statements in the constitution about supporting good governance and development. The Good Governance and Anti-Corruption Commission has been established and is made responsible for 'the consolidation of principles of transparency, integrity and accountability'. This provides for the values of truth and ethics in administering the country's affairs, which are core to the spirit of the shari'a. The constitution lays out principles for enabling a better quality of life for Tunisians. It speaks of social justice and sustainable development, thus drawing on contemporary concepts that fit well with the shari'a's primary objectives. The enhancement of the lives of people is to be carried out by ensuring their rights to participate in various aspects of the country's development. Also in consonance with the Prophet's Sunna, the state promises to enable various classes of vulnerable group to participate in national life. The integrity of the 2014 Tunisian constitution will depend on the way in which the government, civil society and citizens implement and protect it.

Civil Society

There is a long tradition in Muslim societies of non-state organisations carrying out activities to sustain and enhance the lives of individuals and the community.[21] Historically, Muslim societies have had several major institutions that were distinct from the state and served to provide for a balance of power, such as the office of the *muhtasib*, the public inspector. There have been numerous sociopolitical Muslim organisations since the early 20th century that have strived to uphold and enhance Islamic values. They have formed organisations that provide social, economic and medical services. This has proved to be of significant value in many Muslim-majority countries where certain public services are unavailable, especially in rural areas, or are of very poor quality. The institutions include hospitals, housing associations, legal clinics and welfare organisations. A major example is that of the Edhi Foundation, a national social welfare organisation in Pakistan. It primarily provides medical care and public health services and, in a country whose government is struggling to meet the needs of a rapidly expanding population, the network of Edhi Centres in urban and rural areas offers support to the generally neglected parts of society.

---

[21] See A.B. Sajoo, ed., *Civil Society in the Muslim Wold: Contemporary Perspectives* (London, 2002); K.H. Karim, 'Muslim Civil Society in Eastern and Western Contexts', in K.H. Karim and M. Eid, ed., *Engaging the Other* (New York, 2014), pp. 153–173.

The privately funded and managed foundation's work has come to be well known among Pakistanis, especially as a result of its large fleet of ambulances.

There is also significant Muslim participation in voluntary associations in western societies that are motivated by Islamic values of service. Several organisations have worked to counter Islamophobia and improve the ways in which Muslims are treated by mainstream institutions and the public. Among the most prominent of these bodies in North America is the Washington, DC-based Council for American-Islamic Relations, whose Canadian counterpart is the National Canadian Council of Muslims. Whereas most major Muslim organisations in western societies tend to be fairly conservative in their religious outlook, there are several that have 'progressive' orientations. The Canadian Council of Muslim Women (CCMW) has a good record of working productively with wider society. Its principles and objectives reflect a desire to interact with other Canadian associations and individuals from Muslim perspectives while upholding the ideals of pluralism, social justice, human rights, the rule of law and inclusion.[22]

The Aga Khans, Imams of the Shi'i Ismaili Muslims, who trace their lineage to the Prophet Muhammad through his daughter Fatima and Ali b. Ali Talib, have been engaged in civil society work since the 19th century. The current Aga Khan, Shah Karim al-Husseini, has established the Aga Khan Development Network (AKDN), which operates as a transnational civil society institution and operates in social, economic and cultural sectors. The AKDN employs some 80,000 people, the majority of whom are based in various developing countries where Muslims are both in majority and minority. It operates in more than 30 countries grouped into eight regions: Eastern Africa, Central and Western Africa, South Asia, the Middle East, Central Asia, the Far East and Southeast Asia, Europe and North America. The Aga Khan Foundation is the lead agency engaged in the AKDN's social development activities, such as education, health and social welfare. Agencies of the Aga Khan Fund for Economic Development are concerned with industrial promotion, tourism, finance, aviation and media. The Aga Khan Trust for Culture runs a historic cities programme, an award for architecture, a music initiative, museum projects, architectural research programmes and a digital archive in various parts of the world.

The AKDN's literature does not mention the shari'a but describes the network's aim as being to 'realise the social conscience of Islam

---

[22] CCMW (Canadian Council of Muslim Women, Le conseil Canadien des femmes musulmanes): http://ccmw.com/.

Sustaining and Enhancing Life   75

through institutional action.[23] The Aga Khan frequently states that improving the quality of life of people is the general goal of the AKDN's agencies. He explains his role in development by referring to Islamic perspectives in which *din* and *dunya* are intertwined. The Imam has coined the term 'the enabling environment' to refer to the fostering of voluntary service to improve social conditions. In all this, he appears to invoke the shari'a's end purposes of sustaining and enhancing human existence.

At an international conference on the Prophet's life held in Karachi, Pakistan, in 1976, the Aga Khan addressed the difficulty of devising ways to ensure that contemporary Muslims could live in peace and prosperity within an Islamic ethos and suggested that the Sunna offers the answer:

> The Holy Prophet's life gives us every fundamental guideline that we require to resolve the problem as successfully as our human minds and intellects can visualize. His example of integrity, loyalty, honesty, generosity both of means and of time, his solicitude for the poor, the weak and the sick, his steadfastness in friendship, his humility in success, his magnanimity in victory, his simplicity, his wisdom in conceiving new solutions for problems which could not be solved by traditional methods, without affecting the fundamental concepts of Islam, surely all these are foundations which, correctly understood and sincerely interpreted, must enable us to conceive what should be a truly modern and dynamic Islamic Society in the years ahead.[24]

The Ismaili Imam finds in the Prophet's life the model for Islamic society in the present and the future. Muhammad developed the institutions of the Muslim state by, in the words of the Aga Khan, 'conceiving new solutions for problems which could not be solved by traditional methods, without affecting the fundamental concepts of Islam'. This approach underlies the problem-solving nature of the shari'a. Whereas the AKDN does not make explicit mention of the shari'a in its ideas about development, the Aga Khan has initiated a research project at the Institute for the Study of Islam of the Aga

---

[23] Aga Khan Development Network: http://www.akdn.org/about-us/akdns-approach-development.

[24] Aga Khan, 'Presidential Address', in Prince Karim Aga Khan, *The Muslim World: Yesterday, Today & Tomorrow* (Karachi, n.d.), p. 28.

76   *The Shari'a*

Khan University to examine its role in issues of governance that lead
to improving the quality of life.

Another major civil society association that is also transnational
in nature and inspired by Islam is Hizmet, also known as the Gülen
Movement. It focuses on the spiritual and intellectual consciousness
of the individual, promoting an inner self that will enable the person
to effect change in society. Emerging in Turkey in the 1960s, it has
spread to various other parts of the world, where it is supported
mainly by members of the Turkish diaspora. It does not have a
formalised institutional structure and is loosely organised. The
movement has around 8 million participants who have built schools,
hospitals, media, relief organisations and interfaith dialogue centres
in some 180 countries on five continents. Its media organs include
television stations (Turkish: Samanyolu TV, Mehtap TV; English:
Ebru TV), newspapers (Turkish: *Zaman*; English: *Today's Zaman*),
magazines and journals (Turkish: *Aksiyon, Sızıntı, Yeni Ümit*; English:
The Fountain Magazine; Arabic: *Hira*), the International Cihan News
Agency and the radio station Burç FM. More than 120 charter schools
in the United States in 25 states, serving mostly underprivileged
students, are operated by participants in the Gülen Movement.[25]

Hizmet stresses the role that technology and new global networks
can play in articulating a Muslim consciousness. Inspired by the
teachings of Fethullah Gülen, the movement is characterised by a
localised set of institutions run by groups of supporters in various
places. They are guided by the Hizmet's media, which carry Gülen's
sermons and commentaries. Influenced by Sufi teachings, he does not
advocate Islamist politics but, nevertheless, holds that religion should
not be marginalised in the public sphere. Since the 1970s, Gülen
has preached a particular Islamic approach to Turkish nationalism,
the free market, contemporary education, democracy and peaceful
coexistence.[26]

In the uneasy politics of Turkey where the interests of religious
and secularist groups have clashed over the last few decades,
Gülen was accused in 2016 of inciting an attempted coup against
the government and previously, in 2000, of wanting to establish an

---

[25] Stephanie Saul, 'Charter Schools Tied to Turkey Grow in Texas', *New York Times*, 6 June 2011: accessible at http://www.nytimes.com/2011/06/07/education/07charter.html?_r=0.

[26] M. Hermansen, 'Who is Fethullah Gülen? An Overview of His Life', in M.E. Marty, ed., *Hizmet Means Service: Perspective on an Alternative Path within Islam* (Los Angeles, 2015).

Sustaining and Enhancing Life   77

Islamic state. Charges were brought against him following a sermon in which he spoke about the shari'a. Explaining his position, he stated

> I talked about ash-shari'a al-Fitriya. God has two collections of laws: one, issuing from His Attribute of Speech, is the principles of religion, also called the shari'a. However, in the narrow sense they mean the political laws of Islam. The other, issuing from His Attribute of Will and Power, is the principles to govern the universe and life, 'the natures of law' that are the subject-matter of sciences. In Islamic terminology, this is called shari'a al-Fitriya. Respecting these two collections of laws will make us prosperous in this world and the next, while opposing them will lead us to ruin. The Muslim world remained behind the West because it opposed shari'a al-Fitriya.[27]

According to Gülen, spiritual and material prosperity comes from adhering to the religious and scientific aspects of the shari'a. He indicates that whereas many Muslims have been striving to follow religious rules and regulations, they have neglected the shari'a al-Fitriya that would enable them to enhance their worldly and spiritual existence. Hizmet is seeking to demonstrate the importance of this aspect of Islam through the success of its development projects, which have improved quality of life in many communities.

Conclusion

Adherence to the notion that the gate of reasoning had closed led to the shrinking of the sources of knowledge among Muslims. Even though this idea was not accepted by all, it affected social growth. Shari'a in the minds of many, the shari'a was reduced from a rich and vibrant resource that provided the tools to deal with ever-changing circumstances to being an ossified body of permissions and prohibitions. As a human construct, it could not be the only path to living a good Islamic life. However, it gained this paramount status over time, even as the perception of its scope narrowed.

The Qur'an's first chapter, Surat al-Fatiha, ends with a prayer beseeching God to guide believers to *al-sirat al-mustaqim*, the straight (i.e. right) path. Here, the *sirat* (path) is not completely synonymous

---

[27] Ibid., p. 33.

with the *shari'a* (path, way), nor with *tariqa* (way). Nevertheless, all three relate to each other. *Sirat* as the straight or right path and the *shari'a* as the path to water appear metaphorically to refer to similar results: material and spiritual fulfilment. *Tariqa* in Sufi parlance also points in the same direction. However, the ideas that constituted the *shari'a* and *tariqa* were formed through the intellectual effort that occurred long after the revelation. They are not as basic to Islamic spirituality as *al-sirat al-mustaqim* by virtue of its clear presentation in the Qur'an. However, this concept has not been developed to the extent of the other two. The *shari'a* has largely stood in for elaborating what is the right path for believers to follow.

Its etymology is indicative of a deep significance that goes far beyond law. The *shari'a* is a guide to the entirety of life. Spiritual and material matters interlace within it in accordance with Islamic views about the symbiotic relationship between them. However, the *shari'a* has been misperceived for centuries as a means to preserve practices from earlier times – times that are seen as being more authentically and more pristinely Islamic. This has produced a conservative attitude to the *shari'a* and has tended to freeze it. Its vast potential for informing the processes of improving human life has been lost for many. In a cruel misuse of its legal elements, unscrupulous authorities have exploited its regime of extreme punishments for political purposes. Such abuses have completely excised the vital aspect of the *shari'a* that highlights mercy and forgiveness, which are replete in the Qur'an and the Sunna.

The sincere endeavour by some actors to engage with Islamic sources to produce integral forms of contemporary Muslim governance gives cause for optimism. In a thoughtful reorientation from the aggressive positions held by several religious parties, the new Tunisian constitution has carved out a circumspect place between modernity and tradition. The constituent assembly evoked the spirit of the *shari'a* but did not inscribe it overtly into the document. Even in a country which is more than 99 per cent Muslim and where the leading political party has been described as being 'Islamist', the constitution is distinct from the formal *shari'a*. Nevertheless, it fosters the sustenance and enhancement of life in a manner that echoes the primary objectives of the latter. The Edhi Foundation, the CCMW, the AKDN and Hizmet, among various other organisations founded by Muslims, are also cognisant of the ethos of the *shari'a* with respect to enabling the improvement of quality of life. They each have long records of success in applying Islamic principles to the work of societal development. These civil society organisations have demonstrated that insightful readings of the Prophet's Sunna can yield some of the most constructive outcomes in realising the purposes of the *shari'a* in our time.

Sustaining and Enhancing Life   79

Further Reading

Bakhtiar, Laleh. *Sufi: Expressions of the Mystic Quest*. London, 1976.

Government of India. *Social, Economic and Educational Status of the Muslim Community of India*. New Delhi, 2006.

Inayatullah, S. and G. Boxwell, ed. *Islam, Postmodernism and Other Futures: A Ziauddin Sardar Reader*. London, 2003.

Karim, Karim H. and Mahmoud Eid, ed. *Engaging the Other: Public Policy and Western-Muslim Intersections*. New York, 2014.

Lapidus, Ira M. *A History of Islamic Societies*, 3rd edn. Cambridge, 2014.

Marty, Martin E., ed., *Hizmet Means Service: Perspective on an Alternative Path within Islam*. Los Angeles, 2015.

Masud, Muhammad K. *Islamic Legal Philosophy: A Study of Abu Ishaq al-Shatibi's Life and Thought*. Islamabad, 1984.

Nasr, Seyyed H. *Ideals and Realities of Islam*. London, 1975.

Sajoo, Amyn B., ed. *A Companion to Muslim Ethics*. London, 2010.

Singer, Amy. *Charity in Islamic Societies*. Cambridge, 2008.

5

Spiritual Refinement

Sa'diyya Shaikh

'Verily, God does not change the condition of a people until they change what is within themselves.'

Qur'an, 13:11

Within Islam, spiritual balance is a foundational impetus in the formulation of law. Islamic law indeed seeks to articulate norms for behaviour and ethical relationships, inspired by a religious cosmology with the God–human relationship at the centre. Generations of Muslim legal scholars have interpreted the implications of this core theological vision, fostering a jurisprudence (fiqh) that is embedded in their understanding of the shari'a. For Muslims, the shari'a itself presents a spiritually vibrant moral vision that fosters ethical, legal and spiritual pathways to human flourishing and well-being within an Islamic cosmology. This chapter aims to illuminate the foundational theological and spiritual dimensions that invigorate the shari'a, and to offer contemporary Muslims the resources to develop formulations of Islamic law and ethics which are both socially relevant and spiritually alive. Critical in these considerations is the interaction between what are considered universal, religiously determined beliefs and norms on the one hand, and changing dynamic ideas about human subjectivity and sociality on the other. In this vein, we engage with essential questions about what constitutes the human being as a religious and social subject from a Muslim perspective.

Recent debates about the ritual leadership of Muslim women shed light on the complex and interweaving relationships of ethics, gender and Islamic law. Especially interesting is an episode in Cape Town in 1994, a historic year for South Africans, who had just triumphed over the apartheid government and ushered in the first non-racial democratic elections. That year, Professor Amina Wadud, a Muslim scholar and courageous activist, delivered a Friday sermon at the invitation of the congregants of the Claremont Main Road Mosque. This sparked intense discussion about women's religious leadership in South Africa and beyond.

82   *The Shari'a*

In 2005, Wadud not only delivered her sermon but also led the Friday
public ritual prayers in New York, in full view of the international
media. Legal opinions about women's leadership of Muslim ritual
prayers (imamate) went viral through social media and internet articles.

Muslim religious leaders responded very differently. On the one hand,
Sohaib Bencheikh, the former Grand Mufti of Marseilles, coming from
an older generation of male graduates from the traditional Egyptian
al-Azhar University, publicly participated in a congregational prayer
service led by another woman in solidarity with the event in New York.
On the other hand, Dr Soad Saleh, a female Islamic law professor also
at al-Azhar, declared that women-led prayers with mixed congregations
constitute apostasy in Islam, an offence punishable by death in classical
interpretations of Islamic law. Among her reasons for rejecting female
imams is that 'the woman's body, even if veiled, stirs desire'. Clearly, debates
about women's public ritual leadership are saturated with contestations
over embodiment and gender, spirituality and leadership, sexuality and
power in Islam. Indeed, these tensions come down to our more basic
understandings of what it is to be 'religious' and 'human', and how these play
out in modern settings that are framed by the dominance of the secular.

Our perspectives on these fraught questions might be unexpectedly
enriched by turning to the refreshing counsel provided by an eminent
13th-century Muslim scholar and Sufi, Muhyi al-Din Ibn al-Arabi
(1165–1240). In a striking contrast to the focus on women's bodies
as the inappropriate provocateur of male desire, Ibn Arabi offers a
very different approach. For him, ungendered and equal access to the
position of imam is ethically driven by the Islamic view that men and
women have identical spiritual potential, a view that I explore in more
detail later in this chapter. Ibn Arabi crisply informs his reader that
spiritual and ontological equality between men and women has clear
social and ritual consequences. It is not simply centuries that divide
Saleh from this pre-modern personality; Ibn Arabi and Saleh also
radically differ with regard to assumptions about the nature of gendered
bodies and human responsibility. Ibn Arabi categorically affirms a universal
and gender-inclusive spiritual map of human nature, where women may
lead a mixed congregation of men and women in ritual prayers.

Ibn Arabi's position highlights a key insight: religious views on
human nature, captured in the term 'religious anthropology', underlie
and saturate legal reasoning.[1] That is, Islamic law is underpinned by

---

[1] For a more extensive discussion of 'religious anthropology', see Sa'diyya
Shaikh, *Sufi Narratives of Intimacy: Ibn Arabi, Gender and Sexuality* (Chapel
Hill, NC, 2012), pp. 6–10.

Spiritual Refinement 83

gendered assumptions about the nature of human beings and interpersonal relationships within a theological worldview. Muslim religious anthropologies are ultimately grounded in particular understandings of the God–human relationship – that is, they necessarily draw on a theological map where the ultimate goal is human refinement and a spiritually imbued existence in harmony with the divine will. Sufis have made subtle and nuanced contributions to these concepts of theology, spirituality and religious anthropology in ways that offer significant insights for contemporary Muslim law and ethics.

This chapter is divided into two main sections. The first makes a case for examining and reimagining the relationship between Sufi spirituality and law. Here I provide a critique and analyses of some dominant legal discourses in the modern period with special regard to the value of engaging Sufi concepts to redress gendered deficits. The second section provides an alternative and constructive vision for rethinking ethics and law on the basis of Sufi spirituality, drawing on Ibn Arabi's ideas in particular. In focusing on gender, it proposes a more inclusive and generous paradigm for contemporary Muslims.

Sufism and the Legal Tradition

Historically, Sufi thinkers have provided a detailed commentary on the spiritual landscape of the human condition, and the ways in which submission to the divine will serve as the basis for law, ethics and sociability. Bringing particular Sufi perspectives to bear on discussions about gender offers fertile spaces to explore the underlying foundations of the law. Such a project directs one to core enquiries about being human, the God–human relationship and the implications for social ethics – all of which underlie fiqh. Such an enquiry also exposes the ways in which partial, historically and culturally conditioned interpretive legacies in fiqh discourses have acquired authority across time and territory. Ultimately, this allows Muslims to critically re-examine the law in the light of the deepest existential and religious priorities within their traditions.

I suggest that particular Sufi discourses present substantial resources for developing more relevant, enriching and benevolent interpretations of the shariʻa and the related understandings of human nature reflected in the Qurʼan than do the prevailing fiqh discourses. It is true that Sufism, like all other traditions of Muslim thought and practice, bears the imprints of its formative history and contexts. Much of the influential legacy of Sufism emerged within androcentric societies, and often mirrors related gender biases. However, Sufi thought concurrently offers resources on the deepest

84   *The Shariʿa*

human imperatives in Islam, which are profoundly gender inclusive
and productive for feminists. In my view the rich relationship between
Sufism and Islamic law has not been sufficiently developed in terms of
its possibilities for rethinking contemporary gender ethics.

Sufis do not hold a singular position on gender; nor is Sufism an
ahistorical remedy that miraculously heralds all things good and
benevolent for women. Even al-Ghazali (1058–1111), who criticised
laws that were not rooted in ethical praxis, envisioned an ethics of
justice saturated with male domination. Sufism as practised in a variety
of historical contexts thus embodies tensions between patriarchal
inclinations and egalitarian impulses.[2]

Yet in some significant ways and instances, Sufi practices have
subverted traditional patriarchal religious anthropology – and, as I
argue later, these subversions invoke egalitarian understandings that
reside at the heart of Sufism, and indeed of Islam. It is these ideas
that I expand and develop here as counter-narratives to the reigning
patriarchal legal narratives of the self and gender.

Rethinking Authority in the Shariʿa

Muslim jurists have drawn on manifold ways of interpreting the sacred
texts, as shown in this volumes' chapters. All too often, however, the
tendency in a male-dominated legal establishment was to select specific
terms from Qurʾanic teachings and to develop these into systematic
foundations for a gender hierarchy. More than anything else this reflected
prevailing social hierarchies of male authority and female obedience.

The Qurʾan itself provides a textured approach to the human being
and gender relations. The more encompassing, generous and egalitarian
visions for imagining the gender-inclusive human being in the Qurʾan
coexist alongside descriptions of male authority. Scholars such as Amina
Wadud and Asma Barlas have attended to the tensions between, on the
one hand, the ways in which the Qurʾan includes women as full human
subjects in relationship with God and society; and, on the other, the
ways in which the Qurʾan describes gender roles characterising the
patriarchal 7th-century context of revelation. These scholars suggest
that essential Qurʾanic teachings on the God–human relationship
reflecting men and women as equal subjects of its worldview have
historically been neglected. Such teachings organically provide spaces
for asserting the ontological equality of every human being.

---

[2] For a discussion of diverse gender narratives in early Sufism, see Shaikh, *Sufi
Narratives*, pp. 38–60.

Spiritual Refinement

A critical reading of pre-modern legal texts reveals the ways in which the legal canon reflects the subjectivities, experiences and ideas of male scholars in particular times and places. Undoubtedly many were sincere scholars with a genuine desire to interpret faithfully the God-given moral pathway, or the shari'a, to the best of their understanding. Their understanding, however, was inevitably influenced by cultural norms of male dominance and gender hierarchy. The 'naturalness' of male dominance in pre-modern legal thought is unremarkable, given the androcentric sociocultural mores of most societies within which they were formulated. Scholars of hermeneutics have made us aware of the historically embedded nature of *all* interpretive endeavours, and how a jurist's pre-understandings and situatedness shape the meanings he or she derives from authoritative texts. Despite historical shifts in the interpretation of gendered concepts in the legal canon, the persistence of gendered binaries of male power and authority over women is evident. Androcentric legal notions of the human condition that derive from particular modes of reading the Qur'an have enduring negative consequences for Muslim women, including broad discrimination in social and legal practice.

Developing a more structural and theologically robust critique requires critical attention to the constructed nature of Islamic juris-prudence, or fiqh, as a human and historically evolving interpreta-tion of the shari'a. The shari'a signifies a moral and religious vision for human fulfilment, while fiqh represents multiple and varied human interpretive attempts to translate that vision into legal norms. A structural critique of the established fiqh canon would involve ask-ing some fundamental questions about the nature of the shari'a and its historical interpretations. What are the ideological implications of using the terms 'shari'a' and 'fiqh' interchangeably? What is the continuing impact of context and historical circumstance on the formation of Islamic law? Indeed, what is meant by the terms 'human being', 'society' and 'God', which underlie dominant stances in the fiqh literature?

Equally promising is a deeper reflection on the very concept of the shari'a as a *path* to be travelled. A path signifies movement and vigour; it presumes a journey where progress defies stagnant or singular conceptions. Suggestively, the image of a path urges one to think of the legal tradition as dynamic – demanding movement and suppleness by travellers who might traverse shifting terrain and varying time periods. It also encourages Muslims to think productively about the fluid and engaged relationship between dimensions of human life that are historical/particular and those that aspire to the transcendental/ universal realms.

On the one hand, a path offers a direction, orientation and ultimate goal towards which one progresses. One might interpret this dimension as the universal purpose of the shariʿa: Muslims in all times and contexts need a compelling existential and spiritual map that provides clear means to achieve the highest goals of engaged surrender to God. On the other hand, depending on its historical and cultural location, a community of believers has to innovatively interpret this existential vision in ways that respond appropriately to a changing social horizon. A responsiveness to location helps move integrated spiritual and social progress on to the ultimate goal of earning divine pleasure. Explicitly recovering the concept of the shariʿa as a path enables one to adopt refreshing approaches to tradition, which in turn allow us to shed attachments to stagnant outer forms. It allows for an embrace of a fluidity nourished by a spiritually vibrant inner core to sustain ethical revival. Such an approach to the shariʿa enables generous and appropriate responses to the invariable changes wrought by culture, history and society, while progressing towards a universal goal of achieving harmony with God's will.

No Muslim project of renewal and revival will develop exclusively on the basis of contemporary social sensibilities. For believers, this must also be informed by metaphysical sensibilities that prioritise the God–human relationship in the development of ethics. Sufism organically addresses these deeper levels of understanding. In holding in view the underlying issues of values, principles and human purpose consistently, Sufism enables the enquirer to arrive at different possibilities from the dominant fiqh discourse.

The debates about the relationship between the shariʿa and the Sufi path (tariqa) have a long history in Islamic thought. In some groups, Sufi practitioners with advanced capacities for ethical judgment exercised their discretion in observing the law. Others insisted that religiously acceptable behaviour should always be determined by the letter of the law. In fact, in the modern period, contestations of the nature of what constitutes proper Sufi teachings and practice resulted in an intensified focus by some major Sufi groups on asserting the primacy of the shariʿa in relation to Sufi practice.[3] Most of these discussions, however, generally accept the dominant fiqh canon, with all of its gendered assumptions, as accurate expressions of the shariʿa. I question such assumptions, particularly some of the problematic presuppositions

---

[3] For detailed discussions of these debates in the modern world, see Elizabeth Sirriyeh, *Sufis and Anti-Sufis: The Defence, Rethinking, and Rejection of Sufism in the Modern World* (London, 2003).

on the nature of men and women that underlie much of the inherited and socially conditioned fiqh canon. While for most legal scholars it is a theoretical commonplace that the fiqh canon represents limited human attempts to express the shari'a and that the fiqh is the product of dynamic human processes, more ideologised and simplistic conflations between the shari'a and fiqh often appear in popular political discourse. This phenomenon continues to have detrimental consequences for gender justice and women's rights in many contemporary Muslim societies.

I also challenge dominant gender constructions underlying much of the traditional fiqh canon as deviating from core ontological assumptions intrinsic to the shari'a. Hence, I am not engaging in the older debate as to whether the shari'a has primacy over the *tariqa* or vice versa. Rather, I argue that certain Sufi discourses offer more refined and penetrating readings of the shari'a and the related assumptions of human nature in the Qur'an than the dominant fiqh discourses. By exploring Sufi metaphysics, this chapter suggests an alternative nexus between Sufism and the shari'a, offering an ontological ground for reshaping gender ethics in emerging feminist fiqh discourses.

Sufi Psychology, Human Nature and Gender

Serious attention to the human being's inner state, together with the belief that people all share the same spiritual imperatives irrespective of whether one occupies a male or a female body, signifies one of the organically genderless assumptions within Sufism.[4] In principle, Sufism and the broader Islamic tradition presuppose that every human being can pursue and achieve the same ultimate goals, and that gender does not constitute an impediment or an advantage to these existential ends. This poses a challenge to the very basis of patriarchy, where the male body is the signifier of social and ontological superiority. Moreover, as detailed below, Sufi psychology inherently promotes vigilance towards assertions of personal and social superiority over others. Such suspicion directed at the spiritual dynamics underpinning interpersonal hierarchy enables a productive space for a critique of gender discrimination. The following exploration of Sufi psychology allows for a deeper dialogue with its gender ideology.

---

[4] Nonetheless, some male Sufis ignored these basic genderless assumptions and integrated misogynist views of the self into their works as evident in a study by Rkia Cornell, '"Soul of a Woman Was Created Below": Woman as the Lower Soul (*Nafs*) in Islam', in Hendrik M. Vroom, ed., *World Religions and Evil: Religious and Philosophical Perspectives* (New York, 2007), pp. 257–280.

88   *The Shariʻa*

Human subjectivity in Sufism may be conceptualised in relation to the tripartite relationship between the soul (*nafs*), the heart (*qalb*) and the spirit (*ruh*), as identified in the Qurʼan.[5] The *nafs*, identified as one's self-awareness, can dynamically range from being dominated by base instincts and cravings to being characterised by a state of peace and submission to God, with varying intermediate possibilities. In its crudest and most unrefined state, it is described as *al-nafs al-ammara*, the commanding soul, or 'the soul that incites to evil' (Qurʼan, 12:53). Dominated by egoistic tendencies, it draws a person to the realm of limited selfhood and transient desires, and is responsible for separation from the original state of harmony between God and humanity. A person governed by *al-nafs al-ammara* perceives worldly, ephemeral attractions such as social power, fame, wealth and physical gratification as meaningful in themselves, and such a person is blind to the true nature of reality.

A central task of the Sufi path is to refine and purify these lower instincts within the self and in so doing establish receptivity to God. The spirit (*ruh*), which is a subtle life-giving entity blown into every human being from God's self (Qurʼan, 15:29), is central to this process of inner refinement. While the *nafs* is associated with the self-centredness and blindness of the devil, the *ruh* has been associated with the angelic qualities of luminosity and discernment, drawing one towards God and the higher echelons of spiritual awareness. The opposing spiritual forces activated by the respective inclinations of *al-nafs al-ammara* and the *ruh* struggle for supremacy within the individual's heart (*qalb*) and give rise to various thoughts, ideas and impulses. Moral choice for the early masters depended on a careful analysis and discernment of these forces and how to respond appropriately to them.[6]

The third constituent, the *qalb*, is the centre of human spiritual receptivity and contingent on the inner state of the individual. Through succumbing to negative or evil impulses and transient desires, most hearts become rusted or opaque. A person removes this rust on the heart by persistent remembrance of God, inner vigilance, abstinence from incorrect behaviour and performance of good actions – including

---

[5]   See the discussion by Annemarie Schimmel, *Mystical Dimensions of Islam* (Chapel Hill, NC, 1975), p. 191.

[6]   Al-Muhasibi (781–857) developed a complex moral psychology providing a seeker with ways to understand egoism and vigilantly monitor his or her responses. For selections from his writings, see Michael Sells, *Early Islamic Mysticism: Sufi, Qurʼan, Miraj, Poetic and Theological Writings* (New York, 1996), pp. 171–195.

Spiritual Refinement 89

service to other human beings and other rigorous spiritual practices. Such forms of spiritual discipline result in the weakening of the commanding soul within the person and the transformation into a different state of being known as *al-nafs al-lawwama*, 'the blaming soul', which desists from evil instincts. This marks the emergence of the conscience, where the striving for good has been integrated and internalised, and where the individual's moral compass is alive and functional. With consistent purification, the heart is cleansed and illuminated by the divine light of the spirit, and the soul of the seeker is satisfied, described as *al-nafs al-mutma'inna*, 'the soul at peace'. Describing such an inner state of attainment, al-Ghazali invokes a *hadith qudsi*, which is particularly popular with the Sufis, where God says: 'The heavens and earth contain me not, but the heart of my faithful servant contains me.'[7] Cultivating this state of receptivity and complete submission to the divine might be seen as the highest theological and existential aspiration for Muslims. For a human being to realise fully the presence of God in the heart, it is necessary to subdue the narcissistic impulses that battle to remain sovereign.

Sufi psychology provides an inherent critique of egotism, which in turn presents an opportunity to challenge notions of male superiority. For Sufis, the constant awareness of God's absolute sovereignty counters the human instinct to claim power over others, including male claims to authority over women. Within this framework, any such claim demands interrogation and may be suspected as a potential trap of the lower self (*al-nafs al-ammara*). This is reflected in a number of classical Sufi narratives where interactions between women and men effectively constitute a penetrating spiritual and social critique of their normative gender assumptions.[8]

One such narrative cited in the famous 13th-century work entitled *Tadhkhirat al-Awliya* (*Memorial of the Saints*) by Farid al-Din 'Attar involves the legendary and influential early Sufi, Rabi'a al-'Adawiyya (ca. 717–801). Narrating this story, 'Attar tells us that some religious men attempted to provoke Rabi'a, saying: 'All the virtues have been scattered on the heads of men. The crown of prophethood has been placed on men's heads. The belt of nobility has been fastened around men's waists. No woman has ever been a prophet.' Rabi'a calmly replies: 'All that is true, but egoism and self-worship and "I am your Lord" have never sprung from a woman's breast ... All these things have

---

[7]   Abu Hamid al-Ghazali, *Ihya 'ulum al-Din* (Cairo, 1909), p. 12.

[8]   For a range of classical Sufi stories reflecting gender critique, see Shaikh, *Sufi Narratives*, pp. 54–56.

90   *The Shari'a*

been the specialty of men.'[9] What might appear to be an acerbic retort also constitutes a formidable spiritual critique of patriarchal power. Rabi'a rejects the men's claims to gender-based superiority by potently associating these with the arch disbeliever in the Qur'an, Pharaoh. The latter's delusional but wilful assertion, 'I am your Lord' (Qur'an, 79:24), reflects the ultimate depths of spiritual disease and desolation.

Rabi'a, invoking a pointed set of Qur'anic associations, denounces men's desire for privilege and authority over women as symptomatic of their severe spiritual deficit. Their chauvinism emerges as the consequence of the deleterious triumph of their *al-nafs al-ammara*. Male subjectivities produced through patriarchy may well be spiritually compromised since implicit assumptions of purely gender-based superiority thwart a fundamental theological imperative in Islam: the ability to discern and surrender to God as the genuine source of power is shrouded when an individual assumes arbitrary superiority over another life. Whatever distracts and misleads an individual from the awareness of God's absolute sovereignty, such as social prestige premised on gender difference, is spiritually detrimental to the individual. Developing this analysis allows us to suggest that patriarchy is reflective of a lack of spiritual discernment. In the above story, central Sufi principles concerning the prioritisation of the inner state and the critique of gender-based hierarchal power are discursively implicit to traditional Sufi insights into spiritual refinement. According to this interpretation, progress on the spiritual path can imply directly challenging patriarchal impulses as they arise. Rabi'a did so with aplomb, and he presents us with a discerning role model for contesting male privilege. While this story encapsulates a penetrating spiritual critique of patriarchy, other Sufi narratives provide generous religious anthropologies with radical implications for rethinking gender, and the 13th-century work of Ibn Arabi is one such resource.

Ibn Arabi: Divine Echoes, Human Reverberations

Muhyi al-Din Ibn Arabi, a legendary Sufi and jurist,[10] offers meaningful ideas about gender that are always situated within a broader Islamic

---

[9]   Farid al-Din Attar, *Muslim Saints and Mystics: Episodes from the Tadhkhirat al-Auliya* (*Memorial of the Saints*), trans. A.J. Arberry (London, 1966), 48.b.

[10]   While there is no evidence that Ibn Arabi was a practising jurist, Eric Winkel [*Islam and the Living Law: The Ibn Al-Arabi Approach* (New York, 1997)] shows that fiqh is integral to Ibn Arabi's entire vision, which is suffused with legal reasoning and jurisprudence.

Spiritual Refinement 91

understanding of universal human nature and purpose.[11] In presenting
a helpful and illuminating ontological map, he draws on the Hadith that
'God created Adam in God's own form', as well as the Qur'anic verse
that states that God 'taught Adam all of the names' (Qur'an, 2:30).[12]
In this context, Adam represents the archetypal human being; he is
neither merely a prophet nor just a male human. The 'names' signify the
attributes or qualities of God – the Qur'an also describes these as 'the
beautiful names' (*al-asma al-husna*). Traditionally, it is held that God
has 99 names, qualities or attributes that reside within His state of unity
(*tawhid*). Creation occurs through a manifestation of these attributes
from the original state of divine oneness.

Ibn Arabi states that among all creation, humanity uniquely reflects
the potential to integrate comprehensively and manifest the totality of
God's attributes – in other words, a microcosm of the divine names.[13]
Humanity unifies and concentrates all God's attributes that are reflected
in a more differentiated manner in the rest of the universe or the
macrocosm. Ibn Arabi presents a particular religious anthropology
through developing the Sufi archetypal human, the *al-insan al-kamil*
('the complete human'), which represents the ideal ethical self and
the exemplary standard for human beings.[14] Those who successfully
embody this archetype in their historical actualities are the prophets
and the friends of God (*awliya*'), as Sufi adepts are called.

In Ibn Arabi's cosmology, human beings all embody the divine
names and are intimately connected to God through these names.
Hence the names form the basis of human existential identity and self-
knowledge. Progressing on the spiritual path demands that one should
strive to purify the self from all false deities, and come to realise
one's state of ontological dependency on God. Given this model,
the question of *how* to integrate the divine names within the self,
the mode of self-cultivation and process of refinement becomes all-
important in the human spiritual journey. Ibn Arabi notes that
progress on the critical path of submission demands that the person

---

[11] Ibn Arabi's more egalitarian gender narratives were at times interwoven
seamlessly with androcentric elements more typical within his context,
reflecting ambivalent formulations of gender that characterise the broader
Muslim legacy. For a full-length exploration of the various gendered dimensions
of Ibn Arabi's thought, see Shaikh, *Sufi Narratives*.

[12] Muhyi al-Din Ibn Arabi, *al-Futuhat al-Makkiyya* (Cairo, 1911), vol. 1,
p. 216; vol. 2, p. 391.

[13] Muhyi al-Din Ibn Arabi, *Fusus al-Hikam* (*Bezels of Wisdom*), trans. R.W.J.
Austin (New York, 1980), p. 50.

[14] Muhyi al-Din Ibn Arabi, *al-Futuhat al-Makkiyya*, vol. 1, p. 216.

92   *The Shari'a*

observes the precise limit of each attribute and does not step outside the related balance between the different names.[15]

For many Muslim thinkers, including Ibn Arabi, the divine names can be divided into two groups that set up several sets of corresponding relationships with one another. These are broadly categorised into names of majesty (*jalal*) and those of beauty (*jamal*). Names of beauty, such as the Loving, the Merciful, the Beneficent, the Gentle and the Forgiver, are closely connected to the concept of God's similarity with creation; those of majesty, such as the Inaccessible, the Bringer of Death, the Overwhelming, the All-High and the Great, are connected to God's incomparability with creation.

Since the human archetype, *al-insan al-kamil*, is comprehensive in reflecting the divine names, the notions of incomparability and similarity are aimed primarily at providing an epistemological guide to the human being. Hence the notion that many of the majestic (*jalali*) qualities belong to the realm of incomparability implies that the sojourner should not make any claims to these qualities at the outset. In relation to God's *jalali* qualities, human beings should adopt a relationship of receptivity and dependency. One cannot respond to God's *jalali* names with one's own ego-based *jalali* qualities, since this will only further distance one from the source and result in misguidance. Satan epitomised misplaced *jalal* when he countered God's command to prostrate before Adam with the claim that 'I am better than he', which reflects arrogance born of a misplaced sense of power and majesty. This plunged him into a state of distance and expulsion from the realm of intimacy with God.

Through receptivity and submission to God's *jalal*, the seeker experiences increasing states of nearness to God, and to the reality of God's beauty (*jamal*). Ibn Arabi suggests that love and submission are the ingredients which yield possibilities of embodying the divine attributes in the correct manner. The epistemological priority accorded to the *jamali* attributes for the seeker is linked to its larger ontological priority within God, who says in a *hadith qudsi*, 'My mercy precedes my wrath.'[16] According to Ibn Arabi, life itself is a reflection of God's all-embracing compassion and is the premise of every other relationship and name attributed to God.

For Ibn Arabi, this pervasive mercy also travels between God and human beings through the realm of human interactions, where he

---

[15]   Ibid., vol. 4, p. 3.

[16]   For a more detailed discussion of this hadith *qudsi*, see William Chittick, *The Sufi Path of Knowledge: Ibn Al-Arabi's Metaphysics of Imagination* (Albany, NY, 1989), p. 23.

Spiritual Refinement 93

highlights the primacy of realising God's *jamali* qualities. Reflecting on the magnitude of these qualities, Ibn Arabi observes that God chooses the merciful ones from among His servants as special recipients of His grace.[17] This does not imply a disregard for Allah's *jalal* but rather the seeker attempting to dissolve the unrefined *jalali* instincts of his or her *al-nafs al-ammara* in the ocean of God's *jamali* attributes. Through this process, the individual's *jalali* dimensions can be safely harmonised, having been purified by receptivity to God, and having maintained the limit demanded by God's incomparability. Hence it can be inferred that God's *jalal* in humanity emerges out of embodying God's *jamal*.

For our purposes, what is clearly illustrated in this ontological framework is that the assumption of *jamali* attributes for human beings occurs in interpersonal and social contexts. One's spiritual transformation occurs significantly through embodying certain types of behaviour in relation to other people. Character is refined through cultivating social interactions based on love, mercy, compassion and gentleness towards our fellow beings. In this framework, spiritual development demands an ethics of care that is socially engaged and not a solitary, individualistic journey.

Ibn Arabi's key understandings of God and humanity have a number of implications for gender ideology. By highlighting the *jamali* aspects of humanity, this approach not only provides a general critique of social hierarchies and discriminatory ideologies but also rejects social structures that prize aggression and other unrefined *jalali* qualities. In our world, this critique is vital, given that these unrefined *jalali* ways of engagement typify the prevalent masculinist ways of being, long tied to destructive violence and suffering.

Over and above providing a critique of these 'macho' social norms, Ibn Arabi's framework directs one to the alternatives, where the qualities of mercy, compassion, care, justice, generosity, patience, forbearance and forgiveness are to be prioritised as what humans ought to embody. It provides a rationale for cultivating societies that value peace and justice as a necessary context for, as well as a predictable result of, the cultivation of individual character. At this level, Ibn Arabi's teachings provide spaces for a powerful, organic and ontologically grounded critique of patriarchal power relations, in relation both to the individual *and* to social formations.[18]

---

[17]   Ibid., vol. 4, p. 409.
[18]   I differ from the approach of contemporary scholars of Sufism, such as Sachiko Murata in *The Tao of Islam* (Albany, NY, 1992), who present spiritual equality between men and women as separate from social realities.

94   *The Shariʿa*

In relation to fiqh, his framework allows one to ask whether our formulations of the law reflect an engagement with the foundational metaphysical principles of Islam. The theological and social prioritisation of *jamali* realities, where majesty (*jalal*) always needs to be contained within an encompassing mercy (*jamal*), offers a crucial insight into the development of a humane legal system that genuinely marries justice with mercy and compassion. Informed by ontological imperatives of mercy, a legal system would need to reflect a deep commitment to an ethics of care, compassion and justice for men and women alike. In the contemporary period, it is clear that traditional Muslim laws seldom meet our current conceptions of care or justice. While the Sufi theological focus on the relationship between *jamal* and *jalal* enables a way to redress the broader contours of traditional Muslim law, Ibn Arabi also presents us with a more detailed elaboration of how gendered religious anthropology impacts sociolegal relationships.

Beyond the Limits of Gender

Ibn Arabi's principal concept of *al-insan al-kamil* presents a pivotal understanding of human purpose that is significant in terms of its explicit gender inclusivity. Ibn Arabi himself repeatedly says that *al-insan al-kamil*, the model for spiritual completion, is ungendered, makes identical demands on men and women, and is attainable equally by both.[19] In an exploration of different forms of sainthood, he draws on the powerful Qur'anic verse 33:35, which explicitly articulates spiritual virtues as gender inclusive:

> For men who surrender to Allah and women who surrender to Allah, for believing men and believing women, for devout men and devout women, for truthful men and truthful women, for men and women who are patient and constant, for men and women who are humble, for men and women who give charity, for men and women who fast, for men and women who guard their modesty, for men and women who are God-conscious – for them, Allah hath prepared forgiveness and a great reward.

Invoking this Qur'anic verse, Ibn Arabi strongly asserts gender-egalitarian and inclusive human possibilities, stating that 'there is no

---

[19]   Ibn Arabi, *al-Futuhat*, vol. 3, p. 89.

Spiritual Refinement 95

spiritual qualification conferred on men which is denied women.[20] In fact, elsewhere he explicitly affirms women's capacity to assume the highest spiritual station – that of the axial saint (*qutb*).[21] The notion that virtue, vice and the whole range of human capacities and responsibilities are equally applicable to men and women is a pivotal teaching on human nature that Ibn Arabi derives from his readings of the Qur'an. This type of religious anthropology has profound possibilities for reconfiguring the gendered legal subject, possibilities that have been inadequately developed by dominant fiqh discourses.

In addition to Ibn Arabi's explicit theoretical positions on the equal capacities of men and women, his autobiography reflects his experiential knowledge and lived experiences of such possibilities. Here we encounter his devotion to female spiritual teachers, his deep companionship with female Sufi peers, and his care and commitment towards his numerous female disciples.[22]

Ibn Arabi's view, reflected in both his theory and his practice, that the cultivation of an integrated balance between *jamal* and *jalal* makes exactly the same demands on male and female aspirants, has significant implications for the understandings of gender in Islam. His position provides an explicitly gender-inclusive notion of religious personhood, where all possibilities of human potential are fully available to men and women alike. Moreover, he prioritises *jamali* interactions between human beings as the basis for spiritual practice and sociability.

Significantly, Ibn Arabi connects women's equal spiritual capacity to equal legal and social competence For example, he points to the figure of Hajar as the initiator of the *sa'i* rites during the *hajj*, noting that her actions create a legal precedent applicable to the entire Muslim community.[23] This sociolegal capacity, he argues, emerges only as a consequence of women's potential for spiritual perfection. The gendered link between spiritual capacity and the ability to set communal legal precedents reflects an explicit connection between spirituality and the law in his framework.

In another discussion, Ibn Arabi begins by informing us of an approach not uncommon among other legal scholars – that despite the

---

[20]   Ibid., vol. 2, p. 35.
[21]   The *qutb* is understood to be the leader of humankind at the cosmic level, a level that saturates every other level of being.
[22]   For descriptions of his female teachers and peers, see Ibn Arabi, *Sufis of Andalusia: The Ruh al-Quds and al-Durrat al-Fakhira*, trans. R.W.J. Austin (Roxburgh, 1988), pp. 142–146, 154–155.
[23]   Ibn Arabi, *al-Futuhat*, vol. 1, p. 708.

96 *The Sharīʿa*

traditional view of restricted female legal testimony, there are situations where in fact one woman's legal testimony is equal to that of two men:

> Usually a judge does not make a definite judgment except with the testimony of two men. Yet in some circumstances the testimony of one woman equals that of two men. For example, the judge's acceptance of her testimony about menstrual cycles as it related to the waiting period after divorce (*ʿidda*), or the husband accepting her statement about his paternity of the child – despite the uncertainty pertaining to such situations. [Another example of this] is the acceptance of her testimony that she is menstruating. So she occupies in such situations, the position of two reliable male witnesses just as the man occupies the position of two women in cases of testimony about debt.[24]

Here Ibn Arabi alerts us that context and experience are principal considerations when determining gender-specific legal capacity. Such an approach suggests that legal rulings appearing to favour men may, in fact, simply be responsive to the realities and pragmatics of the social arena. Within his context, the ordinary woman's experience was limited primarily to the private realm of their bodies, while men were active in the public arena of commerce. The weight of their respective testimonies is evaluated in relation to their respective experiential and knowledge bases. Such a reading of the law resists the notion that male testimony is inherently superior. Given the vast historical changes in gender relations, this approach demands a legal system that is responsive to shifts in human social experience.

With his pragmatic reading, Ibn Arabi disrupts some of the normative gender assumptions in traditional Muslim legal discourses, notably with regard to notions of intrinsic male superiority in matters of testimony. His examples also focus on women's agency and legal capacity, in contrast to more patriarchal representations of men as primary subjects. In illuminating the contextual nature of traditional legal rulings, he urges the reader towards a dynamic, socially engaged formulation of the law.

In a pragmatic yet capacious view on issues of dressing, modesty and the covering of nakedness (*ʿawra*), Ibn Arabi states:

> Some people say that all of a woman's body, with the exception of her face and hands, constitutes the *ʿawra* ... In our opinion, the only parts of her body that are *ʿawra* are her genitals. God, the Exalted, says: 'When they tasted of the tree, their shameful

---

[24] Ibid., vol. 3, p. 89.

Spiritual Refinement 97

parts became manifest to them, and they began to sew together the leaves of the Garden over their bodies.' God put Adam and Eve on equal footing regarding the covering of their shameful parts, which are their genitals. If women are still ordered to cover their bodies, it is for the sake of modesty, and not because their bodies are shameful.[25]

Ibn Arabi rejects the ubiquitous ideas that women's bodies inherently require greater concealment than men's bodies, or that their bodies are a source of shame. Moving from the primordial into the historical, his statement, 'If women are still ordered to cover the rest of their bodies, this is for the sake of modesty' suggests that once the spiritual boundary of covering genitals has been established, notions of modesty are then not ontologically driven but rather socially produced. The element of social contingency is also reflected in the conditional 'if' with which he begins this statement regarding the command for modesty. This logic also addresses the religious rationale underlying the *hijab* debate, and in my view it offers contemporary Muslims significant flexibility and dynamism to harmonise religious requirements with cultural and social sensibilities on questions of physical modesty.

Ibn Arabi also asserts a bold position in terms of women's leadership of ritual prayers (*salat*), a controversial debate even in contemporary times:

Some people allow the imamate of women absolutely before a congregation of men and women. I agree with this. Some forbid her imamate absolutely. Others permit her imamate in a congregation exclusively of women. How to evaluate this? The prophet has testified about the [spiritual] perfection (*kamal*) of some women just as he witnessed of some men, even though there may be more men than women in such perfection. This perfection is prophethood. And being a prophet is taking on the role of a leader. Thus women's imamate is sound. The basic principle is allowing women's imamate. Thus whoever asserts that it is forbidden without proof, he should be ignored. The one who forbids this has no explicit text. His only proof in forbidding this is a shared [negative opinion] of her. This proof is insubstantial and the basic principle remains which is allowing women's imamate.[26]

---

[25] Ibid., vol. 1, p. 408.
[26] Ibid., p. 447.

98   *The Shari'a*

Ibn Arabi links a public communal role of the imam with an individual's spiritual capacity, an approach described by contemporary scholar Eric Winkel as 'spiritual legal discourse'.[27] Winkel observes that Ibn Arabi's spiritual legal discourse is about discerning divine guidance in ways that 'illuminate the crossover from outward ritual to inward truth' in every moment to ensure the dynamic search for divine guidance.[28] Winkel notes precisely this approach in Ibn Arabi's views regarding women's imamate.[29]

Ibn Arabi explicitly connects the Prophet's affirmation of women's spiritual capacity to ritual leadership and explicitly disregards the position of scholars who reject women's imamate. In this case, complete spiritual realisation implies equal and ungendered access to ritual leadership, a radically egalitarian position. While a few scholars had taken this position on the issue of women's imamate, including the much earlier al-Tabari (839–923), it was certainly not a popular viewpoint.[30] There are very few historically documented examples of women's imamate. Nevertheless, Ibn Arabi's discussion of this issue and his reference to other scholars' opinions prompts the question of whether women's imamate was perhaps an undocumented occurrence in certain communities. Whatever the case, discussions of these possibilities by leading Muslim intellectuals of the time illustrate that women's imamate was never relegated to the realm of the unthinkable. The Islamic legacy holds counter-narratives of gender that destabilise patriarchal norms. In addition, implicit in Ibn Arabi's argument regarding women's imamate is the assumption and reality that communal prayer can and should occur in gender-inclusive mosque spaces, an idea that remains contested in many contemporary Muslim settings.

In reviewing Ibn Arabi's various legal stances, I am not simply making the case that Muslims have a precedent for choosing gender-egalitarian options on matters such as legal testimony, dressing or leadership of congregational prayers. Rather, Sufi concepts relating to human nature offer us resources to address structural issues in the formulation of fiqh, as a human venture in traversing the shari'a.

---

[27] Winkel, *Islam and the Living Law*, p. vii.

[28] Ibid., pp. 23–24.

[29] Ibid., pp. 40–41.

[30] In *Bidayat al-Mujtahid* (Cairo, 1983), vol. 2, p. 289; Ibn Rushd, an Andalusian contemporary of Ibn Arabi, states that among the various legal positions on women's leadership of congregational prayer, one such position permitted women to lead mixed congregations.

Creatively engaging the relationship between Sufism and Islamic allows contemporary Muslims to draw on some of the most profound Islamic understandings of the God–human relationship, deepening the approaches to addressing social justice and gender equality. By carefully examining the assumptions about human nature employed in the dominant legal discourses, and by holding the law accountable to the inclusive spiritual imperatives for submission to God as outlined in Sufism, Muslims are able to develop a more holistic approach to ethics and jurisprudence. For Muslims today, Ibn Arabi's framing of religious personhood inspires practice that is enriched by ever-deepening forms of justice and beauty.

Further Reading

Ali, Kecia. 'Progressive Muslims and Islamic Jurisprudence: The Necessity for Critical Engagement with Marriage and Divorce Law', in *Progressive Muslims: On Gender, Justice, and Pluralism*, Omid Safi, ed., pp. 163–189. Oxford, 2003.

Barlas, Asma. *Believing Women in Islam: Un-reading Patriarchal Interpretations of the Qur'an*. Austin, 2002.

Chittick, William. *The Sufi Path of Knowledge: Ibn al-Arabi's Metaphysics of Imagination*. Albany, NY, 1989.

Helminski, Camille Adams. *Women of Sufism: A Hidden Treasure*. London, 2003.

Hirtenstein, Stephen. *The Unlimited Mercifier: The Spiritual Life and Thought of Ibn 'Arabi*. Oxford, 1999.

Mir-Hosseini, Ziba, Mulki al-Sharmani and Jana Rumminger. *Men in Charge? Rethinking Authority in Muslim Legal Tradition*. London, 2014.

Murata, Sachiko. *The Tao of Islam: A Sourcebook on Gender Relationships in Islamic Thought*. Albany, NY, 1992.

Safi, Omid, ed. *Progressive Muslims: On Gender, Justice, and Pluralism*. Oxford, 2003.

Schimmel, Annemarie. *Mystical Dimensions of Islam*. Chapel Hill, NC, 1975.

Shaikh, Sa'diyya. *Sufi Narratives of Intimacy: Ibn Arabi, Gender and Sexuality*. Chapel Hill, NC, 2012.

al-Sulamī, Abū 'Abd al-Raḥmān. *Early Sufi Women (Dhikr al-Niswa al-Muta'abbidāt aṣ-ṣūfiyyāt)*, translated by Rkia Cornell. Louisville, KY, 1999.

Wadud, Amina. *Qur'an and Woman: Rereading the Sacred Text from a Woman's Perspective*. New York, 1999.

Wadud, Amina. *Inside the Gender Jihad*. London, 2006.

6

Women's Equality

Ziba Mir-Hosseini

'[J]ustice is at once a prerequisite for and a requirement of religious rules. A rule that is not just is not religious. Justice, in turn, aims to fulfil needs, attain rights, and eliminate discrimination and inequity.'

Abdolkarim Soroush, *Reason, Freedom, & Democracy in Islam* (Oxford, 2000)

Understanding gender in Islam calls for exploring history and revisiting its texts to unveil an egalitarian vision for Muslims today. I focus in this chapter on two themes: marriage and divorce, and women's participation in society, notably the idea of hijab as seclusion. These themes are sides of the same patriarchal coin that has historically legitimated and institutionalised the control of women. By highlighting the theological and philosophical assumptions at play, I aim to expose the basis of inequality in the 'legal shari'a' – rooted in the social, cultural and political conditions within which Islam's sacred texts were understood and turned into law.

There are three interconnected elements to my argument. First, assumptions about gender in Islam, as in any other religion, are necessarily sociocultural, changing and negotiated in the course of history. Second, Islamic legal tradition contains neither a unitary nor a coherent concept of gender, but rather a variety of ideas that rest on different theological, juristic and social assumptions. In part, this reflects a tension in Islam's sacred texts between ethical egalitarianism as an essential part of its message and the patriarchal context in which this message unfolded. This tension (which is shared by other scriptural traditions) enables both proponents and opponents of gender equality to claim textual legitimacy for their respective positions. Finally, gender equality became inherent in conceptions of justice in the course of the 20th century, and acquired a clear legal mandate through international human rights instruments, notably the Convention on the Elimination

102   *The Shariʻa*

of All Forms of Discrimination Against Women (CEDAW). These
philosophical and legal developments, coupled with the shifting status
of Muslim women and their growing demand for legal equality, present
a deep challenge to established patriarchy from within Islam.

Approach and Framework

I come to this subject as an anthropologist as well as a Muslim woman,
and I locate my analysis within the tradition of Islamic thought –
invoking two vital distinctions. These classical distinctions have been
obscured in modernity by the emergence of national legal systems that
selectively reform and codify Islamic family law, as well as by a new
political Islam that uses the shariʻa as ideology.

The first distinction is between the shariʻa and fiqh. This underlies
the emergence of various schools of Islamic law and within them a
multiplicity of positions and opinions. The shariʻa, literally 'the path
or the road leading to the water', for Muslims is the totality of God's
will as revealed to the Prophet Muhammad. As Fazlur Rahman notes,
'in its religious usage, from the earliest period, it has meant "the
highway of good life", i.e. religious values, expressed functionally
and in concrete terms, to direct man's life'.[1] Fiqh, 'understanding',
denotes the process of human endeavour to discern and extract
legal rules from the sacred sources of Islam – that is, from the Qurʼan
and the *Sunna* (the practice of the Prophet, as contained in Hadith,
traditions). Throughout this chapter, then, the shariʻa is understood as
an ideal that embodies the spirit and trajectory of Islam's revealed texts,
a path that guides us in the direction of justice; while fiqh includes not
only the legal rulings (*ahkam*) and positive laws (enacted or legislated)
that Muslim jurists claim to be rooted in the sacred texts, but also
the vast corpus of jurisprudential and exegetic texts produced by
the scholars.

Justice is rooted in Islamic teaching at large, and is integral to
the outlook and philosophy of the shariʻa. This is where the juristic
consensus ends. What justice allows and requires, its scope and its
manifestation in laws, and its basis in the sacred texts, are the subject
of contention and debate. In essence, there are two main schools
of theological thought. The prevailing Ashʻari school holds that our
notion of justice is contingent on revealed texts and is not subject to
extra-religious rationality. The Muʻtazili school, on the other hand,

---

[1]   F. Rahman, *Islam* (Chicago, 2002), p. 100.

Women's Equality   103

argues that justice is innate and has a rational basis, independent of revealed texts. I adhere to the latter position, as developed by contemporary Muslim thinkers such as Abdolkarim Soroush and Nasr Hamid Abu Zayd. From this perspective, our understanding of justice, like that of the revealed texts, is tied to the field of our knowledge and is shaped by extrareligious forces. As Soroush notes, any religious text or law that defies our notion of justice should be reinterpreted in the light of an ethical critique of their religious roots.

My second distinction, which I also take from Islamic jurisprudence, is between the two main categories of legal rulings (*ahkam*): between '*ibadat* (ritual/spiritual acts) and *mu'amalat* (social/contractual acts). Rulings in the first category, '*ibadat*, regulate relations between God and the believer, where jurists contend there is limited scope for rationalisation, explanation and change, since they pertain to the spiritual realm and divine mysteries. This is not the case with rulings on *mu'amalat*, which involve relations between humans and respond to social context, to which most rulings concerning women and gender relations belong. Since human affairs are in constant flux, there is always a need for fresh interpretations of the texts, in line with time and place. This is the rationale for *ijtihad* ('self-exertion', 'endeavour'), which is the jurist's method of finding solutions to new issues in the light of the guidance of revelation.

Let me stress that I do not seek to emulate the jurists (*fuqaha*), who extract legal rules from the sacred sources by following juristic methodology (*usul al-fiqh*). Nor is my approach the same as that of the majority of Muslim feminists who revisit the sacred texts in order to 'unread patriarchy'.[2] Rather, I seek to engage with juristic constructs and theories to unveil the theological and rational arguments, and legal theories, that underlie them. Above all, I seek to understand the conception of justice and the notion of gender that permeate family law in Islamic legal tradition, which I contend is a social construction, like other laws in the realm of *mu'amalat*, and is shaped in interaction with political, economic, social and cultural forces, and with those who have the power to represent and define interpretations of Islam's sacred texts.

---

[2]   See, for example, A. Barlas, *Believing Women in Islam: Unreading Patriarchal Interpretations of the Qur'an* (Austin, TX, 2002); N. Barazangi, *Women's Identity and the Qur'an: A New Reading* (Gainsville, FL, 2004); R. Hassan, 'Feminist Theology: Challenges for Muslim Women', *Critique: Journal for Critical Studies of the Middle East*, 9 (1996), pp. 53–65; A. Wadud, *Inside the Gender Jihad: Women's Reform in Islam* (Oxford, 2006).

Gender in Classical Fiqh: The Sanctification of Patriarchy

In fiqh texts from the formative period of Islamic thought, gender inequality is a tenet that reflects how the authors related to the sacred texts, and to the world in which they lived. Inequality between men and women was the natural order of things, the way to regulate relations between them. Classical fiqh's assumptions about gender are encapsulated in two sets of legal rulings: those that define marriage and divorce, on the one hand, and women's covering and seclusion, on the other. In these matters, the various fiqh schools all share the same inner logic and patriarchal conception. If they differ, it is in the manner and extent to which they have translated this conception into legal rules.

Marriage: From Contract to Control

Classical jurists defined marriage as a contract of exchange, whose prime purpose is to legitimise sexual relations between a man and a woman. The contract is called *'aqd al-nikah* (contract of coitus) and has three essential elements: the offer (*ijab*) by the woman or her guardian (*wali*), the acceptance (*qabul*) by the man, and the payment of dower (*mahr*), a sum of money or any valuable that the husband pays or undertakes to pay to the bride before or after consummation.

Jurists often used the analogy of the contract of sale, and alluded to parallels between the status of wives and female slaves to whose sexual services husbands/owners were entitled, and who were deprived of freedom of movement. Al-Ghazali, the great 12th-century Muslim philosopher, in his monumental work *Revival of Religious Sciences*, echoed the prevalent view of his time:

> It is enough to say that marriage is a kind of slavery, for a wife is a slave to her husband. She owes her husband absolute obedience in whatever he may demand of her, where she herself is concerned, as long as no sin is involved.[3]

Likewise, al-Muhaqqiq al-Hilli, the renowned 13th-century Shi'i jurist, wrote:

> It has also been said that [marriage] is a verbal contract that first establishes the right to sexual intercourse, that is to

---

[3]   Abu Hamid al-Ghazali, *Ihya 'Ulum ad-Din* (Revival of Religious Sciences), trans. M. Holland (Hollywood, FL, 1998), p. 89.

Women's Equality   105

say: it is not like buying a female slave, when the man acquires the right of intercourse as a consequence of the possession of the slave.[4]

Ishaq ibn Khalil, a prominent 14th-century Maliki jurist, was equally explicit when it came to dower and its function in marriage:

When a woman marries, she sells a part of her person ... As in any other bargain and sale, only useful and ritually clean objects may be given in dower.[5]

I am not suggesting that classical jurists conceptualised marriage either as a sale or as slavery. Certainly there were significant differences and disagreements about this among the schools, and debates within each, with legal and practical implications. Even statements such as those quoted above distinguish between the right of access to the woman's sexual and reproductive faculties (which her husband acquires) and the right over her person (which he does not). Rather, what I want to communicate is that the notion and legal logic of sale and ownership (*tamlik*) underlie their idea of marriage, and define the parameters of laws and practices where a woman's sexuality, if not her person, becomes a commodity, an object of exchange. It is also this logic, as we shall see, that defines the rights and duties of each spouse in marriage.

Classical jurists, aware of possible misunderstandings, were careful to stress that marriage resembles sale only in form, not in spirit; they drew a clear line between free and slave women in terms of rights and status. The marriage contract is among the few contracts in fiqh that crosses the boundary between its two main divisions: *'ibadat* and *mu'amalat*. The jurists spoke of marriage as a religious duty, lauded its religious merit and enumerated the ethical injunctions that the contract entailed for the spouses. But these ethical injunctions were eclipsed by those elements in the contract that concerned the exchange and sanctioned men's control over women's sexuality. What jurists defined as the prime 'purposes of marriage' separated the legal from the moral in marriage; their consensus held these purposes to be the gratification of sexual needs, procreation and the preservation of morality. Whatever

---

[4]   al-Muhaqqiq al-Hilli, *Sharayi al-Islam*, vol. II, Persian trans. by A.A. Yazdi, compiled by M.T. Danish-Pazhuh (Tehran, 1985), p. 428.
[5]   F.H. Ruxton, *Maliki Law: A Summary from French Translations of Mukhtasar Sidi Khalil* (London, 1916), p. 106.

served or followed from these purposes became duties incumbent on each spouse, which the jurists discussed under *ahkam al-zawaj* (laws of matrimony). The rest, though still morally incumbent, remained legally unenforceable, left to the individual conscience.

For each party, the contract entailed a set of defined rights and obligations, some with moral sanction and others with legal force. Those with legal force revolve around the twin themes of sexual access and compensation, embodied in *tamkin* (obedience; also *ta'a*) and *nafaqa* (maintenance). *Tamkin*, defined in terms of sexual submission, is a man's right and thus a woman's duty; whereas *nafaqa*, defined as shelter, food and clothing, is a woman's right and a man's duty. A woman becomes entitled to *nafaqa* only after consummation of the marriage, and she loses her claim if she is in a state of *nushuz* (disobedience). There is no matrimonial regime: the husband is the sole owner of the matrimonial resources, and the wife remains the possessor of her dower and whatever she brings to or earns during the marriage. She has no legal duty to do housework and is entitled to demand wages if she does. The procreation of children is the only area the spouses share, but even here a wife is not legally required to suckle her child and can demand compensation if she does.

Among the default rights of the husband was his power to control his wife's movements and her 'excess piety'. She needed his permission to leave the house, to take up employment, or to engage in fasting or forms of worship other than what is obligatory (i.e. the fast of Ramadan). Such acts might infringe on the husband's right of 'unhampered sexual access'.

A man could enter up to four marriages at a time, and terminate each contract at will: neither grounds for termination nor the consent or presence of his wife were needed. Legally, *talaq*, repudiation of the wife, is a unilateral act (*iqa*) which acquires effect by the declaration of the husband. A woman may secure her release by offering him inducements – *khul'*, often referred to as 'divorce by mutual consent'. As defined by classical jurists, *khul'* is a separation claimed by the wife as a result of her extreme 'reluctance' or 'dislike' (*karahiya*) towards her husband, and the essential element is the payment of compensation (*'iwad*) to the husband in return for her release. This can be the return of the dower, or any other form of compensation. Unlike *talaq*, *khul'* is a bilateral act because it cannot take legal effect without the consent of the husband. If the wife fails to secure his consent, then her only recourse is the intervention of the court and the judge's power either to compel the husband to pronounce *talaq* or to pronounce it on his behalf. In defining *talaq* as the exclusive right of the husband, jurists used the analogy of manumission – a right that exclusively rested with the master of a slave.

The Hijab: Covering to Confinement

Unlike marriage, classical fiqh texts contain little about the dress code for women. The prominence of the hijab in Muslim discourse is recent, dating to the 19th-century Muslim encounter with colonial powers. It is only from then that we see literature in which the veil acquires a civilisational dimension, and becomes both a marker of Muslim identity and an element of faith.

Early legal texts did not use the term 'hijab', nor such descriptors as *burqa*, *chador* and *parda* (*purdah*). Rather, they referred to *sitr* (covering) to discuss the issue of dress for both men and women, but in two contexts only: rulings on covering the body during prayers, and rulings that govern a man's 'gaze' at a woman prior to marriage.

The rules are minimal but clear-cut. During prayer, both men and women must cover their *'awra* or private parts. For men, this is the area between knees and navel, while for women it is all but the hands, feet and face. With regard to the 'gaze', it is forbidden for men to look at the uncovered body of women to whom they are not closely related; this can be waived when a man wants to contract a marriage and needs to inspect the woman he intends to marry. The rulings on covering during prayer fall under the category of *'ibadat* (ritual/ worship acts), while those on gaze are to do with *mu'amalat* (social/ contractual acts).

There is, however, another notion of the hijab that remains implicit in these texts: confinement. This rests on two interrelated juristic constructs that cut across *'ibadat* and *mu'amalat*. The first defines a woman's whole body as *'awra*, a sexual zone, that must be covered both during prayers (before God) and in society (before men). The second construct considers a woman's sexuality to be *fitna*, a source of danger to public order, and consequently grants men the right to control women's movements. The rulings on segregation (forbidding interaction between unrelated men and women) have their logic in this second construct.[6]

Unveiling Patriarchal Premises

Whether the fiqh norms above actually corresponded to practices of marriage and gender relations is an enquiry that Muslim feminist scholars have begun to undertake. Yet some scholars and Islamists

---

[6] See K. Abou El-Fadl, *Speaking in God's Name: Islamic Law, Authority and Women* (Oxford, 2001), pp. 239–247.

continue to deem those norms to be immutable and divinely ordained, thus seeking to legitimate patriarchy on religious grounds. Such claims have to be challenged on their own terms. Among important questions to ask are: How far do these rulings reflect the principle of justice that is inherent in the shari'a? Why and how does classical fiqh define marriage and covering in such a way that they deprive women of free will, confine them to the home and make them subject to male authority? These questions become even more crucial if we accept, as I do, the sincerity of the classical jurists' claim that they derive their ideal model of gender relations from Islam's sacred sources.

Muslim feminist scholarship points to two interwoven trends in history. The first has to do with the ethos that informed readings of the sacred texts, the exclusion of women from the production of religious knowledge, and the scarcity of female voices in law-making. The second is about how social norms and practices were sanctified and turned into fixed entities. That is, rather than considering them as temporal, earthly matters, the jurists treated them as 'divinely ordained', thus immutable.

The model of marriage and gender roles in the fiqh tradition is grounded in the patriarchy of pre-Islamic Arabia, which continued into the Islamic era, though in a modified form. There is an extensive debate in the literature on this, into which I shall not enter. But there are two points of consensus among the students of Islam and gender. The first is that the revelatory texts and the Prophet altered some of the existing patriarchal practices of the time (e.g. burying infant girls alive and coercing women into unwanted marriages) but left others intact (e.g. polygamy and men's right to unilateral divorce). The Qur'an and the Hadith set in motion a reform of family laws in the direction of justice, which halted after the Prophet's death. What the Prophet did was to rectify injustice and introduce justice as these were understood in his day. Second, the further we move from the time of revelation, the more women are marginalised: their voices are muted and their public presence is curtailed.

Many verses in the Qur'an condemn women's subjugation, affirm the principle of gender equality and aim to reform existing practices in that direction.[7] Yet this subjugation is reproduced in fiqh, though in a mitigated form. The model of marriage here is based on a type prevalent in pre-Islamic Arabia, known as 'marriage of dominion'. It closely

---

[7]   See H. Muhammad, F.A. Kodir, L.M. Natsir and M. Wahid, *Dawrah Fiqh Concerning Women: Manual for a Course on Islam and Gender* (Cirebon, Indonesia, 2006).

Women's Equality

resembled a sale, by which a woman became her husband's property.[8] The jurists redefined and reformed aspects of the marriage of dominion to accommodate the Qur'anic call to reform, and to enhance women's status within a patriarchal institution. Women became parties to, not subjects of, the contract, and recipients of the dower or marriage gift. Likewise, by modifying the regulations on polygamy and divorce, the jurists curtailed men's scope of dominion over women in the contract, without altering the essence of the contract or freeing women from the authority of fathers or husbands.

In producing these rulings, the jurists based their theological arguments on a number of assumptions: 'women are created of and for men', 'God made men superior to women', 'women are defective in reason and faith'. These became theological tenets for jurists seeking to discern legal rules from the sacred texts, despite the absence of any support in the Qur'an, and in the face of women's active role as transmitters of the Hadith.

The moral and social rationale for women's subjugation is found in the theory of difference in male and female sexuality, which goes as follows: God gave women greater sexual desire than men, but this is mitigated by two innate factors, men's *ghayra* (sexual honour and jealousy) and women's *haya*' (modesty and shyness). What jurists concluded was that women's sexuality, if left uncontrolled by men, creates havoc, and is a real threat to social order. Feminist scholarship on Islam gives vivid accounts of the working of this theory in medieval literature, and its impact on women's lives in contemporary Muslim societies.[9] Women's *haya*' and men's *ghayra*, seen as innate qualities defining femininity and masculinity, became tools for controlling women and the rationale for their exclusion from public life. The sale contract, as discussed, provided the juristic basis for women's subjugation in marriage, and the legal construction of women's bodies as '*awra* (pudenda), and of their sexuality as a source of *fitna* (temptation), removed them from public space and thus from political life.

It is not my contention that male jurists conspired to subordinate women. Rather, in discerning the terms of the shari'a, jurists were constrained by a set of gender assumptions and legal theories that reflected

---

[8]   J. Esposito, *Women in Muslim Family Law* (Syracuse, NY, 1982), pp. 14–15.

[9]   F. Mernissi, *Beyond the Veil: Male-Female Dynamics in Muslim Society*, rev. edn (London, 1985); Z. Mir-Hosseini, 'Sexuality, Rights and Islam: Competing Gender Discourses in Post-Revolutionary Iran', in G. Nashat and L. Beck, ed., *Women in Iran from 1800 to the Islamic Republic* (Chicago, IL, 2004), pp. 204–217. For an example of the forthright avowal of this rationale today, see A.A. Maududi, *The Laws of Marriage and Divorce in Islam* (Kuwait, 1983).

the social and political realities of their age. Subsequent generations treated the assumptions, theories and rulings as though they were part of the shari'a. This is what a modern scholar regards as a crisis of epistemology in the traditional approach to Islamic legal heritage:

> Muslim jurists, by exercise of their rational faculty to its utmost degree, recorded their reactions to the experiences of the community: *they created, rather than discovered, God's law*. What they created was a literary expression of their aspirations, their consensual interests, and their achievements; what they provided for Islamic society was an ideal, a symbol, a conscience, and a principle of order and identity.[10]

Gender equality as understood today was 'unthinkable' in these classical ideas of justice and was absent from all pre-modern legal theories and systems. Indeed, until the 19th century, women's rights were far better protected in Islamic than in western legal traditions. Muslim women, for instance, could retain their legal and economic autonomy in marriage, while in England it was not until 1882, with the passage of the Married Women's Property Act, that women acquired the right to retain ownership of property after marriage. The assumptions that animated English family law in the 18th century show striking parallels with those of classical fiqh.[11]

Gender in Modernity: Modified Patriarchy

With the rise of western hegemony over the Muslim world and the spread of secular systems of education in the 19th century, the ideological hold of fiqh conceptions of gender relations began to wane. At the same time, the colonial encounter turned the 'status of women in Islam' into a contested issue, a symbolic political battleground between the forces of traditionalism and modernity, a situation that has continued since.

---

[10] A. Sachedina, 'The Ideal and Real in Islamic Law', in R.S. Khare, ed., *Perspectives on Islamic Law, Justice and Society* (New York, 1999), pp. 15–31 (emphasis added).

[11] D. Wright, 'Legal Rights and Women's Autonomy: Can Family Law Reform in Muslim Countries Avoid the Contradictions of Victorian Domesticity?', *Hawwa: Journal of Women of the Middle East and the Islamic World*, 5(1) (2007), pp. 33–54.

Women's Equality

A vast literature on 'women in Islam' dates from the start of the 20th century. Produced by religious publishing houses in both Muslim and western domains, this literature is available (much of it now on the internet) in various languages, including English.[12] It consists of highly varied texts, which range from outright polemic to sound scholarship, and which fall into two broad genres. The first, comprising the majority of available texts and views, advocates a modified version of classical rulings. Authors in this genre, which I term 'Neo-Traditionalist', reject legal equality between the sexes as a western idea that has no place in an Islamic worldview. They argue for 'complementarity of rights', sometimes called 'gender balance'. The second genre, which I call 'Reformist' or 'Feminist', advocates gender equality on all fronts. It emerged in the last two decades of the 20th century and constitutes a small part of the literature.

Gender Balance: Inequality Redefined

The roots of the first new discourse can be traced to the 19th century and the Muslim world's encounter with western colonial powers, but its impact is linked with the emergence of modern nation-states in the 20th century and the creation of modern legal systems. In many Muslim states, fiqh provisions on the family were selectively reformed, codified and grafted onto unified legal systems inspired by western models. With the exceptions of Turkey and the Muslim-majority Soviet Central Asian states, which abandoned fiqh in all spheres of law and replaced it with western-inspired codes, and Saudi Arabia, which preserved classical fiqh as a fundamental law and sought to apply it in all spheres of law, most Muslim states retained fiqh only with regard to family and inheritance laws. The extent and impetus for reform varied from one country to another, but, generally, reforms were introduced through procedural rules, notably on registration of marriages and divorces, which left the substance of the classical law more or less unchanged. Tunisia stands out for incorporating gender equality in its 1956 family law.

Hence, family law moved from being the concern of private scholars operating within a particular fiqh school to the legislative assemblies of

---

[12] For a discussion of such writings in the Arab world, see Y. Haddad, 'Islam and Gender: Dilemmas in the Changing Arab World', in Y. Haddad and J. Esposito, ed., *Islam, Gender and Social Change* (Oxford, 1998), pp. 1–29; for Iran, see Z. Mir-Hosseini, *Islam and Gender: The Religious Debate in Contemporary Iran* (Princeton, NJ, 1999); for Muslims in Europe and North America, see A. Roald, *Women in Islam: The Western Experience* (London, 2001).

states. Statute books replaced fiqh manuals and texts in regulating the status of women. This led to the creation of a hybrid family law that is neither classical fiqh nor quite western, and to a new gender discourse that is ambivalent on equality in the family. Though commonly termed 'Islamic Modernism', this discourse is better described as 'Neo-Traditionalism' because it shares the basic classical understanding of gender. Where it differs is in its implementation through the machinery of a modern nation-state that gives new legal force to patriarchal interpretations of the shari'a.

The Neo-Traditionalist gender discourse is found not only in legal codes of Muslim countries but also in new kinds of text that are not necessarily juristic in their reasoning, thus making them more accessible to the general public. Published by religious publishing houses and largely written by men (at least until recently), the aims of these texts are to shed new light on the status of women in Islam, and clarify 'misunderstandings about the law of Islam'. The main themes through which the authors of these texts address gender relations are women's covering, marriage and divorce laws, and women's rights to education and employment. While these writings are diverse in their sociocultural origins, they share an oppositional stance and a defensive or apologetic tone: oppositional, because their concern is to resist change and voices of dissent from within, which they cast as 'alien'; apologetic, because by going back to classical fiqh and upholding its rulings, they have to defend its inherent and anachronistic gender biases.

Neo-Traditionalist texts lack the coherence and sense of conviction that imbue classical texts. Keen to distance themselves from overtly patriarchal language and concepts, their authors keep silent on the juristic theories and theological and other assumptions that underlie these rulings in classical texts. For instance, they ignore the parallels in the legal structures of the contracts of marriage and sale, and in views such as those of al-Ghazali (see p. 104) which see marriage as a type of enslavement for women. Yet the patriarchy implicit in their texts is ultimately inescapable – as in Abul Ala Maududi's explanation of why women cannot have equal rights to divorce:

> If she were to be given this right, she would grow over-bold and easily violate the men's rights. It is evident that if a person buys something with money, he tries to keep it as long as he can. He parts with it only when he cannot help it. But when a thing is purchased by one individual, and the right to cast it away is given to another, there is little hope that the

latter will protect the interest of the buyer, who invested the money. Investing man with the right to divorce amounts to the protection of his legitimate rights. This is also checks the growth of the divorce rate.[13]

Maududi's *Purdah and the Status of Women in Islam* (1998), like Morteza Mutahhari's *System of Women's Rights in Islam* (1991), has been influential.[14] Both authors were ideologues whose anti-colonial and anti-western discourses became seminal for Islamist groups and movements. For Maududi in South Asia, Muslims had come to adopt western and to some extent Hindu values that corrupted their own civilisational ethos. The solution was an 'Islamic state' with the capacity and inclination to enforce the Islamic way of life, where women's seclusion and control by men are foundational. Mutahhari, writing in Iran as part of the religious opposition to the Shah's secularising policies, was less adamant in his opposition to modernity and less overtly patriarchal. However, along with Maududi, he embraced key premises about the 'naturalness' of laws in Islam and the 'innate difference' between women and men. Properly understood, fiqh rules were in line with human nature (*fitra*), taking into account the biological and psychological differences between the sexes, and reflected the shari'a as a divine blueprint for society.

Ironically, this stance accentuates the internal contradictions and anachronisms in classical rulings. For example, if, as the classical theory holds, women's sexual desire is greater than men's, and if laws in Islam work with the grain of nature, then why allow men but not women to contract more than one marriage at a time? Surely God would not give women greater sexual desire yet allow men to be the polygamists and make covering obligatory for women? Neo-traditionalists resolve such contradictions by modifying the classical theory in order to eliminate its conflict with the newly advocated theory of the naturalness of fiqh-based law. Women's sexuality is now explained as passive and responsive, and men's as active and aggressive, a theory that has little precedent in classical texts. In arguing for such a theory, Maududi and Mutahhari do not draw on Islam's sacred texts but on western psychological and sociological studies. Their readings of these (long-outdated) sources are selective, and they cite as 'scientific evidence' only those that are consistent with fiqh views of marriage.

---

[13]   A.A. Maududi, *The Laws of Marriage and Divorce*, p. 27.
[14]   For a reading of both authors' works, see L.R. Shehadeh, *The Idea of Women in Fundamentalist Islam* (Gainesville, FL, 2003).

114   *The Shariʻa*

They are also selective in their readings of the sacred texts and in their use of classical notions.[15]

Gender Equality: Questioning Patriarchal Premises

With the rise of political Islam in the second half of the 20th century, and the rallying cry of 'return to the shariʻa' as embodied in fiqh rulings, Neo-Traditionalist texts and their gender discourse gained prominence. The 1979 popular revolution in Iran that brought Islamic clerics to power was a milestone in this regard; women's covering and gender segregation in public space became mandatory. The same year saw the dismantling of reforms introduced earlier in the century by modernist governments in Iran and Egypt, and the introduction of fiqh criminal punishments (*hudud* ordinances) as part of Pakistan's national laws. It was also the year when the United Nations adopted the CEDAW.

The slogan of 'return to the shariʻa' and the importation of fiqh notions of gender into policy became the catalyst for a critique of this venture, and it spurred Muslim women's activism. Classical fiqh texts were brought out and exposed to critical scrutiny and public debate. A vital element of this new phase has been to place women themselves, rather than the abstraction of 'the status of woman in Islam', at the heart of the battle between the forces of traditionalism and modernism. By the early 1990s, a new way of thinking about gender had emerged: a discourse that was 'feminist' in its aspiration yet 'Islamic' in its language and sources of legitimacy. Some versions of this new discourse came to be labelled 'Islamic feminism', which many Islamists and secular feminists found unsettling. I have written and spoken at some length about this, and I regard it as futile to categorise neatly and label the diverse and evolving voices across the Muslim world and beyond. They all seek gender justice and equality for women, though they do not always agree about what constitutes 'justice' or 'equality' and the best ways of attaining them.[16]

What merits recognition here is the potential of a brand of feminism, which takes Islam as the source of its legitimacy, to challenge the hegemony of patriarchal interpretations of the shariʻa and the authority

---

[15] See K. Ali, *Sexual Ethics and Islam: Feminist Reflections on Qurʼan, Hadith and Jurisprudence* (Oxford, 2006).
[16] For example, Z. Mir-Hosseini, 'Beyond "Islam" vs "Feminism"', *IDS Bulletin* 42(1) (January 2011), pp. 67–77.

Women's Equality 115

of those who speak in the name of Islam. This certainly enables Islamic Feminism to expose the inequalities embedded in current interpretations of the shari'a as constructions by male jurists, with all that this entails in the search for fresh responses in modernity beyond old dogmas. This builds on the work of earlier reformers, such as Mohammad Abduh, Muhammad Iqbal and Fazlur Rahman, in insisting that human understanding of Islam is tied to time, space and experience.[17]

Rather than searching for an exclusively Islamic genealogy for gender equality, human rights and democracy (which was the concern of earlier reformers), the new thinking emphasises how religion is understood and how religious knowledge is produced. A primary aim is to revive the rationalist approach that was eclipsed historically when legalism became dominant, giving precedence to the form over the spirit of the law. In this respect, the works of contemporary Muslim thinkers such as Mohammad Arkoun, Khaled Abu El-Fadl, Nasr Abu Zayd, Mohammad Mojtahed Shabestari and Abdolkarim Soroush are critical.[18] The questions they ask and the assumptions that inform their readings of the sacred texts differ radically from those of classical jurists. In the process, they also expose the contradictions inherent in earlier discourses on family and gender rights.

Conclusion

A growing body of texts under the rubric of 'women in Islam', and the intensity of the debate in this regard, are indications of a radical shift in thinking about Islamic law, gender and politics. Even those who see classical fiqh rulings as an unchanging part of the shari'a itself invoke 'women's rights' and 'gender equity' in Islam but are silent on the juristic theories and theological assumptions that underlie them. Such theories and assumptions are repugnant to modern sensibilities and

---

[17] For a textual genealogy, see C. Kurzman, ed., *Liberal Islam: A Sourcebook* (Oxford, 1998).

[18] See U. Gunther, 'Mohammad Arkoun: Towards a Radical Rethinking of Islamic Thought', pp. 125–167; N. Kermani, 'From Revelation to Interpretation: Nasr Hamid Abu Zayd and the Literary Study of the Qur'an', pp. 169–192; F. Vahdat, 'Post-Revolutionary Modernity in Iran: The Subjective Hermeneutics of Mohamad Mojtahed Shabestari', pp. 193–224, in S. Taji-Farouki, ed., *Modern Muslim Intellectuals and the Qur'an* (Oxford, 2004); K. Abou El-Fadl, *Speaking in God's Name: Islamic Law, Authority and Women* (Oxford, 2001). On Soroush's ideas on gender, see Z. Mir-Hosseini, *Islam and Gender: The Religious Debate in Contemporary Iran* (Princeton, NJ, 1999), pp. 217–246.

116   *The Shari'a*

ethics, and alien to the experience of marriage among a growing body of
contemporary Muslims.

The secularisation of law and legal systems in the 20th century did
not yield an egalitarian family law in Muslim societies. Setting aside
fiqh as the source in all areas of law except the family only reinforced
the religious tone of provisions about gender, turning them into the
last bastion of Muslim legal tradition. At the same time, deprived of the
power to define and administer family law, fiqh and its practitioners
were confined to the ivory tower of seminaries; they lost touch with
changing political realities and were unable to meet the deeper
challenges of modernity. The rise of political Islam in the 1970s reversed
this process, bringing religion back into politics and law, but it had the
paradoxical and unintended result that patriarchal interpretations of the
shari'a were desanctified. Women were incentivised to demand equality
and had the language to argue for it from within the tradition. In the
new century, this egalitarian challenge can no longer be ignored.

Further Reading

Abou El-Fadl, Khaled. 'The Place of Ethical Obligations in Islamic Law',
    UCLA Journal of Islamic and Near Eastern Law, 4(1) (2004–2005),
    pp. 1–40.
Abu Zayd, Nasr Hamid. *Reformation of Islamic Thought: A Critical
    Analysis.* Amsterdam, 2006.
Ahmed, Leila. *Women and Gender in Islam: Historical Roots of a Modern
    Debate.* New Haven, CT, 1992.
Ali, Kecia. *Sexual Ethics and Islam: Feminist Reflections on Qur'an,
    Hadith and Jurisprudence*, rev. edn. Oxford, 2016.
Lampe, Gerald, E., ed. *Justice and Human Rights in Islamic Law.*
    Washington, DC, 1997.
Mernissi, Fatima. *Women and Islam: An Historical and Theological
    Enquiry*, trans. Mary Jo Lakeland. Oxford, 1991.
Mir-Hosseini, Ziba, Mulki Al-Sharmani and Jana Rumminger, ed. *Men
    in Charge? Rethinking Authority in Muslim Legal Tradition.* London,
    2015.
Sharma, Arvind and Katherine Young, ed. *Feminism and World
    Religions.* Albany, NY, 1999.
Sonbol, Amira El Azhary, ed. *Women, Family and Divorce Laws in
    Islamic History.* Syracuse, NY, 1996.
Stowasser, Barbara. 'Women's Issues in Modern Islamic Thought', in
    Arab Women: Old Boundaries, New Frontiers, Judith Tucker, ed.
    Bloomington, IN, 1993.

Taji-Farouki, Suha, ed. *Modern Muslim Intellectuals and the Qur'an.* Oxford, 2004.

Wadud, Amina. *Inside the Gender Jihad: Women's Reform in Islam.* Oxford, 2006.

Welchman, Lynn. *Women and Muslim Family Laws in Arab States: A Comparative Overview of Textual Development and Advocacy.* Amsterdam, 2007.

7

Family Law to Finance

Mohamed M. Keshavjee and Raficq Abdulla

At the core of the shariʿa, as various chapters in this volume have shown, is the idea of an ethical commitment to the good, in its communal as well as individual understandings. Historically, this came to be captured by two interlocking practical tools that would undergird both the moral and the legal development of the shariʿa. *Maslaha* sought to ensure that serving public welfare, carefully defined, would guide jurists and theologians in adjudicating the everyday choices faced by the faithful. *Maqasid* facilitated such adjudication by identifying the 'higher purposes' of the shariʿa as a normative framework, tied to the fundamentals of being Muslim. These tools become vital in orienting the shariʿa as a purposive, rather than passively traditionalist, framework.

This chapter enquires into the modern-day relevance of *maslaha* and *maqasid*, including in contexts where Muslims may be a minority of the population, as the shariʿa intersects with secular frameworks of normative authority. In particular, we focus on three specific situations that call for mediating the demands of faith and everyday socio-economic realities: (a) cross-border child abduction following the breakdown of cross-cultural marriages; (b) the production of new financial instruments in Malaysia in a globalised environment of banking and commerce; and (c) fresh approaches to family law disputes in the United Kingdom, with reference to contemporary human rights norms. These varied situations bring to the fore the challenges of fostering a purposive shariʿa today, of balancing fidelity to deeply held socio-cultural traditions with evolving norms of ethical propriety. Yet it is important to recognise that this balancing act did not commence with modernity: Muslims have a long historical record of grappling with local exigencies and imperatives (*darura*), as the shariʿa gave rise to a potent tradition of law-making or fiqh. Indeed, it was this quest that saw the emergence of the tools of *maslaha* and *maqasid*.

Historical Background

Maqasid al-shari'a, as a 'system of values that could contribute to a desired and sound application of the shari'a,[1] has been used as a tool of legal interpretation since the 9th century.[2] It is based on the principle that Islamic law is *purposive* in nature and is meant to serve particular aims, such as promoting welfare and avoiding harm. *Maqasid* has a rich presence in Islamic legal history, from the works of early commentators such as al-Juwayni (1028–1085) and al-Shatibi (1320–1388) to modern-day ones such as Rashid Rida (1865–1935), Ibn Ashur (1879–1973), Taha Jabir al-Alwani (1935–2016) and Yusuf al-Qaradawi (b. 1926).[3]

Some Muslim scholars in the pre-modern period recognised fully that the definitive list of all the *maqasid* or *masalih* did not exist in the Qur'an and the Sunna, and that *masalih* are potentially limitless, evolving according to time and context.[4] However, the majority of Muslim scholars, for complex reasons that are beyond the remit of this chapter, restricted the scope of the *maqasid* to matters falling outside the realm of 'duties toward God' (*'ibadat*, as opposed to matters relating to fellow men, *mu'amalat*), and some explicit and unambiguous injunctions from the sacred texts.[5] Generally, over time, most legal scholars followed this very restricted approach. A noteworthy exception was Najm al-Din al-Tufi (1276–1316), a Hanbali scholar who considered *maslaha* as having a regulatory function over all established sources of law. This gave it 'a universal and humanist status in the [Islamic] law' by privileging public interest (*maslaha*) over a clear meaning of the text and thereby 'subordinating the text to the divination of the universal institutions and purposes of the shari'a'.[6]

Al-Tufi was preceded by al-Ghazali (1058–1111), who, while not initially accepting the principle of *maslaha* as one of the sources

---

[1] J. Auda, 'A Maqasidi Approach to Contemporary Application of the Shari'ah', *Intellectual Discourse* 19 (2011), pp. 193–217, 194.
[2] I. Nyazee, *The Outlines of Islamic Jurisprudence* (Islamabad, 2000), pp. 162–175.
[3] See J. Auda, *Maqasid al-Shariah as Philosophy of Islamic Law* (London, 2008).
[4] M.H. Kamali, *The Principles of Islamic Jurisprudence* (Cambridge, 1991), p. 235.
[5] A. Duderija, ed., *Maqasid al-Sharia and Contemporary Reformist Muslim Thought, an Examination* (New York, 2014), pp. 3, 10.
[6] E. Moosa, 'The Poetics and Politics of Law after Empire: Reading Women's Rights in the Contestations of Law', *UCLA Journal of Islamic and Near Eastern Law* 1 (2001–2002), pp. 1– 28, 11.

of *usul al-fiqh* (principles of jurisprudence), considered in several instances that the *maslaha* doctrine 'secures the purpose of revelation'.[7] Al-Shatibi, a Maliki scholar from Muslim Spain, who is recognised as one of the most systematic theoreticians of this concept, considered *maqasid* to be 'the fundamentals of religion, basic rules of the laws, and the universals of belief'.[8] Contemporary figures such as the Egyptian professor of philosophy Hassan Hanafi (b. 1935), the Moroccan professor of philosophy Muhammad Abed al-Jabri (1935–2010) and the Indonesian intellectual Nurcholish Madjid (1939–2005) viewed the *maqasid* and *maslaha* dimensions of Islamic law as the essence of the Qur'an, and held that interpretations founded on these mechanisms can take precedence over clear Qur'anic texts. For the Afghan Islamic scholar Mohammad Hashim Kamali (b. 1944), the early formulations of *usul* had not significantly addressed this dimension of the law 'until al-Shatibi who developed his major theme on the objectives and the philosophy of shari'a (*maqasid al-shari'a*)'. Kamali makes the further point that al-Shatibi's contribution occurred 'too late to make a visible impact on the basic scheme and methodology of *usul*'.[9] This sentiment is echoed by Othman Auda, among other scholars today. Thus an increasing number of contemporary scholars have become aware of this gap in the pre-modern theories of law with regard to the hermeneutical employment of *maqasid* and *maslaha* approaches to Islamic law that present an important possibility for its reform.

However, modern scholars have expanded the scope of the five traditional *maqasid*: the protection of life, intellect, property, offspring and religion. Rashid Rida, for example, included women's rights. The Egyptian cleric Muhammad al-Ghazali (1917–1966) added justice and freedom. Yusuf al-Qaradawi included human dignity, and Ibn Ashur added equality, orderliness and freedom. Taha Jabir al-Alwani included the concept of developing civilisation on earth, and Gamal Eddin Attia included 24 essential ones which he put into four realms: the individual, the family, the umma and all of humanity.[10] This burgeoning scholarship not only helps to fill a gap but also builds on earlier formulations, and expands the scope of *maqasid* and *maslaha* approaches. In a few cases, it

---

[7]   Ibid., p. 5.

[8]   Auda, *Maqasid*, p. 21.

[9]   M.H. Kamali, 'Methodological Issues in Islamic Jurisprudence', *Arab Law Quarterly*, 11 (1996), p. 5.

[10]   See G.E. Attia, *Toward Realisation of the Higher Intent of Islamic Law (Maqasid al Shari'ah): A Functional Approach*, trans. N. Roberts (Kuala Lumpur, 2010), pp. 116–151.

elevates hermeneutically these approaches above the clear *nusus* (texts) found in the Qur'an and the Sunna. While discourses continue to take place at the academic level, practical considerations are pulling Muslims today in a similar direction, as we shall see in the next two sections.

Responding to International Child Abduction

Across the global Muslim diaspora there are growing numbers of marriages among people of different cultures, ethnicities, faiths, languages and nationalities.[11] To address this issue, the Hague Convention on the Civil Aspects of International Child Abduction (hereafter called the 1980 Hague Convention) was adopted in October 1980. To date, over one-third of the countries of the world have signed up or have adhered to this convention. Most Muslim countries have not become party to it, citing, among other things, the clash between the convention and the shari'a as it is understood in their respective jurisdictions.[12]

To deal with this problem, a number of creative approaches have been embarked on over the past decade between a few western countries and some Muslim countries. Some civil society institutions in European Union (EU) countries took a much greater proactive stance and in 2009 set up a training programme in Brussels, jointly sponsored by the German organisation Internationales Mediationszentrum für Familienkonflikte und Kindesentführung (MiKK), Child Focus of Belgium and the Catholic University of Leuven. The main objective of the programme was to prepare mediators and others dealing with this issue in the 27 EU countries to be better equipped to engage with the 1980 Hague Convention. This entailed working with the central institutions established under the Convention, and exploring how mediation could be used as a process of dispute resolution complementary to the legal framework of each country and the Convention. The training was not restricted to mediators but included lawyers, academics and personnel responsible for running the central institutions under the 1980 Convention in each participating country.

---

[11] M. Keshavjee, 'Cross-Border Child Abduction Mediation in Cases Concerning Non-Hague Convention Countries', in C. Paul and S. Kieswetter, ed., *Cross-Border Family Mediation: International Parental Child Abduction, Custody and Access Cases*, 2nd edn (Frankfurt, 2014), p. 91.
[12] The 1980 Hague Convention is basically a procedural agreement which does not in any way affect a state's internal law, such as family law, whether civil or religious.

Family Law to Finance 123

As part of this programme, MiKK commissioned trainers, judges and academics to contribute to a manual, with specific input on the Islamic dimension of child abduction, including shari'a-related perspectives.[13] The manual provided an anonymised case study which was used for role-play. The trainers emphasised that the notion of child abduction was fully amenable to mediation in Islam, based, inter alia, on the verses of the Qur'an that exhort or extol negotiated settlement (*sulh*), the Sunna of the Prophet Muhammad, Muslim juridical history, Ottoman court practice and the family statutes of most Muslim-majority countries. This principle of negotiated settlement cuts across both branches of Islam, Shi'i and Sunni. The trainers emphasised that as an integral part of the Islamic legal tradition, arbitration and mediation were more significant than litigation, which is usually seen as the last resort.

Even where the 1980 Hague Convention applied, the trainers noted, mediation among western disputants was regarded as the preferred option once all the legal safeguards were in place. Since mediation is the preferred option in Islamic juridical thought, it was explained to the trainees that mediation could play an important role in addressing the problem where one of the parties to the dispute was a Muslim who had unlawfully removed a child of the marriage to a Muslim country that was not party to the convention. The role-play case study involved an engagement with stakeholders and mediators, the language to be used in such situations, and shari'a-related issues with regard to different Muslim communities.

In this practical endeavour, mediators were motivated to use the shari'a itself to address a problem affecting children where the shari'a was being projected as an inhibitor to changing the national laws of Muslim countries, with regard to the global principle of advancing the best interests of the child. This principle is hardly unknown in Muslim jurisprudence. While Muslim governments themselves have registered their reservations and exceptions to the convention (and its associated protocols), judges from western countries are in ongoing consultation with their counterparts in some Muslim

---

[13] A contribution to this dimension was provided by Mohamed M. Keshavjee, co-author of this chapter. He and Rukhsana Abdulla, a mediator with the UK National Conciliation and Arbitration Board of the Ismaili Muslim community, also participated in a training session in Brussels on the principles of the 1980 Hague Convention. In turn, they provided training on the cultural dimensions of family mediation in the context of faith-based Muslim communities to participants in the MiKK Child Focus programme noted above.

countries to explore how issues might be resolved at the level of the judicial officers of their respective countries. An endeavour promoted by the Canadian government and the Hague Conference on Private International Law in 2009 resulted in a working committee under the joint chairmanship of a Canadian diplomat, William Crosbie, and a Pakistani supreme court judge, Tasadukh Hussain Jillani. The working committee was made up of representatives from 22 countries, split equally between western and Muslims countries, including Morocco, Malaysia, Jordan and Egypt. It was mandated to develop mediation structures that could assist parents in resolving cross-border family disputes over the custody of or contact with their children, in situations where the 1980 and 1996 Hague Conventions do not apply.

Under the auspices of the Permanent Bureau of the Hague Conference, the working committee has built cooperation between contracting and non-contracting states to the two conventions. It has called for the setting up or designation of a Central Contact Point (CCP) for international family mediation in each state, to assist parents who are involved in cross-border family disputes over children. The primary role of the CCP is to provide information about legal and mediatory services to parents, as well as to provide guidance to mediators on how to ensure that agreements are enforceable by the legal systems of the countries concerned. As of 2016, 12 Muslim countries had either formally designated or established their CCPs for international family mediation. Other countries have established entities in their jurisdictions that could take on this responsibility. In addition the EU, through its Euromed Justice Project, has elaborated the CCP structure in its handbook of good practice concerning cross-border family conflicts. Moreover, regional seminars co-hosted by Canada with the Islamic International University of Malaysia and the Doha Institute of the Qatar Foundation have sought to advance cooperation in and education about these issues, including child abduction.

Of late, Morocco has become a party to the 1980 Hague Convention, and various other Muslim countries' representatives are taking steps to ensure that their countries endeavour to sign up to it. There is growing appreciation that the Convention is fully compatible with the shari'a. This approach eschews abstract philosophical arguments or the taking up of ideological positions in favour of the 'higher purposes' (maqasid) of the shari'a, including the need to address the primary interests of the child, which are enshrined in the shari'a. It is also noteworthy that the success of this pragmatic approach has relied on civil society actors, from independent legal experts to social service institutions, working in partnership with states.

Islamic Finance in Malaysia

In Malaysia in the early 1980s, the government felt the need to enhance the socio-economic status of the Malay component of the country's population, which was seen as historically disadvantaged. Wealth creation as well as the preservation of the 'national patrimony' were broad objectives in this regard. New financial products to stimulate investment and economic growth were envisaged, in keeping with the ethos of the nation's Muslim identity.[14]

Among those new products were *bai al-murabaha* and *al-musharakah* for contracts of sale for vehicles and properties; *ijara* for commercial financing; *bai al-inah* and *tawarruq* for personal financing; and *bai al-dayn* for sale of debt. These were not entirely new creations but had historical antecedents. However, they were not all regarded positively by many religious scholars, who were concerned about shari'a norms with regard to the charging of interest, opaque financial transactions that pass risk to one party at the expense of the other, gambling and uncertainty. Essentially, financial contracts that fail to create 'real' wealth and are not based on the 'real' economy are viewed with disapproval. The debate about the validity of the products enumerated above, and others, continues: some Muslim countries take a hard line and regard them as illicit, while others allow their use under government oversight on the basis of their contribution to the public good, or *maslaha*.

To deal with this matter pragmatically, the Malaysian government sought to engage with legal scholars, socialising and educating them to understand the needs of a modern economy, while also acquainting economists and bankers with the principles of Islamic ethics and values at the heart of 'shari'a finance'. This novel approach to enable the shari'a to play an authentic and essential role in creating a modern financial system required creative thinking that was acceptable to all the relevant parties. Fortunately, at this time, two important Islamic jurisprudential figures, the late Dr Mohamed Zaki Badawi, a graduate of Islam's most prestigious classical university, al-Azhar, and Dr Mohammad Hashim Kamali, one of the world's leading scholars on Islamic law reform, were working in Malaysia and were approached for their opinions. They both played a seminal role in the evolution of thinking towards a new

---

[14] This section has benefited from the generous and invaluable advice of Professor M. Iqbal Asaria and Mushtak Parker, editor of *IslamicBanker* magazine. On financial instruments in Muslim settings at large, see Rodney Wilson, 'Economy', in A. B. Sajoo, ed., *A Companion to Muslim Ethics* (London, 2010), pp. 131–150.

126   *The Shari'a*

paradigm on the use of the shari'a in finance. Badawi had previously been involved with 'modernist' issues in Egypt, Northern Nigeria and Saudi Arabia, and he was later to become the leading Islamic scholar in the United Kingdom (on which more in the next section). He had a keen eye for 'purposive' law (its *maqasid*) and for its need to be relevant to contemporary realities.

In his numerous works, Kamali unequivocally expressed the need for Islamic law to reform for a number of reasons, both internal and external to the faith tradition. He wrote:

> The increased isolation of shari'a from the realities of law and government in contemporary Muslim societies accentuates the need for fresh efforts to make the *Shari'a* a viable proposition and a living force in society. Our problems over *taqlīd* [literal and imitative readings and practice of texts and commandments] are exacerbated by the development of a new dimension to *taqlīd* as a result of Western colonialism which had led to indiscriminate imitation of the laws and institutions of the West. The prevailing legal practice in many Muslim countries, and indeed many of their constitutions, are modelled on a precedent that does not claim its origin in the legal heritage of Islam.[15]

With regard to the possibility of effecting reform of Islamic law and legal theory in particular, Kamali provides various examples of how the Qur'an, the Sunna and the relationship between revelation and reason create space for the reform of the law. Hence

> reason is the torchlight which illuminates man's path in the material world of observation and investigation ... whereas revelation is the source of transcendental knowledge ... of the world beyond perception. One is the realm of investigation and the other of faith and submission to divine providence. Islam's vision of reality, truth, and its moral values of right and wrong are initially determined by revelation and then elaborated and developed by reason.[16]

The Malaysian products noted above were developed through a national process of consultation and cooperation among various civic and

---

[15]   Kamali, 'Methodological Issues in Islamic Jurisprudence', p. 4.
[16]   Ibid., p. 14.

religious sectors, with a view to arriving at a consensus that served 'traditional' and pragmatic expectations. Consider the financial product of *bai al-dayn* (sale of debt), whereby a debt can be sold for debt. Such a transaction is regarded as involving *riba* or interest, and is frowned on in countries in the Middle East, which were then also developing their particular system of shari'a finance. Malaysia, which follows the Shafi'i school of law, chose to allow such transactions on the basis of *maslaha*: it enables the setting up of mortgages, which is a need recognised in modern times. A variation of the *bai* product is the *bai al-inah*, which allows the use of credit cards. These financial products were deemed to be acceptable by shari'a scholars in Malaysia, influenced by Badawi and Kamali, who helped the scholars to view the innovations as being backed by, or based on, receivables or tangible goods. Accordingly, they were not solely exchanging money for money but filling a gap in shari'a finance which needed this type of product. Promissory notes, for example, could be sold on to provide a vehicle for cash management. Another shari'a contract developed by the Malaysian government was *tawarruq*. This is loosely classified as a commodity *murabaha*, whereby, for instance, the customer of a bank enters into a transaction similar to that of a mortgage. However, in this case, the bank purchases the property or entity directly, which, in turn, is sold to the customer over a period of time at a higher price that can be paid in instalments. This instrument is especially useful for cash management, which allows banks to raise money for clients. *Tawarruq* requires a client of a bank who requires cash to agree to sell a commodity to a third party at a discount. Technically, the third party must not be connected to the bank in any way. In practice, however, this condition is dispensed with, even in Saudi Arabia, which adopted it from Malaysia.

Malaysia also developed *tawarruq sukuk*. These *sukuk* are fixed-income instruments by which money can be raised for business, working capital and expansion, for example. They are a response to shari'a finance's inability to work in equity financing and venture capital projects because of the long gestation period, and the lack of expertise to evaluate risk. The authorities sought alternatives and created a trust certificate which is not a bond as such but is backed by an asset, or by the use of an asset or usufruct. This structure is being developed further so that assets do not have to be tangible entities. They may also be intangibles that produce revenue-like marketing income, or petrochemical contracts, airtime, electricity meter readings, receivables due on insurance contracts, and income received from rights over intellectual property such as royalties. These certificates, in turn, can be securitised and traded on exchanges, thus unlocking liquidity. *Sukuk* are actively traded in the United Kingdom and Malaysia, though not in the Gulf, where owners of certificates generally hold them until maturity.

In the interest of *maslaha*, Malaysia has introduced a regulatory framework for socially responsible investments, green and social *sukuk*, thus further widening the reach of the instrument. The educational, banking and institutional framework set up by the government provides a degree of confidence for investors who are able to have recourse to legal sanctions if necessary. There is also a degree of consumer protection for those investing in shari'a products, which gives Malaysia a degree of sophistication not commonly found in other Islamic countries. It is worth noting that, to date, about 70 per cent of the uptake of *sukuk* in Malaysia has been by non-Muslims who regard the product as safe and competitive.

As we have seen, shari'a finance in Malaysia has been more innovative. It has also been more engaged with the wider, communally responsible obligations entailed by the shari'a than other Muslim countries, where a more conservative and restricted understanding of the role of the shari'a prevails. The authorities, the financial system and scholars have been concerned as much with *tayyib* or ethically commendable products as with the halal or permitted conditions that make financial products shari'a compliant or shari'a based. In effect, Malaysia is able to marshal continuous change in its shari'a finance system because it looks to the *maqasid*, which in turn depends on interpretation that is sensitive to temporal and social context. Shari'a finance, at least in Malaysia, is outside the paradigm of 'Islamisation'.

Yet the innovatory stance taken by Malaysia is not without tensions between theory and practice. These require proper accountability on the part of policy-makers, regulators whose remit is problematic in an open-market system, and legislators. Innovation which is driven by financial engineering invites risk, and risk in general is regarded with great wariness by the shari'a, most notably when the excesses of risk verge on gambling (*maysir*) and uncertainty (*gharar*). Above all, the shari'a expects risk to be shared by *all* stakeholders in any commercial venture. But even the conventional banking system, as recent experience has shown, is precarious and can injure the fabric of society. Regulators have to play a role in preventing this, yet tend to act after the event. Bankers themselves, driven by the profit motive and maximising shareholder value, by the pursuit of pricing advantages and competitiveness, by their own bonuses and the fear of failing to keep up with the competition, are routinely prone to exceeding both legal and ethical constraints.

What we see, then, is how *maslaha*, aligned with *maqasid*, gives the shari'a a progressive stance with regard to society's well-being, while striving to uphold core principles. It does not allow for the creation of derivatives which are regarded as tools for gambling, or which fail to contribute to the real economy. At the same time, shari'a finance often responds to the form rather than the substance of the ethics of the shari'a. The idea of the public good is necessarily capacious; and its guardians are not always clearly delineated, though in Malaysia this problem is allayed by legal and institutional structures set up in conjunction with the banks and shari'a scholars. Evidently, a *maqasid*-based approach driven by necessity and public interest (*darura* and *maslaha*) has its challenges. Through exchanges of best practice, what is learnt in one part of the Muslim world is now beginning to influence other parts, such as through international conferences held in London and Dubai under the aegis of Islamic finance organisations from Malaysia and the Middle East.

The Muslim Law (Shariah) Council in the United Kingdom

With the civil justice system globally under severe stress, the social movement known as alternative dispute resolution (ADR) emerged in the 1970s through the work of a leading Harvard-trained jurist, Frank Sander. It is true that the idea of negotiated settlement is hardly new. However, ADR in its contemporary form was gaining traction in many of the countries across the western world. In the United Kingdom, this was largely in the area of family law, spearheaded by the family-mediation practitioner John Haynes. Mediation was also beginning to be recognised in commercial and other disputes through the work of institutions such as the Centre of Effective Dispute Resolution. This trend in ADR as a way of resolving disputes in the United Kingdom was propitious for the growing population of Muslims who were making their homes in the country and needed methods of dealing with their own disputes apart from the expensive, often culturally painful and complicated, formal legal solutions dispensed by UK courts. In the field of faith-based resolution of conflicts, the issue of Muslim methodologies and processes, particularly in the United Kingdom, could be perceived as quite accidental and opportunistic. The example of the Muslim Law (Shariah) Council (MLSC) in the United Kingdom serves as a valuable case in point.

In the mid-1970s, a Muslim woman from the Indian subcontinent, belonging to the Hanafi school of law, found herself in a difficult

130   *The Shariʿa*

situation: an English Court granted her a divorce, while her Muslim husband refused to grant her a *talaq*, which only a husband may grant his wife.[17] Without a *talaq* – that is, an Islamically valid repudiation of the marriage by her husband – she found herself unable to marry again within the Muslim community, while her husband entered into another marriage. The English court could do nothing further: she was fully entitled to contract another marriage under English law, but English courts did not have any jurisdiction over the shariʿa aspects of the case. So the woman approached the London Central Mosque, a major UK institution, to seek advice from the imams about any relief she might be able to obtain under the shariʿa. The imams at the mosque felt unable to help her for the converse reason that the English courts were unable to be of assistance. Since England is not a Muslim-majority country, the imams lack judicial authority as Muslim legal functionaries to grant her a change of status, which would allow her to enter into a fresh marriage with another Muslim.

At the time, Dr Mohamed Zaki Badawi, who was both an imam and a legal scholar, was based in the United Kingdom and looked into the matter. He examined the texts of the Hanafi school of jurisprudence and found in the philosophy of the eponymous founder of the school, Abu Hanifa, the principle that the shariʿa does not countenance any harm (*darar*) to a Muslim. Hence, if a Muslim found him or herself in a situation that was outside a Muslim context, the principles of necessity (*darura*) and public interest (*maslaha*) would entitle the knowledgeable among their community to constitute themselves in a type of court to ensure that justice was done. The present situation, referred to as a 'limping marriage', was regarded as a matter of public interest (*maslaha*) which needed addressing.

Badawi invited the woman's husband to come forward and explain his reasons for not granting a *talaq* to his wife and thereby placing her in a state of suspension with regard to her marital status, something contrary to the spirit of the shariʿa. After all, protecting the individual from harm (*darar*) was the fundamental moral purpose of the shariʿa. At first the husband was intransigent, but subsequently he relented on condition that his former wife reimbursed the funds that he had expended on her. In the computation of the sum, Badawi drew on the principles of a 'negotiated settlement' or *sulh*, and he prevailed on the husband to accept a sum that was equitable. Finally, the matter was resolved and the group of imams involved endorsed the new status of

---

[17]   M. Keshavjee, *Islam, Sharia and Alternative Dispute Resolution: Mechanisms for Legal Redress in the Muslim Community* (London, 2013), p. 1.

Family Law to Finance 131

the woman by passing a fatwa (judicial opinion) which granted her a divorce. Thus began the MLSC, which, since its inception, has helped more than 25,000 women, mostly in the United Kingdom but also elsewhere in Europe, to obtain Islamically valid divorce certificates outside a Muslim-majority setting.[18]

This procedure has not been challenged so far, either in countries of the western diaspora or in the Muslim world where parties have contracted new marriages. This does not rule out important 'conflict of law' issues which could arise in the future. However, for the moment, this form of relief appears to fit within the framework of alternative justice. In this regard, the procedure is not purely mediatory in the strict sense of the term, for the parties are not actually constructing their own mediated settlement but are seeking the assistance of an imam to obtain a certificate attesting to the dissolution of the marriage Islamically.

Such an agreement is largely by way of a declaration. While the MLSC limits itself to declaratory judgments, it is estimated that there are some 85 shariʿa councils operating in the United Kingdom applying the shariʿa at various levels. These councils have diverse approaches to the shariʿa. Some use formal, literal interpretations, while others look at the wider picture and apply *maqasid* and maslaha principles. Some civil society organisations in the United Kingdom, individual activists and, at times, even government institutions are concerned about this development. In 2016 the then home secretary, Theresa May, set up a commission to investigate the procedures of the various shariʿa councils with the specific remit to examine how women and children are dealt with. This action reflects the ongoing concern of the role of the shariʿa in the United Kingdom, which resonates with similar and often more vociferous concerns elsewhere (e.g. Canada) about the role of the shariʿa in civil society, especially in family disputes.[19] Concerns about the terms of reference with regard to the UK commission have been expressed recently, but the authors take issue with the assertions of journalist

---

[18] Ibid., p. 3.
[19] The Canadian context is discussed in Jennifer Selby's contribution to this volume (Chapter 12). More generally, see R. Griffith Jones, ed., *Rights, Responsibilities and the Place of Shariʿa* (Cambridge, 2013); J.R. Bowen, 'How Could English Courts Recognise the Shariah?', *University of St. Thomas Law Journal*, 7(3) (2011), pp. 411–435; S. Bano, *An Exploratory Study of Shariah Councils in England With Respect to Family Law* (2012): accessible at www. reading.ac.uk/web/files/law/An_exploratory_study_of_Shariah_councils_in_ England_with_respect_to_family_law_.pdf.

132   *The Shari'a*

Melanie Philips in a piece in *The Times*.[20] This newly conceived role
of shari'a councils exemplifies the creative approach undertaken by
a Muslim legal scholar, in collaboration with a team of imams, in a
diasporic setting where the *maqasid al-shari'a* was not academically
debated but in fact taken for granted in attempting to understand
the very purpose of the law in providing justice to a woman who was
being unfairly treated by her Muslim husband. It has certainly created
a new opportunity for women, taking into consideration the social
dimension and public interest aspect of the situation where thousands
of Muslim women would find themselves either remaining single or
living in relationships in which they would feel a sense of religious
discomfort.[21]

Muslim juridical exegetes and ADR institutions in the United
Kingdom would do great service to Muslim ADR bodies by ensuring
that the principles of ADR are strictly adhered to and that their
deliberations accord with the public laws of the United Kingdom. In
addition, proper training services informing disputants of their rights
and obligations, as well as making sure that they seek independent legal
advice, would ensure that ADR does not degenerate into an inferior
form of justice but plays a meaningful complementary role to the legal
system that currently operates in the United Kingdom. One example of
this is the National Conciliation and Arbitration Boards of the Ismaili
Muslim community that have developed a culturally sensitive model
which is used in more than 20 countries, which combines contemporary
mediation practices with ethical values enshrined in the shari'a and
which operates within the framework of the public laws of the various
countries where these boards function.

Conclusion

The understanding of *maqasid* and *maslaha*, as we have argued,
is potentially limitless. It is being redefined by some scholars in a
globalised context: Muslim societies and civil society institutions are
becoming sensitive to the interconnectedness of issues and the need
to work collaboratively both within and beyond local settings. In

---

[20]   M. Phillips, 'May Needs to Wake Up to the Reality of Sharia', *The Times*,
2 August 2016, p. 26. In the autumn of 2016, debates commenced in the UK
parliament with regard to the role of such councils and their relationship with
the national laws of that country.
[21]   S.N. Shah-Kazemi, *Untying the Knot: Muslim Women, Divorce and the
Sharia* (London, 2001).

Family Law to Finance   133

some instances, such as regarding international child abduction, the initiative has been generated largely from outside the Muslim world but it has traction with a number of civil society institutions in Muslim countries.

In other cases, such as financial products, the Malaysian government has co-opted religious functionaries and redefined the idea of *maqasid* as it applies in the context of the country's perceived needs. Here, the impetus originated from high-ranking officials within the government, working in close cooperation with both state institutions and theological organisations. The result has been the development of financial instruments that are beginning to play an important role in global finance. Thus the shari'a is becoming a significant participant in the world financial system. In the case of the United Kingdom's shari'a councils, while the development was largely accidental and opportunistic, a great deal still remains to be done to shape this institution in a manner that is compatible with the principles of *maqasid*, which was the reason in the first place for the councils coming into existence in non-Muslim societies, and is within the law of the land. A rigid approach to the shari'a is unlikely to serve the evolving needs of cosmopolitan Muslim communities, not only in the western diaspora but also in Muslim-majority societies. *Maqasid*, for its part, must find expression within the contours of a globalising world.

Further Reading

Abdalla, Amr. 'Principles of Islamic Interpersonal Intervention: A Search from within Islam and Western Literature', *The Journal of Law and Religion* 15 (2001), pp. 151–184.

Duderija, Adis. *Maqasid al-Sharia and Contemporary Reformist Muslim Thought, An Examination.* New York, 2014.

Griffith-Jones, Robin, ed. *Islam and English Law: Rights, Responsibilities and the Place of Shari'a.* Cambridge, 2013.

Keshavjee, Mohamed M. 'Cross-Border Family Mediation', in *International Parental Child Abduction, Custody and Access Cases*, C. Paul and S. Kieswetter, ed. Frankfurt, 2014.

Keshavjee, Mohamed M. *Islam, Sharia & Alternative Dispute Resolution: Mechanisms for Legal Redress in the Muslim Community.* London, 2013.

Kortweg, Anna and Jennifer Selby, ed. *Debating Sharia, Islam, Gender Politics and Family Law.* Toronto, ON, 2012.

Kuran, Timur. *Islam and Mammon: The Economic Predicaments of Islamism.* Princeton, NJ, 2004.

Othman, Aida. 'And Amicable Settlement is Best: Sulh and Dispute Resolution in Islamic Law', *Arab Law Quarterly*, 21 (2007), pp. 64–90.

Roberts, Simon and Michael Parker. *Dispute Processes: ADR and the Primary Forms of Decision Making*. Cambridge, 2005.

Shah-Kazemi, Sonia Nurin. *Untying the Knot: Muslim Women, Divorce and the Shariah*. London, 2001.

8

Bioethics

Amyn B. Sajoo

In modern bioethics, reasoning has centred on identifying key governing principles, which are then applied to fact situations in order to elicit suitable outcomes. This 'principlism' has the appeal of appearing rational and transparent. It allows for something close to an objective approach in a field which is open to a range of subjective moral convictions, including faith-based ones. Here, bioethics functions rather like law, where principlism has long enjoyed near-global hegemony. One expects of the law that it will offer a high degree of consistency and predictability. In practice, four principles – autonomy, non-maleficence, beneficence and justice – lay claim to universal application across the full spectrum of biomedical issues.

Of late, critiques of this stance have come to the fore, not only in bioethics but also in the larger context of ethical reasoning. 'Narrative' approaches point to the inadequacy of reducing complex fact situations, such as around reproductive and end-of-life choices, to tidy trade-offs over selected principles. There is also scepticism about the expertise of professional bioethicists in dealing with such complexities, which extends to Muslim settings. Christian ethicists have also questioned the practical value of the quartet of principles.

These critiques form part of the larger concern that ethical reasoning generally has fallen under the spell of legalism, straying from its roots in enquiring about the character of the acting agent. This was how Aristotelian ethics matured into a rigorous tradition, where the virtues are of the essence in guiding decisions which are the outcome of and a reflection on individual character.[1] In this view, decisions about matters such as abortion, organ donation and euthanasia begin with the values that ought to govern one's choices, mindful of the actual circumstances

---

[1] L. Groarke, *Moral Reasoning: Rediscovering the Ethical Tradition* (New York, 2011); A.E. Hooke, ed., 'What Is Virtue Ethics?', in *Virtuous Persons, Vicious Deeds* (Mountain View, CA, 1999), pp. 133–185.

136   *The Shari'a*

in which decisions are to be made. It will not do to force the individual into a system of prefabricated principles that 'deliver' proper choices, and to leave it to the actor to ask, incidentally, what the choice might say about the individual.

Virtue ethics found robust favour in early Islam, down to the Middle Ages when scores of Muslim jurists and philosophers embraced the stance of the 'First Master', the title they gave to Aristotle.[2] Given that the medical sciences were a field of excellence in the Muslim world from the 9th century to the 14th, it is no surprise that guidelines on ethical practice emerged in *bimaristans* (hospitals) from Iran and Syria to Iraq, Egypt and Tunisia.[3] But how would the character-centric outlook of Muslim neo-Aristotelianism, glossed by the influence of the physician Galen (ca. 129–200 CE), square with the shari'a? The latter was being shaped into a legalistic code in the hands of the ulama (theologians and jurists), who had much to say about health choices, often because they were themselves also adept in the sciences. Still, what they had to say was generally the outcome of a juristic mode of reasoning in which the fatwa was a typical outcome, in all its formalism.

There was a reaction to this legalism, rather like the critiques of principlism in modern secular ethics. Whether in medicine, philosophy or theology, many felt that sensitivity to context must trump a mechanistic mode of reasoning. A vital space was thus carved out in which public welfare, *maslaha*, could, under certain conditions, override the orthodox rules of the shari'a. Conservatives were only comfortable doing this if they could ground this in the text of the Qur'an, or at least the Sunna (the body of Prophetic conduct and rulings). Others went further: when necessary, one should venture beyond the text while preserving its spirit. Thus was born *maslaha mursala*, reasoning 'torn from scripture' in pursuit of the general welfare. For all its practical appeal, though, *maslaha mursala* raises some hard questions. How can it resist becoming a relativist ethos that bends to the zeitgeist? If fact situations are unique in being tied to the particulars of the agents involved, can a faith-based framework offer guidance that is overarching and distinctive?

This chapter argues that a hybrid of principlist and narrative ethics is best suited to contemporary challenges, especially in view of rapid

---

[2] G. Hourani, *Reason and Tradition in Muslim Ethics* (New York, 1985), pp. 11–13.

[3] A. Dallal, 'Science, Medicine, and Technology: The Making of a Scientific Culture', in J.L. Esposito, ed., *The Oxford History of Islam* (New York, 1999), pp. 155–213.

Bioethics 137

advances in biotechnology, whether in Muslim-majority or diasporic contexts in a globalised world. No less pressing is the need to fashion appropriate ethical responses to biosocial problems such as female genital mutilation (FGM) and honour crimes. Yet the pragmatism of this hybrid approach can hardly assure its 'Islamic' legitimacy, a critical element in enabling change. This is where *maslaha mursala*, embedded in the traditional discourse of the shari'a, serves as a valuable field of justification and validation. To do so effectively, *maslaha* will itself need to take into account individual rights as an integral aspect of public welfare. Autonomy becomes all the more important in a discourse that stresses collective (public) welfare. This is not quite as radical an idea in a Muslim context as might be thought.

Modernist reformers have already drawn on *maslaha mursala* in grappling with colonial and post-colonial laws across Asia and the Middle East. Recently, Muslim countries played an active part in drafting UNESCO's Universal Declaration on Bioethics and Human Rights, which highlights the nexus between individual autonomy and moral traditions.[4] At the same time, the narrative-virtue ethics discourse has something to learn from the emphasis on collective welfare in the tradition of *maslaha*, on issues ranging from new reproductive technologies and stem-cell therapies to advance directives on end-of-life questions.

I begin by setting forth some of the problems with the quartet of principlist bioethics today, and with alternative stances that stem from the critiques of narrative-virtue ethics. Next I address the principlism of Muslim ethics, including in biomedical issues, with specific regard to *maslaha* as an ethicolegal response. Finally, I suggest how the confluence of narrative-virtue ethics and *maslaha mursala* would have much to offer in addressing challenges in bioethics today. 'Muslim ethics' is conceived of as a major aspect of the theological as well as lived experience of communities, from the very foundations of Islam in the 7th century. I shall discuss the unfolding of this ethical dimension in broad outline, drawing out strands that relate particularly to what we today regard as biomedicine.

Principalism and Its Discontents

The primacy of individual autonomy in mainstream bioethics is a response to the long history of medical paternalism, amid the

---

[4] UNESCO, Universal Declaration on Bioethics and Human Rights (Paris, 2005): accessible at http://www.unesco.org/new/en/social-and-human-sciences/themes/bioethics/bioethics-and-human-rights/.

138 *The Shariʿa*

post-World War II rise of the discourse on human rights. One's physical and psychological well-being are felt to be matters that require informed consent before any biomedical intervention. In what has become the most widely applied model of 'principlism' since the late 20th century, autonomy is coupled with non-maleficence – do no harm – as a practical guide to making bioethical choices. 'Beneficence' and 'Justice' – doing good, and fairness – round off the model.

In the hands of its best-known proponents, Thomas Beauchamp and James Childress, the model has evolved over the years to make space for a sophisticated 'reflective equilibrium'. This draws on the liberal philosophy of John Rawls, where conflicting principles can be reconciled.[5] The four principles are not intended to be mechanistic in the model's application, at least in the more refined form that it takes today after various criticisms. So wide is the impact of this principlist model that it is seen as both the most rational and the most intuitively informed way to deal with ethical problems in contemporary biomedical practice. Some scholars have gone so far as to assert that the model resonates not only with modern Muslim approaches to bioethics but also with medieval Islamic medicine, regardless of the formal packaging.[6]

While lauding the role of reflective equilibrium in allowing for 'thinking outside the box', critics increasingly find the Beauchamp and Childress model to have acute limitations in decision-making. One set of criticisms is about the failure to recognise the role of institutional culture. Clinics, hospitals, laboratories and nursing homes all have their normative preferences, as do communities and individuals, but in an asymmetrical relationship with the former. Paternalism can remain very much intact as professional rules frame how patient autonomy, for example, is exercised. What is called for, say the critics, is 'empirical enrichment' in understanding how choices are made. This is especially so in terms of the particular experience that the individual brings to his or her encounter with health practitioners.[7]

A further criticism, which strikes at the very foundation of the principlist model, concerns its idea of individual autonomy. For

---

[5] T.L. Beauchamp and J.F. Childress, *Principles of Biomedical Ethics*, 6th edn (New York, 2009), notably pp. 368–397, also on Rawls's approach to the principle of justice, pp. 246–250.

[6] S. Aksoy and A. Elmai, 'The Core Concepts of the "Four Principles" of Bioethics as Found in Islamic Tradition', *Medicine and Law* 21 (2002), pp. 211–224.

[7] H. Lindemann, M. Verkerk and M. Walker, ed., *Naturalized Bioethics: Toward Responsible Knowing and Practice* (New York, 2009), pp. 8–13; A.Z. Newton, *Narrative Ethics* (Cambridge, MA, 1995).

Bioethics 139

Beauchamp and Childress, this is about affirming that each of us has 'unconditional worth', and 'the capacity to determine his or her own moral destiny', as set forth in the philosophy of Immanuel Kant (1724–1804).[8] As an antidote to medical paternalism, in which the physician or the system dictates choices to the patient, who can argue with the importance of the individual's worth and agency? Yet Kant was willing only to affirm the exercise of that agency if it conformed to a universal 'moral rationality', rather than mere impulses or desires. This idea of autonomy might well require the physician or the system to reprove the patient for abusing his or her exercise of agency, where harm ensues to the individual or to others.[9] In short, bioethical choices are tied here to an understanding of ethical value that for Kant is not overridden by a claim to 'doing it my way'.[10]

Principlism, then, seems to fall short on its attention to both context and the quality of individual agency. There is serious neglect of the social and individual narratives in which institutions interact with people: these relationships need to be localised, something that principlism, with its top-down framework, is hard pressed to accomplish. Other critics ask how judgments about, say, responding to a foetus or child with Down's syndrome are subject to the 'moral expertise' of professional bioethicists. Should the client allow the judgment of the expert substitute for their own? Or does this amount to a perilous submissiveness?[11] What does the bioethicist, whose institutional ties may shape the advice offered, bring to such choices? The issue is further shaded by the fact that training in bioethics is generally in the mould of mainstream principlism.

No less troubling is the role of the market in informing the decisions of professional bioethicists. Consumerism too often creates the expectation that the ethicist will serve as an advocate for market-driven desires as 'entitlements'. Corporate influence on decisions with regard to treatment options is strong, and growing globally, in ways that are mirrored in other aspects of biomedical practice, from pharmaceuticals and technologies to the politics of public policy. Virginia Sharpe offers

---

[8] Beauchamp and Childress, *Principles of Bioethics*, p. 103. Kant's account of autonomy is developed in his *Groundwork of the Metaphysics of Morals*, trans. M. Gregor and J. Timmermman (Cambridge, 2012), Section II.

[9] A.E. Hinkley, 'Two Rival Understandings of Autonomy, Paternalism, and Bioethical Principlism', in H.T. Engelhardt, ed., *Bioethics Critically Reconsidered: Having Second Thoughts* (Dordrecht, 2012), pp. 85–95.

[10] Ibid., p. 93.

[11] J.L. Nelson, 'Trusting Bioethicists', in L. Eckenwiler and F. Cohn, ed., *The Ethics of Bioethics: Mapping the Moral Landscape* (Baltimore, MD, 2007), pp. 47–55.

140   *The Shari'a*

several examples of industry-driven initiatives, not only in medicine but
also in environmental and food-related public policy, where particular
ethical outcomes are manipulated.[12] In noting that 'money tends to
encourage conformity and to obscure moral obligations', her criticisms
bring us back to the concerns of those for whom principlism is urgently
in need of sensitivity to context, beyond the 'cool' application of
normative rules.

It is not in bioethics alone that principlist reasoning is subject to
trenchant criticisms. The two dominant normative traditions in ethics
today are utilitarianism, with its calculus of majoritarian satisfaction,
and Kantian deontology, in which duties drive choices.[13] Both can
be seen as catering to the demand in modernity for systemic modes
of ethical governance and decision-making, where consistency and
rationalism are prized. Indeed, both traditions have left their mark on
contemporary legal and political systems. They have also found their
way into bioethics, seeking to shape institutional as well as individual
choices.[14] Like the principlism of Beauchamp and Childress, utilitarian
and Kantian ethics have also raised concerns about the loss of context
and individual subjectivity in the name of objective processes.

'Virtue ethics' has in recent years become the major critical response
to utilitarian and Kantian modes of reasoning, harking back to the
Aristotelian tradition in placing character and its cultivation at the
very core of moral action.[15] Here the acting agent is the starting point,
with a disposition committed to the virtues not for their pragmatic
but rather for their inherent value. This disposition needs practical
wisdom in the habitual exercise of these virtues, finding a middle
way between extremes. The reward for this striving is *eudaimonia*,
commonly rendered as 'happiness', but not to be confused with pleasure
or satisfaction; rather, it is the ideal of exemplary living.[16] Traits such as
courage, integrity and restraint are prized as integral to excellence in
character. This is what makes them virtues.

---

[12]   V. Sharpe, 'Strategic Disclosure Requirements and the Ethics of Bioethics', in
Eckenwiler and Cohn, *The Ethics of Bioethics*, pp. 170–180.
[13]   S.M. Cahn and P. Markie, ed., *Ethics: History, Theory, and Contemporary
Issues*, 4th edn (New York, 2009); R. Shafer-Landau, ed., *Ethical Theory: An
Anthology* (Oxford, 2007).
[14]   H. Kuhse and P. Singer, ed., *A Companion to Bioethics* (Oxford, 2001),
pp. 72–79, 80–85.
[15]   Aristotle, *Ethics* [*The Nicomachean Ethics*], trans. J.A.K. Thomson (London,
1976).
[16]   L. Groarke, *Moral Reasoning*, in C. Oakley and D. Cocking, ed., *Virtue Ethics
and Professional Roles* (New York, 2006).

Bioethics 141

Against those who would dismiss this as too broad to be useful in practice, virtue ethicists have drawn out specific ways in which the approach can shape decisions on matters such as abortion, euthanasia and patient care.[17] The approach has found resonance in 'care-based' and feminist stances in bioethics, which share the conviction that mainstream principlism is too removed from the economic and social contexts that frame everyday choices. It should be pointed out that virtue ethics does not eschew principles as such; the individual is expected to strive towards ideals that are universally recognised. What the various critiques from this perspective aim to do is *situate* principles or values in the context of acting well.

Principlism, the Shari'a and *Maslaha*

Virtue ethics sits quite comfortably within all the major faith traditions, where the quest for individual and communal salvation is at stake.[18] A special and enduring esteem developed in the Islamic Near East, and later in Andalusia, for the Hellenic philosophical heritage as embodied in the works of Aristotle, Plotinus and Proclus. They had created a systematic body of thought that centred on character – not only of the individual but also of governors and their societies. While Asian texts such as those of Confucius and Manu had ventured into this earlier, with elaborate codes of conduct, the Hellenic heritage was more amenable in terms of the availability of translations, and in offering modes of justification that lent them to appropriation.

Muslim thinkers such as al-Kindi (ca. 805–873), al-Razi (ca. 854–925) and al-Farabi (ca. 870–950) set the trend in embracing Hellenic ideas as vital building blocks in the making of the virtuous community or umma. Aristotelian ideas were especially vital in the hands of the foundational figures in Sunni and Shi'i ethical thought – Ibn Miskawayh (ca. 932–1030), al-Ghazali (1058–1111) and al-Tusi (ca. 1201–1274). The upshot was a conspicuous role for discursive reason in the making of Muslim ethics, at a time that also witnessed the rise of an energetic scientific tradition across the Middle East. Physicians were already

---

[17] E.D. Pellegrino, and D.C. Thomasma, ed., *The Virtues in Medical Practice* (New York, 1993); R. Hursthouse, 'Virtue Theory and Abortion', *Philosophy and Public Affairs* 20 (1991), pp. 223–246; P. Foot, 'Euthanasia', *Philosophy and Public Affairs* 6 (1977), pp. 85–112; J. Oakley, 'A Virtue Ethics Approach', in H. Kuhse and P. Singer, ed., *A Companion to Bioethics*, pp. 86–97.

[18] W. Schweiker, ed., *The Blackwell Companion to Religious Ethics* (Oxford, 2008).

142   *The Shariʿa*

adopting codes of proper conduct (*adab*), drawing heavily on Galen and Hippocrates – whose famous oath was appropriated – but soon adding an overlay of regional Judeo-Christian and Islamic precepts.[19]

The development of these practices in medicine tapped into a larger ethos. 'Healthcare' in the medieval Islamic world was located within the domain of human responsibility, extending to matters from personal hygiene and sanitation to the obligation to seek remedies to illness. The *Qanun fi al-Tibb* (Canon of Medicine) of Ibn Sina (ca. 980–1037) was to eventually take this rationalism to the West in Latin and Hebrew, but that was long after it had spread in Muslim cities. Here is an account by the historian al-Maqrizi after a visit to one of the world's largest hospitals at the time, Cairo's al-Mansur hospital, built in 1285:

> I have found this institution for my equals and for those beneath me, it is intended for rulers and subjects, for soldiers and for the emir, for great and small, freemen and slaves, men and women ... Every class of patient was accorded separate accommodation: the four halls of the hospital were set apart for those with fever and similar complaints; one part of the building was reserved for eye-patients, one for the wounded, one for those suffering from diarrhoea, one for women; a room for convalescents was divided into two parts, one for men and one for women. Water was laid on to all these departments ... even those who were sick at home were supplied with every necessity.[20]

Contagion and infectious disease were to be understood in the same vein as facets of public health, and the waves of the plague which repeatedly struck the Mediterranean and northern Europe were not taken with resignation as curses from above. There is a telling admonition on the subject by a leading scholar and politician of Granada, Ibn al-Khatib, in his treatise on the Black Death of 1349:

> One principle that cannot be ignored is if the senses and observation oppose traditional evidence, the latter needs to be interpreted, and the correct course in this case is to interpret

---

[19] M. Levey, 'Medical Ethics of Medieval Islam with Special Reference to Al-Ruhāwī's "Practical Ethics of the Physician"', *Transactions of the American Philosophical Society* 57(3) (1967), pp. 1–100.

[20] Quoted in W. Osler, *The Evolution of Modern Medicine* (Whitefish, MT, 2004), pp. 73–74.

Bioethics 143

it according to what a group of those who affirm contagion say. In the Law there are many texts that support this, such as [the Prophet's] saying: 'The sick should not be watered with the healthy' ... God protect us from nonsense and grant us success in speech and action.[21]

As it turned out, the bubonic plague that afflicted the region was not in fact contagious, though many other forms of the plague can be. The issue was not settled until the late 19th century, and the point is that Ibn al-Khatib was keen to proceed on the best empirical evidence.

'Traditional evidence' was certainly not good enough for Ibn al-Nafis (1213–1288), the Syrian physician and legal scholar who moved to Cairo and uncovered details of the pulmonary circulation of the blood. Al-Nafis wrote critical commentaries on Galen as well as on Ibn Sina's *Qanun*, and there can be little doubt that his anatomical observations were the result of careful cadaver dissection.[22] Moreover, al-Nafis has been alone in this, given the flourishing of empirically based rather than philosophical science at the time across the Middle East. Damascus witnessed the establishment of among the first schools dedicated entirely to the teaching of medicine, and its founder was none other than al-Nafis's teacher, al-Dakhwar.

It is significant that al-Dakhwar's school attracted the support and participation of leading religious scholars in Damascus, that al-Nafis (like Ibn al-Khatib, Ibn Sina and a host of other physicians) was also adept in Islamic jurisprudence, and that learned texts conventionally made reference to scripture. Far from being a purely secular endeavour, science and particularly medicine served the ideal of *islah*, social reform and doing good, which harked back to the earliest teachings of the Prophet. Belief itself is coupled with good works so that mere profession of the faith without constructive social action is seen as empty; believers are not only properly guided but are 'possessors of minds' with moral agency (Qur'an, 39:17–18; 81; 82:5). *Islah*, then, is understood as a rational ethical task for the faithful individual and umma alike.[23]

---

[21] Quoted in J. Stearns, 'Enduring the Plague: Ethical Behavior in the Fatwas of a Fourteenth-Century Mufti and Theologian', in J.E. Brockopp and T. Eich, ed., *Muslim Medical Ethics: From Theory to Practice* (Columbia, SC, 2008), pp. 39–40.

[22] A. Dallal, 'Science, Medicine, and Technology', *The Oxford History of Islam*, pp. 205–207; G. Saliba, *Islamic Science and the Making of the European Renaissance* (Cambridge, MA, 2007), p. 239.

[23] A.K Reinhart, 'Origins of Islamic Ethics: Foundations and Constructions', in Schweiker, *The Blackwell Companion to Religious Ethics*, pp. 244–253, p. 247.

144   *The Shari'a*

Islah comes from the same root as *maslaha*, the pursuit of the public good or welfare, in matters of Islamic law as well as ethics. As noted throughout this volume, a coupling of ethics and law constitutes the shari'a. Historically, a vast body of practical normative guidance, fiqh, was derived from the principles of the shari'a. The common reduction of the shari'a to 'Islamic law' obscures this difference. Yet a culture of legalism gradually prevailed in the common understanding of the shari'a, for reasons that are explored elsewhere in this book: fiqh, in short, came to stand for the shari'a at large. But this was not always so, and the trend never ceased to have its critics.

Al-Nafis's dissection of cadavers could, on a strict reading of the shari'a and fiqh, be regarded as problematic because it went against the canonical tenet of burying the deceased promptly and with the body intact – widely affirmed in Muslim practice. Yet there is no record of any allegations that al-Nafis's actions amounted to desecration. Nor for that matter was autopsy unconditionally forbidden in the classical period. Likewise, despite the customary segregation of gender roles in the shari'a, male physicians commonly treated female patients (as can be seen in medieval illustrations). We might also recall Ibn al-Khatib's protest against 'traditional evidence' in the face of sound public health concerns, and Ibn Rushd's rebuke of those who would downplay rigorous and informed discourse in the name of a narrow orthodoxy. These are best regarded as paradigm cases in the driving role of *maslaha mursala* in the evolution of Muslim ethics.

Modern Legacy – and Prospect

Amid public debate about conducting post-mortems in Egypt, the noted reformer Rashid Rida (1865–1935) pushed in 1910 for this to be deemed in the public interest and not a violation of shari'a tradition. Like his more prominent Cairene collaborator, Muhammed Abduh (1849–1905), Rida argued that colonial laws in this regard should be seen pragmatically rather than as necessarily anti-Islamic.[24] The fact that a concurring opinion on this matter was still needed in the 1940s, and yet again in the 1980s, is telling. This entire debate was in the form of fatwas, couched in proper juristic logic, drawing on foundational sources. What a contrast with the experience of al-Nafis on cadavers and dissections.

For many of today's Muslim reformers, a retrieval of ethical reasoning is the only way forward for a shari'a that speaks to modern challenges.

---

[24] V. Rispler-Chaim, 'The Ethics of Postmortem Examinations in Contemporary Islam', *Journal of Medical Ethics* 19 (1993), pp. 164–168, p. 165.

Bioethics   145

Fazlur Rahman (1919–1998) was surely right to lament a double diminution: ethics plays a minor role at best within fiqh methodology, while also losing the stature it once enjoyed as a discourse in its own right. Others such as Abdolkarim Soroush (b. 1945) and Mohammed Shahrur (b. 1938) have little patience for traditionalist fiqh, and they advocate the fullest use of methodologies from the sciences and humanities in approaching scripture and its social implications.[25] Likewise, Tariq Ramadan (b. 1962) calls for robust collaboration between secular and religious expertise in adopting an integrative approach to decision-making on the practical application of the shariʿa.[26]

Arguably, nowhere is the disjunction between traditionalist legal methodology and contemporary needs more evident than in the field of bioethics. The combination of new biotechnologies, health systems tied to market economics, and the array of individual choice serves to create a setting in which rigid principlism is of increasingly limited value. Consider, for example, the challenges posed by the matter of organ donation and transplant, notably with regard to kidneys. Complex issues such as informed consent and advance directives, fixing the time of demise for cadaver donations (around brain/cardiac death), and the commercialisation of donations and transplants have proved especially vexing in Muslim settings where cultural understandings of the shariʿa are highly varied.[27] Numerous fatwas have been issued by authoritative national muftis and international councils to the effect that donating kidneys affirms the classical Islamic principle of saving a life, provided that no undue hardship is suffered by the donor. In diasporic settings such as Canada and the United Kingdom, health institutions have duly invoked these rulings.[28]

---

[25]   M. Sadri and A. Sadri, ed., *Reason, Freedom and Democracy in Islam, Essential Writings of Abdolkarim Soroush* (New York, 2000); M. Shahrur, *The Qurʾan, Morality and Critical Reason*, trans. A. Christmann (Leiden, 2009).

[26]   T. Ramadan, *Radical Reform: Islamic Ethics and Liberation* (Oxford 2009), p. 167.

[27]   F.A. Shaheen, M. Al Jondeby, R. Kurpad and A.A. Al-Khader, 'Social and Cultural Issues in Organ Transplantation in Islamic Countries', *Annals of Transplantation* 9(2) (2004), pp. 11–13; F. Moazzam, *Bioethics and Organ Transplantation in a Muslim Society: A Study in Culture, Ethnography and Religion* (Bloomington, IN, 2006).

[28]   Canadian Council for Donation and Transplantation, *Faith Perspectives on Organ Donation and Transplantation* (Edmonton, 2006): accessible at http://www.legacyoflife.ns.ca/other_questions/Faith-Perspectives.pdf; National Health Service (UK), Organ Donation: What Does My Religion Say? Islam, available at: https://www.organdonation.nhs.uk/about-donation/what-does-my-religion-say/islam/.

146   *The Shariʿa*

Yet the supposed authority of these fatwas has settled very little in practice, any more than it did a century earlier on the matter of post-mortems. Sherine Hamdy's fieldwork shows how Egypt's popular shaykh Muhammad al-Shaʿrawi (1911–1998) succeeded in trumping the collective will of the Al-Azhar academy, as well as the state, in insisting that 'our bodies belong to God' and organ donations violate shariʿa tradition.[29] In a country with an acute shortage of donated kidneys and an appalling rate of commercial trafficking, repeated attempts at national legislation have failed in the face of popular opposition. Hamdy notes that, for many, al-Shaʿrawi's stance was in contrast to official muftis 'who went so far as to "sell the religion" in order to facilitate the aims of the government'.[30] The appeal to *maslaha* has been taken up by non-governmental actors such as the Coalition for Organ-Failure Solutions, which is now actively campaigning in Egypt and across the Muslim world.[31]

Similar disjunctions between conflicting fatwas and popular social practice have been well documented on a range of other biomedical issues.[32] For Ebrahim Moosa, this signals an epistemic dissonance between jurisprudence and contemporary science. Judging by the modes of reasoning in sample fatwas on organ transplantation in Pakistan, Egypt and the Academy of Islamic Jurisprudence, he finds little prospect of convergence anytime soon.[33] And consider how DNA evidence of paternity and the ensuing responsibility for the welfare of a child is caught in traditionalist legal approaches to the shariʿa.[34] Again,

---

[29] S. Hamdy, *Our Bodies Belong to God: Organ Transplants, Islam, and the Struggle for Human Dignity in Egypt* (Berkeley, CA, 2012).

[30] Ibid., p. 117.

[31] D. Budiani and O. Shibly, 'Islam, Organ Transplants, and Organ Trafficking in the Muslim World: Paving a Path for Solutions', in J.E. Brockopp and T. Eich, ed., *Muslim Medical Ethics*, pp. 138–150, 147–148.

[32] M. Clarke, 'Science and Social Change', in A.B. Sajoo, ed., *A Companion to Muslim Cultures* (London, 2012), pp. 103–115; B. Krawietz, 'Brain Death and Islamic Traditions: Shifting Borders of Life?', in J.E. Brockopp, ed., *Islamic Ethics of Life: Abortion, War, and Euthanasia* (Columbia, SC, 2003), pp. 194–213; S. Hamdy, 'Blinding Ignorance: Medical Science, Diseased Eyes, and Religious Practice in Egypt', *The Arab Studies Journal* 13(1) (2004), pp. 26–45.

[33] E. Moosa, 'Interface of Science and Jurisprudence: Dissonant Gazes at the Body in Muslim Ethics', in T. Peters, M. Iqbal and S.N. Haq, ed., *God, Life, and the Cosmos: Christian and Islamic Perspectives* (Aldershot, 2002), pp. 329–355.

[34] H. Bahgat and W. Afifi, 'Egypt', in R. Parker, R. Petchesky and R. Sember, ed., *SexPolitics: Reports from the Frontlines* (Rio de Janeiro, 2011), pp. 53–89: accessible at http://www.sxpolitics.org/frontlines/book/index.php.

Bioethics   147

ethical critique is trumped by a straightforward claim that it is law
which determines religious legitimacy, no matter that the outcome turns
on technical reasoning that is vindicated by nothing more than the
politics of patriarchy.

Where does all this leave health practitioners and institutions
with regard to everyday bioethical decisions which they and/or their
patients must undertake in view of their religious convictions? Calls
for sensitivity to and accommodation of such convictions abound, not
least in diasporic secular settings.[35] Can the prevalence of traditionalist
reasoning with frequently polarised claims to authoritativeness continue
to be relevant, whether in western or Muslim-majority societies?

I propose three broad conclusions in the light of the foregoing, which
will return us to the discussion that began this chapter, on the narrative-
virtue critique of principlism. First, the negotiating space offered by
maslaha mursala matters above all for the legitimacy that it confers,
both in Muslim-majority societies and the western diaspora. Bioethics
negotiation that abjures faith-related considerations may be expedient,
but it can be deeply unsatisfactory for clients and practitioners alike.
The locus of *maslaha* in a long tradition of shari'a discourse allows for
an evaluation that is tied to ground realities and a rational appreciation
of public welfare, yet attuned to fundamental Islamic values. Clearly,
the demands of modern human rights, built around autonomy,
must fit into a weighing of the good. Historically, one recalls that
al-Ghazali rejected the use of torture, even where its results might serve
the public interest, because of the competing interest in not injuring
an individual who might turn out to be innocent.[36] In this vein, there
is much to be said for a recent exercise in applying traditional Jewish
ethics to contemporary problems of abortion, capital punishment, the
environment, homosexuality and gender.[37]

Second, *maslaha* cannot mount to utilitarian evaluation. Some
Muslim thinkers argue that a permissive approach to *maslaha mursala*
would open the floodgates to expediency. This is not an unreasonable

---

[35]   C. Seale, 'The Role of Doctors' Religious Faith and Ethnicity in Taking
Ethically Controversial Decisions during End-of-Life Care', *Journal of Medical
Ethics* 36(11) (2010), pp. 677–682; A.S. Daar and A. al-Khitamy, 'Healthcare',
in A.B. Sajoo, ed., *A Companion to Muslim Ethics* (London, 2010), pp. 119–130;
I.H. Jaffer and S.M.H. Alibhai, 'The Permissibility of Organ Donation, End-of-
Life Care, and Autopsy in Shiite Islam: A Case Study', in J.E. Brockopp and T.
Eich, ed., *Muslim Medical Ethics*, pp. 167–181.
[36]   A. Emon, 'Natural Law and Natural Rights in Islamic Law', *Journal of Law
and Religion* 20 (2004), pp. 351–395.
[37]   R.E. Friedman and S. Dolansky, *The Bible Now* (New York, 2011).

148   *The Shari'a*

concern.[38] No faith tradition can be expected to ignore 'red lines' in ethical choice. Yet those lines are a matter of interpreting broad foundational principles in present-day settings. For example, FGM is deemed by many Muslim activists as crossing a red line.[39] Others insist that its value as a traditional rite of passage must be preserved, notwithstanding its patriarchal roots. The persistence of the practice despite forceful campaigns and legislation attests to the weakness rather than the strength of the current understanding of *maslaha*. Thus in Egypt, where FGM is notoriously widespread, the Muslim Brotherhood has sought to reverse the national campaign against the practice, claiming in the face of all evidence (including formal rulings by the al-Azhar establishment) that it is religiously endorsed.

And consider the debate over FGM in Malaysia, where a conservative religious establishment endorsed the practice in a 2009 fatwa. This stance has been assailed by Malaysian medical practitioners and youth empowerment activists on the grounds that it is a harmful cultural practice with no justification in public health or indeed in Islamic theology.[40] With the prevalence of FGM in Malaysia, the task of reform is surely a long-term one. *Maslaha* aids in fostering such change as an avenue with a strong tradition of safeguarding public welfare.

Another example in this vein is the practice of honour killing. This is no more an Islamic practice than is FGM, but rather a sociocultural ritual which pervades regions that may be predominantly Christian, Hindu, Jewish, Muslim or animist. Nevertheless, it is widespread in some Muslim societies, including Afghanistan, Egypt, Indonesia, Jordan, Pakistan and Turkey, and is frequently unpunished by the full force of criminal law. Ayse Onal observes that religious authorities have not only failed to use their influence in this regard but also 'remained silent even when religion is cited as a motivation for such killings'.[41] The prospect, then, of having red lines drawn around the practice is far greater through the exercise of *maslaha*, in a context where it is framed as gravely harmful to the collective welfare and thence to the faith.

That traditional religious institutions, from mosques to jurists' panels, have failed to deal with these practices effectively might be

---

[38]   W. Hallaq, *Shari'a: Theory, Practice, Transformations* (New York, 2009), pp. 511–514.

[39]   Z. Kassam, 'Gender', in A.B. Sajoo, ed., *A Companion to Muslim Ethics* (London, 2010), pp. 105–118.

[40]   Asri. A, 'Muslim Doctors against Female Circumcision', *FMT News*, 17 October 2016: accessible at http://www.freemalaysiatoday.com/category/nation/2016/10/17/muslim-doctors-against-female-circumcision/.

[41]   A. Onal, *Honour Killing* (London, 2008), p. 254; Kassam, 'Gender', pp. 112–115.

Bioethics 149

dismissed as the result of sociocultural codes overriding the shariʿa. The cost of such resignation is borne by an enormous number of Muslims, especially women. Patriarchy is a pervasive feature of the traditionalism that historically underlies how the shariʿa has been understood. Is it a surprise that a male juristic elite, as the custodian of the shariʿa within and beyond state-run institutions, has with rare exceptions proved less than enthusiastic about gender justice? Kwame Appiah's critique of cross-cultural honour codes, in their resistance to and enabling of radical shifts in moral perspective, is a reminder of how inclusive the methods and social actors need to be in this regard.[42] With specific regard to honour crimes among the Pashtun communities of Afghanistan and Pakistan, he tracks the religious and secular 'coalition of insiders and outsiders' which is all too gradually, yet surely, undermining the association of gender and honour that drives the practice. Appiah acknowledges that such coalitions occur less in rural than urban settings, where women's networks and shelters have been growing. But this conforms to historical patterns in transforming patriarchal honour, from Chinese foot-binding and marriage practices to English gentlemen's codes of exclusion. The prospective role of *maslaha* is to spread the responsibility for change beyond the confines of jurists and other traditional actors.

Finally, if it is not to fall victim to the legalistic principlism from which it offers sanctuary, *maslaha* merits treatment as an ethical discourse in its own right. This includes sensitivity to the actual realities of various stakeholders, through appropriately broad consultation.[43] The fiqh/shariʿa tradition within which it developed historically has always staked a claim to the ideal of being more than a corpus of rules: faith and its ethical imperatives are said to be foundational, and the rules merely the means to those ends. It was a tradition 'constructed on the assumption that its audiences and consumers were, all along, moral communities and morally grounded individuals'.[44]

Decisions with regard to stem-cell therapies and pre-natal genetic diagnosis, no less than humane animal slaughter and the proprieties of adoption, are subject to a values analysis that partakes not only of scripture and its various traditional cognates (Sunni and Shiʿi) but also

---

[42] K.A. Appiah, *The Honor Code: How Moral Revolutions Happen* (New York and London, 2010), pp. 139–172.

[43] A. Padela, I. Shanawani and A. Arozullah, 'Medical Experts and Islamic Scholars Deliberating over Brain Death: Gaps in the Applied Islamic Bioethics Discourse', in B. Arda and V. Rispler-Chaim, ed., *Islam and Bioethics* (Ankara, 2010), pp. 55–75.

[44] Hallaq, *Shariʿa*, p. 583.

of the cultural politics thereof, including that of gender. Matters are not made any easier when the state becomes the keeper of the shari'a. A flourishing ethical discourse in its own right becomes all the more vital as the law grapples with the moral challenges of new technologies and choices, mindful that 'hard cases make bad law'.

Mainstream bioethics thrives on a paradigm that draws on utilitarian and deontological modes of reasoning, which came to break away from Aristotelian virtue ethics. In prizing the autonomy of the individual, the principlist model has dispensed with the Kantian insistence that autonomy should be ethically grounded. This orientation has serious implications for a deeper personhood, which sits at the core of moral choices at both ends of life. Muslim ethics, too, built on the character-centred discourse of Aristotle, coupled with an abiding concern for the public good. At its best, this has served as the raison d'être of the shari'a. *Maslaha*'s engagement with the narrative-virtue critique of principlist bioethics is edifying in its recognition of the need to balance individual and public interests. As such, it may also contribute to dealing sensibly with the tensions of culture and secular-religious polemics, which often get in the way of appreciating the shared nature of the stakes at hand.

Further Reading

Arda, Berna and Vardit Rispler-Chaim, ed. *Islam and Bioethics*. Ankara, 2010.

Benatar, Solomon and Gillian Brock, ed. *Global Health and Global Health Ethics*. Cambridge, 2011.

Brockopp, Jonathan E., ed. *Islamic Ethics of Life: Abortion, War, and Euthanasia*. Columbia, SC, 2003.

Engelhardt, H. Tristam, ed. *Bioethics Critically Reconsidered: Having Second Thoughts*. Dordrecht, 2012.

Lindemann, Hilde, Marian Verkerk and Margaret U. Walker, ed. *Naturalized Bioethics: Toward Responsible Knowing and Practice*. New York, 2009.

Messer, Neil, ed. *Theological Issues in Bioethics*. London, 2002.

Moazzam, Farhat. *Bioethics and Organ Transplantation in a Muslim Society: A Study in Culture, Ethnography and Religion*. Bloomington, IN, 2006.

Sachedina, Abdulaziz. *Islamic Biomedical Ethics: Principles and Application*. New York, 2009.

Sajoo, A.B., ed. *A Companion to Muslim Ethics*. London, 2010.

Schweiker, W., ed. *The Blackwell Companion to Religious Ethics*. Oxford, 2008.

Setta, Susan M. and Sam D. Shamie, 'An Explanation and Analysis of How World Religions Formulate their Ethical Decisions on Withdrawing Treatment and Determining Death', *Philosophy, Ethics, and Humanities in Medicine* 10(6) (2015): accessible at https://peh-med.biomedcentral.com/articles/10.1186/s13010-015-0025-x.

Statman, Daniel. *Virtue Ethics: A Critical Reader.* Edinburgh, 1997.

9

Legitimising Authority: A Muslim Minority under Ottoman Rule

Amaan Merali

In the summer of 1571 the imperial chancery in Istanbul received the following missive from officials in Baghdad regarding the shrines of Ali ibn Abi Talib at Najaf and his son Husayn at Karbala, two of the most revered Shi'i imams:

> It has become known to the caretaker of the shrines that heretics who come here on pilgrimage have altered the carpets to include names [of Shi'i imams] like those from the frontier that are banned, and are covering the floors of the auspicious shrines and respectable sanctuaries of noble Imam Ali and noble Imam Husayn ... It is necessary to change these for several imperial carpets from the royal, glorious mosques of Anatolia.[1]

This seemingly mundane change of carpets highlights many of the issues which the Ottoman Empire had been confronting for decades. The state was eager to promote its image as the defender of Islamic orthodoxy. This identity, defined in contrast to its main Muslim competitor, the Shi'i Safavids in Iran, would do much to legitimise Ottoman authority. Sometimes the measures taken to protect and promote this image could be innocuous, as in the replacement of carpets. More often than not, the state arrested, tried, imprisoned and tortured, even executed, its subjects who fell outside Ottoman orthodoxy.

The imperial legal system positioned itself as the vanguard of this orthodoxy. By the 16th century, the Ottoman legal system had a centralised network of judges (*kadıs*) and jurisconsults (muftis) through

---

[1] C. Şener, *Osmanlı Belgeleri'nde Aleviler-Bektaşiler: 78 Orjinal Belge* (Istanbul, 2002), pp. 64–65.

154   *The Shariʻa*

whom the investigation and prosecution of transgressing religious
norms took place. The Ottomans were well aware of the legitimising
effect on imperial authority. Their adoption and elaboration of the
Hanafi school of Islamic law was integral to justifying that authority:
state intervention in doctrine was politically expedient and expanded
the bases of Ottoman power. It became lawful to equate challenges
to political authority with heresy. Indeed, the interplay between
religious legitimacy and political authority was not specific to the
Ottomans. These dynamics were a well-worked trope in the Muslim
world, and they included the literary genre of 'mirrors for princes'.
This genre, the bulk of which consisted of manuals of statecraft,
advocated a just relationship between the ruler and the ruled. The
best way to attain universal justice was through the preservation
of established regulations and institutions – namely, those of the
shariʻa. Sovereignty was conceptualised as a circle of equity whereby
the ruler guaranteed justice for all his subjects through the total
implementation of the shariʻa, and, in turn, subjects were expected
to obey the law of the land by observing religious norms and
paying taxes. It was incumbent on both the ruler and the ruled to play
their respective roles lest social order and religious injunctions were
to be compromised.[2]

The 19th-century era of reforms (Tanzimat) and the reign of Sultan
Abdulhamid II (r. 1876–1909) witnessed the expenditure of much
effort on legal standardisation and the promotion of egalitarian rhetoric
for all subjects, regardless of religion. The crowning achievement was
the first-ever codification of the shariʻa between 1869 and 1876. The
Ottoman civil code (*mecelle*) emphasised legal reasoning and procedure
while remaining thoroughly within the traditions of the Hanafi school.[3]
For our purposes, however, earlier state intervention in Hanafi doctrine
had more of an impact. What the learned class (*ilmiye*) comprising
individuals like judges and scholars (ulama) had defined in the 16th
century as Ottoman orthodoxy – an orthodoxy that positioned the
sultan-caliph as the guardian of Hanafi interpretations of the Qurʼan
and Prophetic traditions (Sunna) – remained relatively unchallenged.
We shall therefore closely follow the opinions of officials who staffed

---

[2]   A. Lambton, 'Justice in the Medieval Persian Theory of Kingship', *Studia
Islamica* 17 (1962), pp. 91–119.

[3]   S. Ayoub, 'The Mecelle, Sharia, and the Ottoman State: Fashioning and
Refashioning of Islamic Law in the Nineteenth and Twentieth Centuries', in K.F.
Schull et al., ed., *Law and Legality in the Ottoman Empire and the Republic of
Turkey* (Bloomington, IN, 2016), pp. 139–149.

imperial institutions and held considerable influence over government and society well into the 19th century.

We are confronted with several important questions when considering legitimacy and authority in the Ottoman context. For example, how did the Ottomans rationalise their power? Which institutions promoted imperial legitimacy and maintained authority? Why did these institutions develop? Who accepted or challenged Ottoman claims to authority? Who defined Ottoman orthodoxy, and at whose expense? In order to understand these dynamics, we require an approach that identifies key concepts and practices of Ottoman governance. We must also attend to the intense competition with the Shiʿi Safavids in Iran. The implications of this imperial rivalry, along with the Ottoman conquest of the Mamluk lands in the Middle East, were important for the consolidation of an Ottoman orthodoxy. This background will help us contextualise the social and political landscape of Greater Syria where the Ottoman Shiʿi Ismailis, also known as the Batiniyya, lived. After a historical survey of the Ismailis, we shall read an Ottoman account of the 1816–1818 Ismaili revolt in al-Kahf and Qadmus. The language of the official summary of the revolt shows just how successful the Ottomans were in promoting a Sunni identity through the confluence of religious legitimacy and imperial authority.

A Just Power

Defining the relationship between legitimacy and authority will allow us to highlight certain concepts and practices that served as the pillars of Ottoman governance. The formation and survival of the Ottoman Empire, both as a concept and as a political entity, were constant processes in legitimising authority. The ways in which officials discussed imperial legitimacy and how they maintained authority fed off one another. That is, the definitions of empire were constructed and challenged by those who shared in Ottoman power. Successful claims to authority legitimised the relationship between those with power and those subject to it. Articulating exactly what was legitimate authority, however, involved saying what it was not. The powerless therefore had an influence on shaping the discourse if only for the fact that any definition of an Ottoman orthodoxy required its heterodox Other. Government policy followed scholarly discourse by attempting to limit the power of those it deemed illegitimate. Marginal groups frequently challenged these claims to authority. The Ismailis, for example, negotiated and engaged with everyday state claims to authority by protesting or revolting against taxes and, later, military conscription.[4]

---

[4]   G. Lowthian Bell, *Syria: The Desert and the Sown* (London, 1907), pp. 195–196.

156   *The Shariʿa*

By the 16th century, the Ottomans had a grand strategy which evinces a more concrete understanding of legitimacy and authority.[5] Ottoman rule was guided by a flexible set of concepts and practices of governmentality. There was an ideology with universal claims emblematised by sultanic epithets such as 'shadow of God on earth'. The strategy shaped domestic and foreign policy and propaganda, and it directed efforts to mobilise human and economic resources, such as the provisioning and protection of the Hajj pilgrimage to Mecca. But how did the state package its grand strategy and market it? The success of government depended on the centre's ability to channel power directly to its institutions, at the expense of independent authority.[6] For the judiciary, as early as the reign of Mehmed I (r. 1413–1421), the Ottomans began to institutionalise a 'learned hierarchy' in order to curtail the avenues of extra-state power and influence of judges and jurisconsults, as well as other scholars.[7] Many individuals were in fact executed for their independent legal authority, such as the renowned Shiʿi jurist of the 16th century, Zayn al-Din al-Amili.[8] Integration through power-sharing was only one way to co-opt elites. Empire could be sold through symbolic articulations as well. Being a member of the Ottoman imperial tradition that claimed a shared heritage with the Caesars of Rome could be quite a selling point.

The Shariʿa and Empire

The confluence of the shariʿa and customary administrative practices illustrates the flexibility of Ottoman governance. True, the legal system drew on the shariʿa. Crucially, however, regional feudal laws governing relationships between elites and tax-paying subjects had an equally rich tradition. So the Ottomans supplemented sultanic edicts issued for administrative purposes (*kanun*) with the shariʿa, adding religious legitimacy to the office of the sultanate.[9] The processes in which these

---

[5]   G. Ágoston, 'Information, Ideology, and Limits of Imperial Policy: Ottoman Grand Strategy in the Context of Ottoman-Habsburg Rivalry', V. Aksan et al., ed., *The Early Modern Ottoman Empire: A Reinterpretation* (Cambridge, UK, 2007), p. 77.

[6]   K. Barkey, *Empire of Difference: The Ottomans in Comparative Perspective* (New York, 2008), pp. 18–19.

[7]   R.C. Repp, *The Müfti of Istanbul: A Study in the Development of the Ottoman Learned Hierarchy* (London, 1986), pp. 118–119.

[8]   D.J. Stewart, 'The Ottoman Execution of Zayn al-Dīn al-ʿĀmilī', *Die Welt des Islams* 48 (2008), pp. 343–346.

[9]   W. Hallaq, *An Introduction to Islamic Law* (Cambridge, UK, 2009), p. 78.

Legitimising Authority   157

feudal laws were systematically codified began under Sultan Bayezid II
(r. 1481–1512), and reached standardisation and reconciliation with the
shariʿa by the reign of Sultan Suleyman I (r. 1520–1566), aptly known as
'the Law-Giver'.[10] The intertwining of the shariʿa and feudal laws can be
evinced in the immediate administrative concerns after Sultan Selim I's
(r. 1512–1520) conquest of Greater Syria in 1516. Having defeated the
Mamluks and triumphantly entered Aleppo, Selim I promptly elicited
the following juridical opinion (*fetva*) with regard to the Shiʿa if they
refused to be taxed and submit to the authority of the Ottomans:

> Those heretics combine all sorts of heresy and evil and
> stubbornness and all sorts of irreligion, bawdry and atheism.
> Whoever says that they are not heretics and atheists and
> should not be fought against is himself an atheist the same as
> they are. The reason for the obligation to fight them and kill
> them is both their atheism and evil.[11]

The persecution of the Shiʿa was not an Ottoman innovation and had
a regional precedent. The Mamluks, like the Ottomans, used heterodoxy
as pretence for the punishment of tax avoidance. The polemics of the
Hanbali scholar Ibn Taymiyya (1263–1328) are cited as an influence on
the anti-Shiʿi atmosphere of Mamluk rule.[12] Ibn Taymiyya's aspersions
on the Shiʿa can be found in many of his writings, notably the *Epistle
on the Transgressions of the Nusayris*, in which he erroneously identified
the Nusayris as Ismailis. In the *Epistle* he claimed that the Shiʿa were
'more heretical than the Jews and Christians', and that 'it was declared
licit to shed their blood and take their property'.[13] In the same year as
the *Epistle*, in fact, the Mamluks massacred thousands of Shiʿa in Mount
Lebanon.[14] Ibn Taymiyya, however, might not have been as influential
as is sometimes thought, and the Mamluks were probably suspicious
of his extreme sectarianism. His anti-Shiʿa cause was directly taken up

---

[10]   C. Imber, *Ebu'ssuʿud: The Islamic Legal Tradition* (Edinburgh, 1997), pp. 40–51.

[11]   Y. Talhamy, 'The Fatwas and the Nusayri/Alawis of Syria', *Middle Eastern
Studies* 46(2) (2010), p. 182.

[12]   E.C. Bosworth, 'Bahāʾ al-Dīn al-ʿĀmilī in the Two Worlds of the Ottomans
and Safavids', *Convegno sul tema (15 April 1991, Roma), La Shiʿa nell'impero
ottomano* (Rome, 1993), p. 117.

[13]   M. St. Guyard, 'Le fetwa d'Ibn Taymiyyah sur les Nosairis: Publié pour la
première fois avec une traduction nouvelle', *Journal Asiatique* 6(18) (1871),
pp. 185–198.

[14]   J.A. Reilly, *The Ottoman Cities of Lebanon: Historical Legacy and Identity in
the Modern Middle East* (London, 2016), pp. 13–16.

158   *The Shari'a*

later by the Damascene Ustuvani Mehmed (1608–1661), leader of the puritanical Kadızadeli movement.[15] The simultaneous use of the shari'a and feudal laws specific to Greater Syria throws into relief the ways in which the Ottoman legal system built on existing traditions to maximise the legitimacy of imperial authority. It was during this formative period that many of the doctrinal incongruities between the Hanafi school and feudal laws were reconciled. This, accompanied by imperial competition, greatly enhanced the legitimacy of the Ottoman Sunni state.

The 15th- and 16th-century Safavid policy of Shi'i messianic activism within Ottoman territory was a significant factor in the creation of an image of an exclusively Sunni state. The Safavid Shah Ismail I (r. 1501–1524), for his part, similarly cultivated the image of an exclusively Shi'i state. Ismail I identified himself as the messiah, who was privy to the same divine knowledge as the Prophet Muhammad, and his son-in-law Ali.[16] This assertion of religious authority attracted many Ottoman Turcoman subjects from Eastern Anatolia. These Turcoman allies of the Safavids, known as the Red Heads (Kızılbaş) because of the colour of their headwear, started a series of revolts against Ottoman authority. The Ottoman state sought out the shari'a and its jurists to combat the Safavid threat by legitimising war against them. The conquest of fellow Muslims is something which the shari'a forbids. Thus, before going to war, Selim I obtained a juridical opinion from the chief imperial jurisconsult of Istanbul (*şeyhulislam*), Sarigorez Nureddin. The Safavids were duly declared to be infidels, and making war with them not only lawful but also necessary: 'Muslim people! Note that this group of Kızılbaş whose leader is Isma'il, the son of Ardabil, disregards the Shari'a and Sunna of our Prophet … To kill them and to destroy their communities is an implicit and essential obligation for all Muslims.'[17] During his march east to confront the Safavids in 1514, Selim I continued to solicit the legal opinions of jurisconsults.[18] The Kızılbaş revolts and the establishment of the Safavid polity had long-lasting detrimental effects on the relationship between the state

---

[15] A.Y. Ocak, *Osmanlı Toplumunda Zındıklar ve Mülhidler Yahut Dairenin Dışına Çıkanlar (15.-17. Yüzyıllar)* (Istanbul, 1998), p. 112.

[16] K. Babayan, *Mystics, Monarchs, and Messiahs: Cultural Landscapes of Early Modern Iran* (Cambridge, MA, 2002), p. 296.

[17] M. Scherberger, 'The Confrontation between Sunni and Shi'i Empires: Ottoman-Safavid Relations between the Fourteenth and the Seventeenth Century', in O. Bengio et al., ed., *The Sunna and Shi'a in History: Division and Ecumenism in the Muslim Middle East* (Basingstoke, 2011), pp. 54–55.

[18] M.C. Şehabeddin Tekindağ, 'Yeni kaynak ve vesikalar ışığı altında Yavuz Sultan Selim'in İran seferi', *Tarih Dergisi*, 17(22) (1967), p. 58.

Legitimising Authority 159

and its Shi'i subjects. This would only worsen when the sultanate became sacralised by the mid-16th century.

Selim I's conquest of Mamluk Egypt, Greater Syria and the Holy Cities of Mecca and Medina was as important for the development of an Ottoman orthodoxy as imperial competition with the Safavids. After this, the Ottoman realm became Muslim-majority for the first time. Selim I also counted Mecca and Medina as imperial possessions, which afforded him great prestige and the honorific title of Servitor of the Two Holy Cities.[19] Caliph was likewise an estimable title which had been claimed by the Ottomans since Mehmed I, but it took on universal significance with Selim I's acquisition of the Two Holy Cities and importantly with the elaboration of Hanafi doctrine under Suleyman I. The articulation of a particularly Ottoman Hanafi doctrine was left to the scholar and chief imperial jurisconsult of Istanbul, Ebussu'ud (1490–1574). For our purposes, Ebussu'ud's greatest contribution to the Ottoman political and legal system was the merger of the offices of the caliphate and the sultanate. Ebussu'ud argued for the merger by claiming that the sultans were divinely appointed, that both offices were hereditary and that the only guarantor for the implementation of the shari'a was Ottoman power.[20] The convergence of the two offices expanded imperial authority, making the sultan 'inheritor of the Great Caliphate' and the 'possessor of the Great Imamate'.[21] The sultans now had interpretive authority in Islamic law and religious sanction to enforce their writ. Thereafter, if ever a legal matter should be left unresolved by the courts, ambiguities in, or conflict between, the shari'a and feudal laws might be referred to the sultan who, as caliph of the Muslim community, could exercise his right to interpretive reasoning (*ijtihad*).

'Shameful Deeds in Light of the Accepted Glorious Shari'a'

Ebussu'ud's mentor and predecessor as chief imperial jurisconsult of Istanbul, Kemal Pashazade (1469–1534), was influential in defining religious and legal norms. In his *Treatise on Exposing the Heresies of*

---

[19] N. al-Tikriti, 'Ibn-i Kemal's Confessionalism and the Construction of an Ottoman Islam', in C. Isom-Verhaaren et al., ed., *Living in the Ottoman Realm: Empire and Identity, 13th to 20th Centuries* (Bloomington, IN, 2016), p. 97.

[20] Imber, *Ebu'ssu'ud*, pp. 98–110.

[21] C. Imber, 'Ebu's-su'ud (d. 982/1574)', ed. O. Arabi et al., *Islamic Legal Thought: A Compendium of Muslim Jurists* (Leiden, 2013), p. 412.

160   *The Shari'a*

the Infidels, Pashazade classified exactly who and what fell outside
correct belief. He went so far as to declare all the Shi'a heretical,
and their being killed and the dispossession of their property and
spouses lawful.[22] Both Pashazade's influence and a context of imperial
rivalry with the Shi'i Safavids are evident in Ebussu'ud's thinking. As
important as Ebussu'ud's argument for the sacrality of the Ottoman
throne was, his legal opinions might have left an even greater imprint,
especially on Ottoman society. The following are representative samples
of Ebussu'ud's opinions involving transgressions of religious norms
(Zeyd and Amr signify person X and person Y):

> *Question:* Whereupon Zeyd says to Amr 'Go and find God
> for me', Amr replies 'You will find Him in the Quran in which
> He has confirmed His works through the Prophet.' If Zeyd
> responds 'What of those works? Without them I can find God',
> or says 'I have found God [outside the Qur'an]', what must be
> done to him?
>
> *Answer:* He is a heretic and his being killed is necessary...
>
> *Question:* According to the shari'a what must be done if, God
> forbid, Zeyd proclaims 'I have no fear of God'?
>
> *Answer:* He is a pure infidel, he can never join the fold of Islam
> and his being killed is allowed.
>
> *Question:* What must be done if Zeyd denies the Day of
> Resurrection by saying 'No-one assembles the believers for
> judgement'?
>
> *Answer:* He must be killed.
>
> *Question:* A certain community does not pray and denies the
> requirements of the month of Ramadan. When Ramadan
> arrives they do not fast and when questioned they say 'Our
> shaykhs tell us that 5 or 6 days of observance is enough' and
> 'as we work manual labour in the vineyards this is allowed'.
> They then continue their errors, make wine and on such days
> this community of infidels honour Ramadan like unbelievers.
> Thus if their actions as such contravene the shari'a, what must
> be done to those at odds with Muslims who have faith and act
> and speak in compliance with the shari'a?
>
> *Answer:* They are infidels and their being killed is permitted.[23]

---

[22] Tekindağ, 'Yeni kaynak...', p. 55.

[23] M.E. Düzdağ, *Şeyhülislâm Ebussuud Efendi Fetvaları: ışığında 16. asır Türk
hayatı* (Istanbul, 1972), pp. 113–114.

Until the late 19th century, Ottoman students of law and judges in court almost always referred to Ibrahim al-Halabi's (1456–1549) compendium of Hanafi law, *Multaqa al-abhur* (*The Confluence of the Seas*). As a source of substantive law, al-Halabi's text was favoured as a didactic and mnemonic tool in Ottoman madrasas and provincial courts.[24] It was a very well regarded legal text on which nearly 70 commentaries were made between the 16th and 18th centuries.[25] The compendium's popularity sheds light on prescriptions to which Hanafi judges referred during adjudication. According to the 'Chapter on the Apostate', individuals who are accused of apostasy ought to be invited back into the fold of orthodoxy, and the killing of such people should only be countenanced after several offers to return to the true faith had been ignored.[26] This appears to be at variance with the majority of Ebussu'ud's opinions, such as the following on the topic of repentance:

> It has been noted that the Prophet ... said 'there are 73 groups who, except for the people of the Sunna, are in the hell-fire' ... From each one there are those who take to evil and corruption, choose to add unbelief and innovation to the shari'a based on their own fancies and they have been exposed as a community of unbelief and perversion. Day after day they wish to increase this. Up until now they continue aware of their shameful deeds in light of the accepted glorious shari'a ... The majority of the great scholars never respect their repentance as acceptable in lieu of their being killed. From the law it is certain they are to be killed ... It has been a plain fact and is agreed upon by the traditions within the people of Islam for those described by shameful deeds. In these cases there is no indecisiveness or doubt ... Regarding this community's terrible corruption and in order to relieve them from their mischief, it is extremely important to wage jihad against them.[27]

Ebussu'ud's opinions were part and parcel of an emerging Ottoman canon of Hanafi jurisprudence which developed alongside the consolidation of an imperial learned hierarchy. The absorption of scholars by

---

[24] Ş.S. Has, 'The Use of Multaqa'l-Abhur in the Ottoman Madrasas and in Legal Scholarship', *Osmanlı Araştırmaları* 7(8) (1988), pp. 393–418.

[25] G. Burak, *The Second Formation of Islamic Law: The Ḥanafī School in the Early Modern Ottoman Empire* (New York, 2015), pp. 123–124.

[26] I. al-Halabi, *Multaqa al-abhur* (Beirut, 1989), pp. 274–277.

[27] Düzdağ, *Şeyhülislâm Ebussuud*, pp. 110–111.

162   *The Shari'a*

state institutions mirrored the development of a relatively centralised
bureaucracy. The state was able to institutionalise the learned hierarchy by the end of the 16th century and to promote a coherent, official
Hanafi doctrine.[28] The Ottoman state institutionalised the learned
hierarchy by assigning to itself the power to appoint its members to
office so that by the 17th century, scholars had become as integral to
Ottoman rule as the military.[29] Those who resisted faced marginalisation by the orthodox establishment and a lack of employment opportunities. If for nothing other than sheer political and legal influence, the
opinions of official scholars such as the chief imperial jurisconsult of
Istanbul provide reliable glimpses into what informed the decisions of
judges in Ottoman courts.[30] It may be tempting to suggest that these
legal responsa had little impact on the historical realities of marginal
groups. To be sure, legal opinions cannot tell the whole story of a
community such as the Ismailis. Yet evidence shows that far from being
confined to the world of ideas, official legal pronouncements addressed
real concerns and affected state policy vis-à-vis the Shi'a well into the
19th century.

It is true that Ottoman society had entered into an ecumenical
bargain whereby the various religious communities (*millet*s) of the
realm knew their place. Later, from the 18th century onwards, the
Greek Orthodox, Armenians and Jews were hierarchically organised
religious and political bodies that were relatively free to govern their
own communal affairs, so long as Ottoman authority was not jeop-
ardised.[31] This degree of communal recognition never applied to the
Shi'a because the Hanafi school did not recognise divisions within
Islam.[32] The relationship between the Ottoman state and the Shi'a was
therefore unique. The term 'Shi'a', in fact, was rarely used and instead
the preferred terms were 'unbeliever', 'heretic', 'atheist' and 'illegitimate
innovator'.[33] In times of social and political turmoil, the interactions

---

[28]   Burak, *The Second Formation*, pp. 155–157.

[29]   Repp, *The Müfti*, p. 28.

[30]   H. Gerber, *State, Society, and Law in Islam: Ottoman Law in Comparative
Perspective* (Albany, NY, 1994), p. 180.

[31]   B. Masters, *Christians and Jews in the Ottoman Arab World: The Roots of
Sectarianism* (Cambridge, 2001), p. 61.

[32]   İ. Ortaylı, 'Les groupes hétérodoxes et l'administration ottomane', in K.
Kehl-Bodrogi et al., ed., *Syncretistic Religious Communities in the Near East*
(Leiden, 1997), p. 206.

[33]   A.Y. Ocak, 'Türk Heterodoksi Tarihinde "Zindîk", "Hâricî", "Râfizî",
"Mülhid" ve "Ehl-i Bid'at" Terimlerine Dair Bazı Düşünceler', *Tarih Enstitüsü
Dergisi* 12 (1982), pp. 518–520.

Legitimising Authority   163

between the state and the Shiʻa generally revolved around accusations of 'heinous acts of worship', 'openly doubting certain religious
commands and proscriptions' and 'spreading propaganda among the
people' or 'disrespect and unbelief towards the Holy Quran and the
Prophet Muhammad'.[34] Scholars constructed an Ottoman identity as
righteous defenders of orthodoxy in large part by defining what it was
not – and it was clearly not Shiʻi Islam.

The Ottoman Ismailis

The Ismaili presence in Greater Syria pre-dates Selim I's conquest
by several centuries. The town of Salamiyya, for example, had been
inhabited by the Ismailis and their imams in the late 9th century
and served as the headquarters for the pre-Fatimid leadership.
Moreover, the community possessed a famous chain of medieval
castles throughout Greater Syria from where the Ismailis concluded
alliances with crusaders and incurred the wrath of those such as the
Ayyubid Sultan Salah al-Din (1138–1193).[35] Ottoman scholars were
aware of the community and their history. Ottomans had written
works about the Fatimids, and made a translation of the theological
treatise by the founder of the medieval Ismaili state of Alamut, Hasan-i
Sabbah (1090–1124), *The Four Chapters*.[36] The Ismailis, along with the
standard pejoratives for the Shiʻa, were referred to as a community
(*taʾife*) in Ottoman administrative documents. This categorisation gave
the Ismailis a degree of autonomy which allowed them to select their
leadership and establish their own communal rules and regulations.[37]

The Ottoman Ismailis lived mainly in Qadmus and Masyaf, both
medieval Ismaili strongholds. Qadmus and its castle were designated
as a subdistrict within the subprovince of Tripoli from the Ottoman
conquest until it was made a district of Sidon in the mid-19th century.
Qadmus reverted to a subdistrict within the newly created province
of Beirut in 1888. Masyaf was a district in the province of Damascus
until 1865, when it was made the district centre of the province of
Syria.[38] There were several Ismaili villages and hamlets around al-Kahf
and al-Khawabi located in the mountains to the southwest and west of

---

[34] Ocak, *Osmanlı Toplumunda*, p. 248.
[35] F. Daftary, *The Ismāʻīlīs: Their History and Doctrines* (Cambridge, 1999),
pp. 107–158, 356–434.
[36] A. Shahrestani, trans., *Tercüme-yi milel ve nihâl* (Istanbul, 1862).
[37] Masters, *Christians and Jews*, p. 62.
[38] T. Sezin, ed., *Osmanlı Yer Adları: Alfabetik Sırayla* (Ankara, 2006), pp. 263, 371.

164   *The Shariʻa*

Qadmus respectively.[39] From the mid-19th century onwards, population growth and competition for resources in these mountainous areas led to the Ismaili resettlement of Salamiyya.[40] In Ottoman times, this was a subdistrict of the subprovince of Hama until 1885, when the town was made a district centre.[41]

Ottoman tax and population surveys labelled Muslim individuals and households as Muslim and did not distinguish between Sunni and Shiʻi. However, we are able to estimate the Ismaili population of Qadmus, al-Kahf and al-Khawabi through a sample of tax censuses dating from the Ottoman conquest until the mid-17th century. A special head tax applied to Ismailis and Nusayris, for which the payments are recorded. The figures refer to households, defined neither as nuclear nor extended, and because these areas were inhabited by both the Nusayris and Ismailis, our population estimate is rather general. With this in mind, Ismaili households in these areas were in the low thousands after the Ottoman conquest but had increased by several thousand by the middle of the 17th century.[42] In contemporary Masyaf, too, we can assume similar numbers of Ismaili households.[43] The Ismaili population declined somewhat, and by the middle of the 19th century it was reported to be in the low thousands in Qadmus, Masyaf, al-Kahf and al-Khawabi.[44] The Ismailis were divided between two factions: the Suwaydani in Qadmus and Masyaf and the Hajjawi around al-Kahf and al-Khawabi.[45] The French consul-general in Aleppo, Jean Baptiste L.J. Rousseau (1780–1831), observed that these groups differed only in 'certain superficial customs'.[46] The origins of the factions are murky, but an influential military family in the region were the Al Suwaydan,

---

[39]   N. Lewis, *Nomads and Settlers in Syria and Jordan, 1800–1980* (Cambridge, 1987), p. 58.

[40]   M. ʻAmin, *Salamīyya fī khamsīn qarn* (Damascus, 1986), pp. 146–157.

[41]   *Suriye vilayet salnamesi* (Istanbul, 1885), vol. 17, pp. 170–171.

[42]   S. Winter, *A History of the ʻAlawis: From Medieval Aleppo to the Turkish Republic* (Princeton, NJ, 2016), pp. 92–95.

[43]   *Haleb livası mufassal tahrir defteri (943/1536)*, (Ankara, 2010), vol. 1, p. 17.

[44]   J.L. Burckhardt, *Travels in Syria and the Holy Land* (London, 1822), p. 153; Rev. W.M. Thompson, 'Tour from Beirût to Aleppo In 1845', *Bibliotheca Sacra and Theological Review* 5(18) (1848), p. 256; F. Walpole, *The Ansayrii, and the Assassins, with Travels in the Further East, in 1850–51, Including a Visit to Ninevah* (London, 1851), vol. 3, p. 302.

[45]   D. Douwes and N. Lewis, 'The Trials of Syrian Ismailis in the First Decade of the 20th Century', *International Journal of Middle East Studies* 21 (1989), p. 217.

[46]   J. Baptiste L.J. Rousseau, 'Mémoire sur l'Ismaélis et les Nosaïris de Syrie, adressé à M. Silvestre de Sacy', *Annales des Voyages* 14 (1811), p. 283.

Legitimising Authority

which may suggest some sort of patron–client relationship with the more affluent Ismaili Suwaydanis.[47] A further division which existed in the community's elite was between those who tended towards political and economic affairs, and those who looked after scholarly and religious duties such as shrine maintenance. The Ismailis in Greater Syria were of the Muhammad-Shahi Nizari line until the disappearance of their 40th imam at the end of the 18th century.[48] After a fruitless search for the Muhammad-Shahi imam in India, in the late 19th century the majority transferred allegiance to the Qasim-Shahi Nizari branch headed by the Aga Khans.[49]

The Ismaili elite in the towns were tax farmers (*mutesellims*) sanctioned by a district governor to collect revenue.[50] Ismaili tax farmers collected the revenue from fiscal units comprising a tax farm, often sublet by individuals who had leased the right to collect taxes directly from the state. Tax farmers were responsible for the provisioning of crops to soldiers and neighbouring towns, but they could also be de facto merchants who profited from the sale of pilfered grain.[51] The Ismaili elite were sometimes guarantors of loans for money put towards a tax farm by individuals from other communities, such as the Nusayris.[52] More commonly, the Ismailis rented tax farms themselves from the state or another individual. Many of the Ismailis were taxed by nomads for protection, which compounded the burden of state-imposed agricultural, punitive, security- and confession-based levies. Although Ismaili settlements were isolated and sparsely populated, the community was nonetheless involved in Ottoman provincial administration.

For the Ismailis of Greater Syria, the Ottoman conquest brought the religious and political conflict with the Safavids directly into their communities and it remained long after the two imperial rivals had agreed peaceful terms. Yet life before the Ottomans was not quite idyllic; many Ismailis under the Mamluks had paid special levies and punitive taxes.[53] Ebussu'ud's sectarianism, however, held sway not only

---

[47] J.A. Reilly, *A Small Town in Syria: Ottoman Hama in the Eighteenth and Nineteenth Centuries* (Bern, 2002), p. 34.

[48] D. Douwes, 'Migration, Faith and Community: Extra-Local Linkages in Coastal Syria', in P. Sluglett et al., ed., *Syria and Bilad al-Sham under Ottoman Rule: Essays in Honour of Abdul Karim Rafeq* (Leiden, 2010), pp. 489–491.

[49] Daftary, *The Ismāʿīlīs*, p. 490.

[50] N. Lewis, *Nomads and Settlers*, p. 59.

[51] Reilly, *A Small Town in Syria*, p. 63.

[52] Winter, *A History of the ʿAlawis*, p. 127.

[53] A. Akgündüz, ed., *Osmanlı Kanunnâmeleri ve Hukukî Tahlilleri* (Istanbul, 1990–1996), vol. 3, p. 500.

over the Ottoman legal system but also over society. Court registers from Aleppo and Hama attest to constant persecution of the Shi'a from the 16th to the 19th centuries. For example, in the mid-16th century, Ismailis were brought to court merely for being Ismaili; and in the early 19th century, some Shi'a were obliged to pay a poll tax reserved for non-Muslims (*jizya*).[54] Like many regional customary laws, the poll tax was not actually an Ottoman imposition, as the Ismailis and Nusayris in Greater Syria had been paying a similar head tax since Mamluk times.[55] In the late 17th century the puritanical Kadızadeli movement, which might have inspired the Wahhabis, counted Ibn Taymiyya and Ebussu'ud as men worthy of emulation.[56] Also, in the 18th century, there was an increase in anti-Shi'i rhetoric inspired by Ebussu'ud's juridical opinions.[57]

'Habitually Mischievous Villains'

The governance of the Ottoman state operated hand in glove with the shari'a, so much so that any challenge to its authority became tantamount to heresy. This was a conscious policy which the Ottomans had crafted for centuries. The 1816–1818 Ismaili revolt and its suppression illustrate the influence of the Ottoman legal system on the state's relationship with its heterodox subjects. For the Ottomans, the Ismailis were, almost by design, given to disobedience because of their heterodoxy. A firm reminder of their inferiority, therefore, was needed every now and again. The mountainous region in which the Ismailis lived had always afforded them some protection from direct government control. So it was not uncommon for the Ismailis to test the limits of state authority by occasionally withholding taxes.

When in 1816 the Ismailis of al-Kahf rebelled against Ottoman authority by refusing to pay their taxes, the state dispatched the deputy

---

[54] M. Salati, 'Shiism in Ottoman Syria: A Document from the Qāḍī Court of Aleppo (963/1555)', *Eurasian Studies* 1 (2002), p. 82; D. Douwes, *The Ottomans in Syria: A History of Justice and Oppression* (London, 2000), pp. 142–143.
[55] M. Salati, *Ascesa e caduta di una famiglia di Ašrāf Sciiti di Aleppo: I Zuhrāwī o Zuhrā-Zāda (1600–1700)* (Rome, 1992), p. 58, n. 42.
[56] S. Evstatiev, 'The Qāḍīzādeli Movement and the Revival of *takfīr* in the Ottoman Age', in C. Adang et al., ed., *Accusations of Unbelief in Islam: A Diachronic Perspective on Takfīr* (Leiden, 2016), pp. 224–225.
[57] S. Winter, *The Shiites of Lebanon under Ottoman Rule, 1516–1788* (Cambridge, 2010), p. 15.

Legitimising Authority 167

governor of Tripoli, Mustafa Aga Berber, an especially violent man. When the official arrived at al-Kahf seeking the taxes, the Ismailis declined to pay.[58] Consequently, al-Kahf was razed and many of the Ismailis fled to Qadmus, where they continued to resist Ottoman authority.[59] The Ismailis were later joined in protest by their Nusayri neighbours. However, by 1818, the revolt had been crushed, its Ismaili instigators executed and their severed heads forwarded to Istanbul. An acquaintance of Mustafa Aga Berber, the adventuress Lady Hester Lucy Stanhope (1776–1839), noted that the deputy governor had considered those he punished to be irredeemable heretics:

> Mustafa Aga Berber at last marched, and, entering the Ansary [Nusayri] mountains, carried fire and sword into their villages. It is supposed that, to the motives furnished him by the cause on which he went, he added personal hatred, on account of their religion … Berber, therefore, was going to a work of faith.[60]

Mustafa Aga Berber had been sent to quash a rebellion against taxes. His 'work of faith', however, highlights how the traditional language of the shari'a had supported the state's claims to authority over its subjects, especially groups whom scholars had never considered normative.

The following official summary about the Ismaili revolt emphasises this point well. The report was sent from the governor of Sidon, Suleyman Pasha, to the Grand Vizier and Sultan Mahmud II (r. 1808–1839). We should pay close attention to the language in the document. The stock pejoratives ('heretics', 'villains') and supplications ('by the grace of God', 'the Sultan's sword') clearly demonstrate how the Ottoman state promoted its orthodox identity by blurring the lines between religious and administrative concerns:

> The tax collecting functions of Latakia should be divided into four tax farms for the Muslims … and the remaining residents of the tax farms from the groups of heretics, one type being the Nusayris and the other type the people of the castles of Kahf and Qadmus, the Ismaili community. The people of the

---

[58] H. 'Uthman, *Tārīkh al-Lādhiqīyah 637/m-1946/m* (Damascus, 1996), p. 65.

[59] I. al-'Awra, *Tārīkh wilāyat Sulaymān Bāshā al-'Ādil, 1804–1819* (Beirut, 1989), pp. 288–290.

[60] H. Stanhope, *Travels of Lady Hester Stanhope, Forming the Completion of Her Memoirs, Narrated by Her Physician C. L. Meryon* (London, 1846), vol. 3, pp. 336–337.

168   *The Shariʻa*

aforementioned communities rely on the mountains, rocky
land and their fortresses in the highlands to continually
oppress the good Muslims. Their daring acts of banditry on the
imperial roads, taking spoils neither forbidden nor permitted,
and violating and damaging public goods can be explained
by their particular habit of following despicably mischievous
paths. Although always in opposition to the office of the
imperial army, this time the aforementioned Ismailis were also
unjust to the Muslims and the sons of the righteous, preying
on them and damaging public property. This caused others
from the groups of heretics, the Nusayris, to unite with them,
breaking from the chain of obedience by endangering and
harming the Muslims. With a strong sense of anticipation
that news of the habitually mischievous villains would spread
if there were patience and calm, it was desired for the sake
of the Empire's fame and glory to end this manner by which
the aforementioned fell from God's grace and dared to rebel.
For this reason the deputy governor of Tripoli, Mustafa Aga
Berber was authorised to determine with a unit from his
column of troops and with men from the imperial army the
arranging of requisite cannons and ammunition. Although the
aforementioned groups of heretics had fortified themselves in
the mountains and their castles, more than 15–20 thousand
shots were fired and with the assistance and grace of God,
strength and fortune on the side of the Sultan, blessings upon
the excellent and benevolent sovereign of auspiciousness,
the vain and conceited fell prey to the Sultan's sword and the
attack left many decimated and ruined. Those who locked
themselves in their castle at Kahf were conquered and along
with that place, demolished. Subjected to these conditions
and finding themselves in a ruinous state, thereafter they were
unable to return to banditry and oppression. On this occasion
the severed heads of 23 of their leaders seized during the battle
were dispatched to the Palace by a pair of my couriers.[61]

The shariʻa lent a great deal of legitimacy to Ottoman power. The state
had succeeded in exploiting its bases of power so that opposition
to taxes was more or less heresy. The blending of religious and
administrative language explains why Mustafa Aga Berber understood
his restoration of order in al-Kahf and Qadmus as a work of faith. The

---

[61]   *Başbakanlık Osmanlı Arşivi* (BOA), Hatt-ı Hümayûn 495/24282 (5 July 1818).

Legitimising Authority 169

language of the report shows that this line of thinking was common enough. Several decades later, for example, officials in Masyaf were alerted to the Nusayris, who had been engaging in brigandage and revolt. After the Nusayris submitted to Ottoman authority by paying their taxes, both the district governor of Masyaf, Rasul Aga and Major Lieutenant Ali Pasha were advised to be wary of the ensuing calm. They were told, moreover, that the Nusayris were to be severely punished the next time they transgressed the bounds of Islamic orthodoxy.[62] The administration's relationship with the Shi'a was framed as a primeval religious struggle. When taxes were paid, the Ismailis were partially tolerated; but if authority was challenged, officials interpreted the economic and political reasons behind most grievances as an essential characteristic of all heterodox groups.

Conclusion: What Ottoman Orthodoxy Was Not

The relationship between the Ottoman state and its Shi'i subjects was more than just persecution. This was due in large part to the state's inability to impose its rule directly in every corner of the empire. The Ottomans were forced to govern in partnership with local elites, many of whom could be Shi'a. Members of the Shi'i Harfush clan were Ottoman administrators in Baalbek and Homs for centuries; and the Shi'i Banu Zuhra dominated the position of chief representative of the descendants of the Prophet Muhammad (*nakibuleşraf*) in Aleppo until the mid-18th century. This is to say nothing of the influential Shi'i families in the Holy Cities, and the power of the Zaydi imams in Yemen.[63] The Ottomans could even favour one 'heretical' group over another. In 1808 the Nusayris took control of the Ismaili town of Masyaf. After the Nusayri attack, a certain Ismaili shaykh, Ali al-Hajj, went to Aleppo and sought a legal opinion from the town's jurists. The scholars subsequently issued a favourable pronouncement which Ali al-Hajj then presented to Ottoman officials.[64] By 1810 both the town

---

[62] *BOA*, İrade-Dahiliye 543/37759, 19 November 1865; *BOA*, Sadaret Mühimme Kalemi Evraki 346/23 (29 November 1865); *BOA*, Sadaret Mühimme Kalemi Evraki 347/16, 26 December 1865.

[63] M. Salati, 'Toleration, Persecution and Local Realities: Observations on Shi'ism in the Holy Places and the Bilad al-Sham (16th–17th Centuries)', *Convegno sul tema (15 April 1991, Roma), la Shi'a nell'impero ottomano* (Rome, 1993), pp. 123–143.

[64] A. Tamir, 'Furū' al-shajara al-Ismā'īlīyya al-Imāmīyya', *al-Mashriq* 51 (1957), p. 592.

170   *The Shariʿa*

and the castle had been restored to Ismaili control through the direct involvement of the governor of Damascus, Yusuf Pasha.[65]

Yet because of the historical developments which went into the making of an Ottoman Sunni identity, official tolerance of the Shiʿa, especially in times of social or political crises, was uncommon. The Ottomans' deep-seated suspicions of the Shiʿa were too entrenched to be rooted out. Wahhabi polemics and violence directed against the Shiʿa led to a massacre at Karbala in 1801, despite Ottoman soldiers being stationed nearby.[66] In Greater Syria, too, a fiery preacher, al-Maghrebi (1764–1827), reiterated Ibn Taymiyya's anti-Shiʿi polemics with the tacit support of provincial officials.[67]

The Ottoman state promoted its image as rightful champion of Islamic orthodoxy through the shariʿa. This made outliers liable to accusations of political and religious deviance. The imperial rivalry with the Shiʿi Safavids proved useful in this regard. It was politically expedient to explain away the conflict in purely sectarian terms. Territorial and administrative expansion required that the Ottomans institutionalise the judiciary to aid in governance, which was a boon for its legitimacy. A remarkable example of this process was the merger of the shariʿa and feudal laws into an imperial legal system. Scholars such as Ebussuʿud were responsible for furthering the Ottoman elaboration of the Hanafi school by making the sultan-caliphs interpreters of its doctrine. The offices of sultanate and caliphate had become so institutionally entwined that imperial survival was a religious imperative. Scholars sought political support for the shariʿa, assuming that it would guarantee the most just application of the law. Administrators knew also that the state needed the shariʿa to maximise its power. Simply put, authority was legitimated by the shariʿa.

The Ottoman legal system highlights a flexible conception of empire and power. The Ottomans used the shariʿa to promote the image of defenders of Sunni Islam. Official scholars, for their part, were responsible for articulating this nexus of legitimacy, authority and power. The relationship largely depended on defining its opposites. The discourse, as we have seen, required juxtaposing an Ottoman orthodoxy which enjoyed legitimacy with certain practices

---

[65]   J.L. Burckhardt, *Travels in Syria and the Holy Land* (London, 1822), pp. 152–153.

[66]   M. Litvak, 'Encounters between Shiʿi and Sunni "Ulama" in Ottoman Iraq', in O. Bengi et al., ed., *The Sunna and Shiʿa in History: Division and Ecumenism in the Muslim Middle East* (Basingstoke, 2011), p. 74.

[67]   Talhamy, 'The Fatwas...', p. 183.

and communities deemed to be illegitimate. An understanding of legitimacy and authority in the Ottoman context demands closer study of those who at first may appear powerless – in this instance the Ismailis. Communities such as the Ismailis, however marginal, were nonetheless integral to the development of an Ottoman identity, if only as a foil for defining orthodoxy.

Further Reading

Baldwin, James E. *Islamic Law and Empire in Ottoman Cairo*. Edinburgh, 2017.

Hallaq, Wael. 'From Fatwās to Furūʻ: Growth and Change in Islamic Substantive Law.' *Islamic Law and Society* 1(1) (1994), pp. 29–65.

Heyd, Uriel. 'Some Aspects of the Ottoman Fetvā.' *Bulletin of the School of Oriental and African Studies* 32(1) (1969), pp. 35–56.

Hourani, Albert. 'From Jabal ʻĀmil to Persia.' *Bulletin of the School of Oriental and African Studies* 49(1) (1986), pp. 133–140.

Imber, Colin. 'The Persecution of the Ottoman Shīʻites According to the mühimme defterleri, 1565–1585.' *Der Islam* 56(2) (1979), pp. 245–273.

Jennings, Ronald C. 'Kadi, Court, and Legal Procedure in 17th C. Ottoman Kayseri: The Kadi and the Legal System.' *Studia Islamica*, 48 (1978), pp. 133–172.

Karateke, Hakan and Marius Reinkowski., ed. *Legitimizing the Order: The Ottoman Rhetoric of State Power*. Leiden, Netherlands, 2005.

Krstić, Tijana. *Contested Conversions to Islam: Narratives of Religious Change in the Early Modern Ottoman Empire*. Stanford, CA, 2011.

Peters, Rudolph. *Crime and Punishment in Islamic Law: Theory and Practice from the Sixteenth to the Twenty-First Century*. Cambridge, 2005.

Schull, Kent F. et al., ed. *Law and Legality in the Ottoman Empire and the Republic of Turkey*. Bloomington, IN, 2016.

Tucker, Judith E. *In the House of the Law: Gender and Islamic Law in Ottoman Syria and Palestine*. Berkeley, CA, 1998.

10

Democratisation and the Shari'a: The Indonesian Experience

Carool Kersten

The relationship between Islam and the state has been the subject of vibrant debate across the Muslim world for well over a century. In the world's most populous Muslim country – a multiethnic archipelago of 16,000 islands with a sizeable presence of many other faith traditions – this debate has a fascinating 20th-century history. But it was the most recent period after the Suharto regime (1967–1998) that fully engaged Indonesia's transition from an authoritarian to a democratic system of governance. It did so amid the quest to accommodate Indonesia's Muslim identity within its political and legal institutional life in a remarkably diverse ethnoreligious setting. This chapter aims to show that contemporary developments, especially with regard to the evolving status of Islamic law, are often obscured by the cavalier use of the word 'shari'a' (*syariah* or *syariat* in Indonesian). The term serves too often as shorthand for Islamic law, or is conflated with fiqh (in Indonesian often spelled *fikih*), a reduction of the shari'a's broader meaning beyond the legal domain.

After setting the historical context of the Islamisation process in independent Indonesia, amid the ongoing democratisation of the political process, this chapter examines three areas that illustrate how the ethicolegal shari'a is evolving in contemporary Indonesia. I have identified the opportunities afforded by administrative decentralisation and a devolution of powers to local and regional state authorities to introduce local Islamic by-laws; a counter-narrative that challenges such initiatives, and proposes a so-called purpose-driven alternative reading of the shari'a and Islamic law; and a pragmatic approach that seeks to negotiate a compromise between these interpretations. The debates in Indonesia about issues pertaining to Islamic law occur in an increasingly antagonistic fashion: formalist and substantive positions have become polarised in the wake of a conservative turn in the leadership of the most important Islamic

174   *The Shari'a*

mass organisations, and under the shadow of an increasingly assertive
ulama establishment.

Background

In the run-up to the formal proclamation of Indonesian independence
on 17 August 1945, the status of Islam (and Islamic law) in the country's
new political constellation was the subject of delicate negotiations.
The key protagonists were Muslim politicians united in Masyumi, the
main Islamic political party which had emerged out of the umbrella
organisation set up by the Japanese during wartime occupation, and
secular nationalists around the president-designate Sukarno and
his deputy, Muhammad Hatta. Recognising that Indonesia's diverse
demographic make-up made the declaration of an 'Islamic state' too
far-fetched, Masyumi politicians had lobbied for a preamble to the
constitution, notably the *Piagam Jakarta* or 'Jakarta Charter'. This
contained the stipulation that Muslim citizens would have to adhere
to Islamic law. Because the Indonesian formulation reads 'dengan
kewajiban menjalankan syariat Islam bagi pemeluk-pemeluknya' ('with
the obligation for adherents of Islam to abide by Islamic law'), this has
become known as 'The Seven Words'.

Considered too contentious for an embryonic state facing the
challenge of holding together a vast geographical space inhabited by
an array of ethnic groups, the nationalists dropped The Seven Words
at the last minute. Instead, Sukarno introduced a quasi-state doctrine
known as the Pancasila or 'Five Principles', one of which stipulates that
all Indonesians would be obliged to believe in a single 'Supreme Being'
(*Ketuhanan Yang Maha Esa*). Muslim politicians associated with the
Masyumi party were dismayed, and lingering resentment continued to
influence their relations with Sukarno's nationalists. The tensions reached
breaking point during the years of 'Guided Democracy' (1957–1965),
when Masyumi was eventually dissolved and its leaders imprisoned.

Away from these confrontations in the political arena during the
early decades of Indonesian independence, important theoretical work
on Islam and Indonesian law was being done in the relative tranquillity
of academia by two Muslim intellectuals, Hasbi Ash Shiddieqy and
Hazairin. Ash Shiddieqy belonged to an ulama family from Aceh in
north Sumatra, historically one of the key centres of Islamic learning in
Southeast Asia. Aside from exposure to a traditional Islamic education,
he was also a member of two Muslim reformist organisations, the
modernist Muhammadiyah and the more puritan Persatuan Islam
(Persis for short). On account of this latter association, Ash Shiddieqy

Democratisation and the Shari'a   175

saw his intellectual labours as a contribution to the purification of Islam, in which regard a 'return to the Qur'an and Sunna' was the proper starting point in transforming a generic understanding of Islamic law into an interpretation that would account for the Indonesian context. As a modernist Muslim, he also advocated the practice of *talfiq* – the selective use of teachings from different schools of law as propagated by Muhammad Abduh (1849–1905) and the Shaykh al-Azhar Mahmud Shaltut (1893–1963). He drew these different strands together into what he called *Fikih Indonesia*, or 'Indonesian fiqh'. The required interpretative endeavour (*ijtihad*) was no longer to be executed by individual scholars but through a collaborative effort (*ijtihad jama'i*) because this offered qualitatively better jurisprudence.[1] Ash Shiddieqy stressed that this revisionist Indonesian *fiqh* was to be restricted to *mu'amalat*, the domain of human interactions, as opposed to the acts of worship or *'ibadat*, which are fixed and eternal.

Ash Shiddieqy's contemporary, Hazairin, had a similar interest in promoting a distinctly Indonesian version of Islamic law. Without formal religious training and as a specialist in Indonesian systems of customary law (*adat*), he was less well equipped for dealing with the substance of Islamic law than Ash Shiddieqy. He therefore focused on formal aspects of Islamic law and the institutionalisation of juridical practice. Where Ash Shiddieqy spoke of Fikih Indonesia, Hazairin proposed the establishment of a *mazhab nasional*, a national school of Islamic law. He also underscored the role of indigenous customs in offsetting those Arab facets of Islamic law that were regarded as alien to local cultures. In this way, legal precepts inherited from the Middle East could be turned into a living legal practice that would better suit the Indonesian situation. Although he was guided strongly by Islamic ethical and legal principles, Hazairin insisted that 'religion was to be the measure of the validity of *adat* and not vice versa'.[2]

The scholarly work of both Ash Siddieqy and Hazairin presents a fusion of Indonesian nationalism and Muslim reformism, envisaged to replace the often divisive colonial legal policies of the Dutch with an instrument for integrating Islamic law into Indonesia's legal system. The work has been instrumental for the 1974 Marriage Act; the establishment of Religious Courts in 1989; and the codification of Islamic legal materials through a presidential decree from 1991

---

[1] Yudian Wahyudi, *Ushul Fikih versus Hermeneutika: Membaca Islam dari Kanada dan Amerika* (Yogyakarta, 2006), p. 41.

[2] R.M. Feener, 'Indonesian Movements for the Creation of a "National Madhhab"', *Islamic Law and Society* 9(1) (2002), p. 104.

176   *The Shariʿa*

on Islamic law compilation, referred to as Kompilasi Hukum Islam (KHI-Inpres).

These measures reflect a different attitude towards Islamic law on the part of the 'New Order' regime, which came to power through a military coup led by General Suharto in 1965. In contrast to Sukarno, who had made every effort to curtail the influence of political Islam, Suharto permitted carefully monitored alternative forms of Islamic activism. While maintaining a ban on the free formation of Islamic political parties, the New Order gave Muslim professionals and intellectuals a role in its development policies. Those opting for such cooperation with the regime not only rejected the idea of Islamic party politics but also encouraged Muslims to adjust to the inevitable need for the secularisation of Indonesian society as part of the modernisation process. Spearheaded by student leader Nurcholish Madjid, and later mentored by the religious affairs minister, Mukti Ali, they were called 'accommodationists' by their detractors.[3] Led by former Masyumi party leader Mohammad Natsir, these other Islamic activists concentrated on religious propagation coordinated through a new body, the Dewan Dakwah Islam Indonesia, which in 1967 was granted government permission.

Another important government initiative within the context of the present discussion was the establishment in 1975 of the Indonesian Ulama Council (Majelis Ulama Indonesia, MUI). Its members were recruited from the country's Islamic mass organisations, mainly the traditionalist Nahdlatul Ulama (NU) and the modernist Muhammadiyah. The MUI became a quasi-government institution responsible for translating the New Order's development policy in Islamic terms through the issuance of fatwas and the government's chief advisory body on religious issues. With the fall of Suharto in 1998 and the ensuing Reformasi that replaced the New Order regime a year later, the MUI began to wrest itself free from government control. Membership was expanded beyond authoritative ulama from the NU, Muhammadiyah and Persis to include representatives of newly emerging political parties, such as the Hizbut Tahrir Indonesia (HTI), and even vigilante organisations such as the Islamic Defenders Front (Front Pembela Islam). As another reflection of autonomy, the MUI invoked the traditional claim of the ulama as 'heirs to the Prophets'.[4] In its Vision 2000 Statement, it also referred to the maxim 'propagation of virtue and

---

[3] C. Kersten, *Cosmopolitans and Heretics: New Muslim Intellectuals and the Study of Islam* (London and New York, 2011), p. 56.
[4] M. Nur Ichwan, "Ulamā', State and Politics: Majelis Ulema Indonesia after Suharto', *Islamic Law and Society* 12(1) (2005), pp. 45, 50.

prohibition of vice' to present itself as the 'guide and servant of the community', and an agent of 'reform and renewal' (employing the Arabic expression *islah wa al-tajdid*).[5] Its independence was further asserted by fatwas and non-legal recommendations or admonitions, known as *tausiyahs*, which shifted from remaining generally supportive of the interim president, Habibie (1998–1999), to increasingly critical during Abdurrahman Wahid's term in office (1999–2001). Most controversial, however, was a series of fatwas issued in 2005, in which the MUI not only opined that secularism, pluralism and liberalism contravened Islamic doctrine but also condemned the practice of communal prayers at interfaith gatherings and declared the teachings of the Ahmadiyya deviant.

With the benefit of hindsight, the assertiveness of the MUI is reflective of a chain of events set in motion by the New Order itself, but which it was no longer able to control and contain. The details of this development are beyond the scope of this chapter, but the so-called 'Reactualisation Agenda' (1983–1993) and the establishment of an Indonesian Association of Muslim Intellectuals (Ikatan Cendekiawan Muslim se-Indonesia, ICMI) in 1990 – both catering to a growing trend towards the Islamisation of Indonesian society – proved too little too late to ward off challenges to Suharto's authority from the mid-1990s onwards. The challenges were spearheaded by Muslim student activists and supported by the leaders of the NU and Muhammadiyah. With Indonesia's transition from authoritarianism to democracy, the public sphere witnessed an unprecedented openness, which also offered an opportunity for the establishment of new Islamic political parties. Some of these, such as the Crescent and Star Party (Partai Bulan Bintang, PBB), which built on the Masyumi legacy, and the Muslim Brotherhood-inspired Justice and Prosperity Party (Partai Keadilan Sejahtera, PKS), actively campaigned to bring back the Jakarta Charter as part of the new constitution. But failing to generate enough traction for this idea, they were forced to explore different avenues to introduce Islamic law into a democratic Indonesia.

A Different Kind of Localisation: The Bottom-Up Introduction of Islamic Law

The post-Suharto government's move towards administrative decentralisation and a devolution of powers from the central government to

---

[5] Ichwan, "'Ulamā', State and Politics', p. 71.

178   *The Shari'a*

local and regional authorities offered parties such as the PBB and the PKS (as well as other advocates of formalist interpretations of Islamic law) an alternative route to achieving their ambitions. They used this new opportunity to introduce Islamic law into Indonesia's legal architecture through local and regional by-laws, which became known as *peraturan daerah syariat* or *perda syariat*.

Developments in the northern Sumatran province of Aceh provide a high-profile case study of the *perda syariat* process, and an instructive example of how the issue is manipulated politically by national and local actors alike. Here, with the threat of secessionism in this historically troublesome and turbulent region, it was the central government that facilitated an initiative that pushed local actors into a reactive role. Neither the Free Aceh Movement (Gerakan Aceh Merdeka), which was waging an armed struggle against Jakarta, nor local religious scholars, critical students and other activists, who were campaigning for a referendum on independence, had the introduction of Islamic law on their agenda. Rather, the Jakarta-appointed governor, police and military commanders – along with local politicians supported by an 'Indonesianised' business middle class, and local ulama, academics and other intellectuals associated with organisations such as the MUI, the Islamic State Institute IAIN al-Raniry, and ICMI – proposed transforming Islamic law into 'Shari'atized [positive] law'.[6] Jakarta responded by issuing presidential decrees instructing the Ministry of Religious Affairs to secure the local situation, by appealing to religious values which resonate in Acehnese culture. This took shape in the form of Law 18/2001 on 'Special Autonomy for the Privileged Province of Aceh as the Nanggroe Aceh Darussalam'. Shortened to 'NAD Act', it provided the statutes for the re-establishment of local shari'a courts, which had first been integrated into the Indonesian legal system in 1970 and then renamed religious courts (*pengadilan agama*) as part of the 1989 Religious Judicature Act, while simultaneously limiting their jurisdiction to matters of family law alone.

Even after the promulgation of a presidential decree instructing the implementation of the NAD Act, the government's precise intentions remained ambiguous. While the new law seeks to uphold the principles of the Religious Judicature Act, conceived as a unified system under the auspices of the supreme court, the transformation of Aceh's religious courts back into shari'a courts is part of a devolution

---

[6] M. Nur Ichwan. 'Official Ulema and the Politics of Re-Islamization: The Majelis Permusyawaratan Ulama, Shari'atization and Contested Authority in Post-New Order Aceh', *Journal of Islamic Studies* 22(2) (2011), pp. 190–191.

Democratisation and the Shari'a   179

of powers to provincial authorities. To Jakarta, the designation 'shari'a' is merely a change of name, but from the perspective of the Acehnese government and religious establishment, renaming the religious courts is an integral part of a significant transfer of power to the province. This reflects an evident 'disconnect between the discourses on the Shari'a for Aceh at the level of the central government and locally in Aceh'.[7] Indeed, when independent ulama established an Association of Regional Acehnese Ulama to act in unison with Aceh's Muslim Youth Organization and academics from IAIN Al-Raniry, within the newly founded Consultative Assembly of Ulama, this initiative for a more proactive local role was frustrated by other scholars associated with the MUI, in close alliance with central government and military leaders who wanted to retain control of the *perda syariat* process.

It only became possible to move this shari'atisation process decisively forward after another crisis situation arose, this time in the form of a natural disaster, the 2004 tsunami. Local chapters of national political parties, such as the PBB and the PKS, began acting as watchdogs to ensure that the government remained sincere in implementing material aspects of Islamic law as an integral part of the massive reconstruction efforts in the wake of the disaster. Both the regional and the national sides agreed to establish a Dinas Syariat Islam, or Shari'a Office, charged with overseeing the introduction of *perda syariat*. From the central level, the Shari'a Office is supported by a working group under the Ministry of Home Affairs, with the participation of the departments of Religion and of Justice and Human Rights, as well as representatives from the police and the supreme court. The actual enforcement of these new regulations was delegated to a special branch of the Shari'a Office, the Wilayatul Hisbah, effectively acting as a kind of religious police. The financial aspects are executed under the auspices of the Baitul Mal Aceh or Acehnese Islamic Treasury. All these institutions are affected by Jakarta's administrative zigzag course, which seems to characterise the whole shari'atisation process. In 2006 the Wilayatul Hisbah was removed from the Shari'a Office's control and merged with the regular police force, while the treasury continues to be poorly managed on both provincial and municipal levels.

---

[7] M. Nur Ichwan. 'The Politics of Shari'atization: Central Governmental and Regional Discourses of Shari'a Implementation in R.M. Feener and M.E. Cammack, ed., Aceh' in *Islamic Law in Contemporary Indonesia: Ideas and Institutions* (Cambridge, 2007), p. 201.

Perda Syariat and Material Law

The mixed signals being emitted from the central government also extend to the material law that is covered under the NAD Act. A contributory factor to this ambiguity is the use of inaccurate terminology. Aside from the term *'perda syariat'* for what is in effect an instrument of fiqh, the word *qanun* has entered the vocabulary too. An Arabic term with a decidedly secular connotation, it is now used to give regional by-laws a more Islamic ring. More serious is the failure in Presidential Decision 11/2003 on Islamic law to clarify how it is supposed to be codified into 'a "comprehensive Shari'a" (*syariat Islam yang Kaffah*)' in Aceh.[8] This not only creates legal uncertainties on the local level, but in accordance with the legal maxim *lex specialis derogate lex generalis* (a law governing a specific matter overrides a law which only governs general matters) it also means that Aceh's *perda syariat* would take precedence over the generally applicable law elsewhere in Indonesia.

Be that as it may, even before the NAD Act had been ratified, provincial authorities had already begun promulgating regional Islamic by-laws. These included a decision declaring the Qur'an and Sunna the main sources of law, and a directive imposing an obligation on all resident Muslims to abide by all aspects of Islamic law. A new set of draft regulations pertaining to creed, worship and religious symbolism was prepared and circulated among academics from Aceh's Syah Kuala University and IAIN al-Raniry, as well as representatives from a number of non-governmental organisations (NGOs), and forwarded to Jakarta for further consideration. Subsequently, it was returned to the regional parliament which approved it in October 2002. The regulations became law through Qanun 11/2002 and received presidential ratification in January of the following year. This has resulted in an exclusivist framing of Islam, along the lines of a conservative understanding of Sunni orthodoxy (*ahl al-sunna wa'l-jama'a*). Hence other Muslims, especially minorities, such as the Shi'a and the Ahmadiyya, are considered to be deviant (*sesat*). This restrictive interpretation has resulted in further stipulations that explicitly forbid the spread of their teachings and that treat blasphemy and conversion from Islam to another religion.

Other pronouncements on acts of worship and religious symbolism are more limited in scope, dealing primarily with prayer and

---

[8]   Ibid., p. 193.

Democratisation and the Shari'a 181

fasting, the use of the Islamic calendar, Arabised Malay script (*jawi*), and dress codes. However, they do have an impact on public life and invade people's privacy. Three further qanuns were issued that prohibit the use of intoxicants (*khamr*), gambling (*maysir*) and unsupervised interactions between unmarried and unmarriageable people (*khalwat*). This last set of regulations also has far-reaching implications for lesbian, gay, bisexual and transgender issues. Transgressions of these regulations carry penalties involving corporal punishment, enacted under the *Qanun Jinaya* or Islamic Criminal Legal Code of 2009. Not everybody in Aceh is in favour of the Islamisation of the legal system from below. In fact, the government of the Autonomous Region at the time regarded it as a political scheme originating from Jakarta. In their view, Aceh is much more in need of clear religious guidance in the fields of education and the economy, rather than legal regulations that pertain to the performance of religious duties or public comportment.

Debating *Perda Syariat*

The examples from Aceh demonstrate that 'state enforcement of Islamic doctrine inevitably presents thorny political and religious issues.'[9] It is no surprise that *perda syariat* initiatives remain controversial, and the subject of fierce debate and disagreement among Indonesia's Muslims. Opponents challenge religious by-laws because they contravene legal uniformity by giving a privileged position to Islamic courts, and because they undermine the non-sectarian intentions of the Pancasila doctrine. Arguably, the doctrine itself has contributed to this difficulty because it has made Indonesia into a country that is neither a religious nor a truly secular state, making it impossible for the government to stay neutral since it cannot officially acknowledge adherence to religious traditions that have not been legally recognised, or allow Indonesians to identify as atheist.

Even without clear coordination between different regional initiatives, the overall rhetoric of proponents of *perda syariat* reflects an attempt to consolidate support on a national level. They maintain that Islamising the legal system is made mandatory by the teachings of Islam. Another argument, tailored more specifically to the Indonesian situation, is that having conceded that the Jakarta Charter will not be part of the constitution, there is nevertheless a democratic right to work towards the implementation of Islamic law. The Islamist intellectual Adian

---

[9] Ibid., p. 205.

182   *The Shariʻa*

Husaini appeals to the very principle of pluralism, which he fought against on other occasions, to argue that Indonesia does not require a unified legal system. In a similar vein, HTI spokesman Ismail Yusanto argues that Pancasila is an open ideology which Indonesians are free to interpret in accordance with their own values.

Such arguments are rejected by opponents such as the economist and former Muhamadiyah executive M. Dawam Rahardjo. Together with other signatories to the 'Declaration of Indonesianess' (*Maklumat Keindonesiaan*), which was issued in reaction to the MUI fatwa against pluralism, secularism and liberalism, he has pointed out that freedom must be interpreted within the context of Pancasila; and further, that while the plurality of Indonesian society may be a fact, true pluralism is to be aspired to as an ideal and should form the basis of a multireligious society. Other advocates of a formalist interpretation of Islam, such as former Masyumi politician Deliar Noer, argue that implementation of Islamic law is not about enforcing its penal code but rather about improving social conditions, poverty relief and educational reform. PBB leader Yusril Ihza Mahendra does not even insist on substituting alternative legislation but suggested during his term as justice minister that Islamic doctrine should be recognised as one of the sources of legal reform.

From Letter to Spirit: *Usul al-fiqh* and *Maqasid al-shariʻa*

This brings the debate from the nuts and bolts of legislation and jurisprudence to the more principled level of *usul al-fiqh*, or 'foundations of jurisprudence', and to the more abstract sub-field of *maqasid al-shariʻa*, the higher objectives of the shariʻa. Such theorising tends to be dominated by Muslim intellectuals who subscribe to progressive interpretations of the shariʻa as a moral or ethical compass. For example, the maverick young NU intellectual Ulil Abshar-Abdalla called for a 'new foundation of jurisprudence', offering a framework for linking legal thinking with other aspects in modern social life.[10] Earlier, important contributions to such a discourse were made by Abshar-Abdalla's teacher, Sahal Mahfudh, and by another of his intellectual mentors, Masdar Farid Masʻudi.

Sahal Mahfudh has helped to advance a contextualised interpretation of fiqh since the 1980s. Insisting that the traditional Shafiʻi text

---

[10]   U. Abshar-Abdalla, 'Apa Setelah Nurcholish Madjid?' in Abdul Halim, ed., *Menembus Batas Tradisi: Menuju Masa Depan yang Membebaskan, Refleksi atas Pemikiran Nurcholish Madjid* (Jakarta, 2006), p. 161.

Democratisation and the Shariʿa   183

tradition must continue to be used, while also drawing attention to the plurality of interpretations found within the respective schools of law, he proposes that fiqh should be regarded foremost as an intellectual exercise rather than normatively fixed jurisprudence. In *Nuances of Social Fiqh*, he explains how contextual perspectives must be teased out through critical but appreciative reassessments of traditional scholarship. Fiqh thus becomes an 'interpretative methodology' (*perangkat hermeutika*).[11] In order to develop such a dynamic understanding, combining intellectual sophistication with the integration of fiqh into the lived reality of Indonesiaʾs Muslim community, he attached central important to the notion of the public good or *maslaha*. This is a concept that has not been extensively elaborated by Shafiʿi legalists. Mahfudh turned to the writings of the North African Maliki scholar Abu Ishaq al-Shatibi (1322–1388), who is regarded as the key classical theorist of *maqasid al-shariʿa*. In Mahfudhʾs reading, *maslaha* plays a double role as a safeguard of orthodox truth claims and as a tool for understanding social reality. In turn, this gives law a dual function as a tool of '*social control* and in *social engineering*'.[12]

These views stand in stark contrast to Sahal Mahfudhʾs later track record as the general president of the NU (1999–2014) and as chairman of the MUI (2000–2014). He presided over the release of fatwas that ruled negatively on interreligious marriage, condemned the Ahmadiyya as heretics, and rejected the concepts of pluralism, liberalism and secularism. These rulings received support from Muslim formalists but met with severe criticism from progressive-minded Muslims, many of whom had been trained in the open-minded atmosphere of the reformed traditionalist study circles which Mahfudh had helped to create in the preceding decades.

Where Sahal Mahfudh had concentrated on unpacking the notion of *maslaha*, Masdar F. Masʿudi focused on the idea of justice (*adala*, or *keadilan* in Indonesian). The notion of justice fits into the category of non-negotiable immutabilities (*qatiʿ*). Applying this to concrete juridical questions, in his book *Religion of Justice*, Masʿudi draws a parallel between the ethical dimensions underlying the obligation of *zakat*, as both an act of worship ('*ibadat*) and redistribution of income, and the abstract notion of economic justice governing *muʿamalat*.[13] Whether

---

[11]   R. Michael Feener, *Muslim Legal Thought in Modern Indonesia* (Cambridge and New York, 2007), p. 169.
[12]   Sahal Mahfudh, *Nuansa Fiqih Sosial* (Yogyakarta, 2011), p. liii (original emphasis).
[13]   M.F. Masʿudi, *Agama Keadilan: Risalah Zakat (Pajak) dalam Islam* (Jakarta, 1991).

184   *The Shariʻa*

dealing with the technicalities of jurisprudence or its epistemological underpinnings, Masʻudi challenges the atomistic approach found in the work of many jurists. He also dismisses the way in which early Muslim modernists had revived ijtihad as lacking in critical reflection, and as being more in the vein of the technical juridical specialism of *tarjih*. Concerned with selecting the right legal position on the basis of the strongest possible evidence, *tarjih* has dominated the legal discourse of the NU's modernist counterpart, the Muhammadiyah. Instead, Masʻudi advocates the methodological coherence that underpins an integral vision of human life, as promoted in *maqasid al-shariʻa*. The preoccupation of legal scholars with the piecemeal fashioning of juridical rulings is thus taken to the level of moral responsibility.

A group of young NU intellectuals who identify themselves as 'Islamic Post-Traditionalists' regard this methodological critique, for all its achievements, as not going far enough.[14] They ask whether the critique has succeeded in turning traditional theology and jurisprudence into a genuinely creative way of thinking. Ahmad Baso, one of the most articulate proponents of Islamic Post-traditionalism, concludes that Masʻudi has failed to offer a real alternative to the paradigm of Sunni orthodoxy, which remains locked in idealism and scripturalism, or to the paradigm of realism found in Muʻtazili thought, and in western humanism. Instead of a new systemic method, Masʻudi's approach is seen as doctrinal-normative and instrumental, driven by pragmatic or utilitarian considerations that serve to justify the status quo and collaboration with those in power. It is an example of what Mohamed Arkoun calls the ahistorical 'sublimation' of Sunni thinking that does not move beyond Ashʻari-Maturidi theology, Shafiʻi fiqh and Ghazalian Sufism; these remain the staple of NU discourse.[15]

Also in terms of the philosophy of law, Masʻudi's understanding of *maslaha* is very different from that of classical scholars such as Najm al-Din al-Tufi, al-Shatibi and Ibn Rushd. His dual interest in fiqh and Sufism is methodologically at odds with the challenges posed by Ibn Hazm, al-Shatibi and Ibn Rushd to the dominance of Shafiʻi *qiyas*, or reasoning by analogy, and the alternative inductive or demonstrative reasoning that characterises *maqasidi* legal thinking. According to Baso, the comparison in *Religion of Justice* of *zakat* with modern taxation

---

[14] C. Kersten. 'Islamic Post-Traditionalism: Postcolonial and Postmodern Religious Discourse in Indonesia', *Sophia: International Journal for Philosophy and Traditions* 54(4) (2015), pp. 473–489.

[15] A. Baso, *NU Studies: Pergolakan Pemikiran Antara Fundamentalisme Islam & Fundamentalisme Neo-Liberal* (Jakarta, 2006), p. 317.

shows a misconstrued grasp of the relationship between religion and this-worldly politics, whereby justice as an attribute of God is turned into an aspect of human viceregency. Referring to the work of the Moroccan philosopher Mohammed Abed al-Jabri (1935–2010), he insists that the economic system in classical Islamic societies was a tributary one, based on the spoils of war and coercion. It is therefore ahistorical to compare *zakat* with modern tax systems. Such blind spots lead to an uncritical legitimation of state hegemony. Mas'udi's identification of the state as the guarantor of the public good likewise reflects an étatist understanding of public interest, shaped by Sunni normativism.

Maqasid al-Shari'a as Islamic Philosophy of Law

Although both Sahal Mahfudh and Masdar Mas'udi make cursory references to *maqasid al-shari'a*, a more consistent argument to treat this idea as a legal doctrine and an epistemological method is made by Yudian Wahyudi, a professor in the philosophy of law at the State Islamic University of Yogyakarta. Inspired by the writings of the Egyptian philosopher Hasan Hanafi (b. 1935), Wahyudi makes *maqasid al-shari'a* part of a sustained advocacy for turning *usul al-fiqh* into a hermeneutics that is philosophical in nature rather than a purely juridical instrument. He has highlighted the significance of *maqasid al-shari'a's* scale of priorities – protecting religion, human life, intellect, property and honour – for thinking about Muslim ethics, law and politics. Wahyudi's efforts fit into a recent trend towards a reappreciation for classical thinking about *maqasid al-shari'a*, which has become perceptible throughout the Muslim world, especially through the writings of the Canadian-Egyptian Jasser Auda (b. 1966). While attention to *maqasid al-shari'a* in Indonesia goes back to the 1960s and 1970s, so far the understanding of this field was reductionist, thus robbing the discipline of *usul al-fiqh* of its philosophical dimension. The quality of thinking of those who have gone on to obtain doctorates in *usul al-fiqh* has shown promise in this regard, as they encounter the hermeneutics of Emilio Betti, Hans-Georg Gadamer and Paul Ricoeur. For Wahyudi, the attention to *maqasid al-shari'a* in the writings of Fazlur Rahman and Khalid Masud did not manage to move the discourse beyond doctrinal engagement, exemplified by the cautionary legal maxim that 'the avoidance of damage takes precedence over obtaining benefit' (*dar' al-mafasid muqaddam 'ala jalb al-masalih*).[16]

---

[16] Y. Wahyudi, *Maqashid Syari'ah dalam Pergumulan Politik: Berfilsafat Hukum Islam dari Harvard ke Sunan Kalijaga* (Yogyakarta, 2007), p. 10.

186   *The Shariʿa*

New theorists take a more proactive stance, promoting a *maqasidi* or purpose-based approach to realise, ensure and preserve the common good for humankind in general, and the Muslim community in particular. They seek to articulate the coherence of Islam's teachings by conceiving of them as a process rather than a teleology. In this reading, what motivated religious scholars to design theories and methods of interpretation was the claim that the text of the Qur'an and the Hadith are limited in a practical sense, whereas human civilisation continues to evolve. In the face of this need to unpack and expand the values encapsulated in the body of sacred texts, there has been a tendency to sacralise such theories and methods, thus 'ensnaring the Muslim community in idolatry' and, ironically, leading 'people to speak of religion in divine language, whereas God speaks to humankind in a human language'.[17] This has also resulted in the atrophy of Islamic law. To escape this quandary, Wahyudi suggests that *maqasid al-shariʿa* must be taken as a surgical scalpel or an optical lens that can be used to interpret the constantly shifting circumstances in which humankind exists, by dissecting or refracting the primary, secondary and tertiary purposes of the human condition. Islamic law is characterised by five parities: it is at one and the same time divine (*ilahi*) and positive (*manusiawi*, man-made) or secular; eternal and temporal; absolute in terms of values but relative in their implementation; universal and local; as well as literal and figurative or spiritual. This is why Islamic law does not propose a simple binary between the permitted (*halal*) and forbidden (*haram*) but recognises intermediate levels of validity, ranging from the recommended (*mandub* or Sunna) and permissible (*mubah*) to the disapproved (*makruh*). It is this realisation that inspired jurists to formulate the levels of priorities in relation to the preservation of religion, human life, intellect, property and honour that make up the *maqasidi* or purpose-based thinking.

Wahyudi argues that *maqasid al-shariʿa* is an integral part of the toolbox for *usul al-fiqh* as a method of thinking, an epistemology that is Islamic in nature and thereby an example of endogenous intellectual creativity. It stresses the need for *usul al-fiqh* always to function as a dialectics between the divine text and custom shaped by history and culture. This creates the degree of relativism that enables *usul al-fiqh* to develop a 'plurality of interpretations' (*pluralitas tafsir*) on the basis of this-worldly historicity.[18]

---

[17] Wahyudi, *Ushul Fikih versus Hermeneutika*, p. 48.
[18] Wahyudi, *Maqashid Syariʿah dalam Pergumulan Politik*, pp. 35–36.

Experimental Compromise: The Family Law Counter Draft

In 2004 a number of Muslim intellectuals from mostly NU backgrounds came together for an exercise in alternative law drafting. Their purpose was to challenge the transformation of the Islamic Law Compilation under Presidential Instruction 1/1991 (KHI-Inpres) into the Material Law Bill of Marriage Law for the Religious Court. The working group had various reasons for targeting this particular piece of legislation. First, it was the most detailed regulation of religious matters at the national level, and it was frequently used by judges of religious courts. Aside from being 'a replica of outdated fiqh' in its approach, KHI-Inpres retained a number of stipulations that contradicted universal Islamic principles such as equality, brotherhood and justice, and which also contravened existing legal regulations and international conventions.[19]

Accordingly, a counter legal draft with a set of concrete amendments to the existing text of the bill was proposed by the working group. The most important amendments concerned interreligious marriage, polygamy, and the definition of marriage as a contract based on agreement between partners instead of a religious covenant – which effectively shifted marriage from the category of *'ibadat* (acts of worship) to *mu'amalat* (human interaction) – and thus subject to change. Other amendments included raising women's qualifying age for marriage from 16 to 19; abolishing the need for women older than 21 to be represented by a guardian, allowing women to act as marriage witnesses; giving women the option of offering a dowry; and equality between the roles, rights and responsibilities of the spouses, including the initiation of divorce. With regard to inheritance law, there could be no discrimination on grounds of religion or being extramarital offspring; the proportions allotted to sons and daughters had to be equal.

This initiative can be regarded as an attempt to find a compromise between the Islamisation of Indonesia's legal system driven by formalists, and the theoretical discussions by Islamic philosophers of law on turning *usul al-fiqh* and *maqasid al-shari'a* into a hermeneutics. For this purpose, the working group collaborated with a number of religious scholars, fellow academics and NGO activists. Alongside the alternative draft bill, they produced a set of documents that included

---

[19] M. Wahid, 'Reformation of Islamic Family Law in Post-New Order Indonesia: A Legal and Political Study of the Counter Legal Draft of the Islamic Law Compilation' in Ota Atushi, Okamoto Masaaki and Ahmad Suaedy, ed., *Islam in Contention: Rethinking Islam and State in Indonesia* (Jakarta, 2010), p. 92.

background discussions about fiqh methodology, and an academic paper on pluralist and democratic Islamic law compilation that outlined 'alternative fiqh standards'. These standards were designed to serve as a future 'fundamental reference for a just society, which upholds values of humanity, respects women's rights, spreads wisdom and kindness, and achieves well-being for all of humankind.[20]

While demands for the formalisation of Islamic law do not necessarily contradict the Indonesian national legal system, there are elements that are discriminatory towards non-Muslims. The authors of the counter legal draft regarded their dossier as the most effective response to the exclusivism that characterised Islamist agendas for the formalisation of the shari'a in terms of safeguarding Indonesian values with regard to nationality and culture, progress towards democratisation, and upholding international human rights standards. The proposed changes enact important global commitments by Indonesia, including the Convention on the Elimination of All Forms of Discrimination against Women, the International Covenant on Economic, Social, and Cultural Rights, and norms dealing with child protection and domestic violence. Thus the Counter Draft Law can be said to shift from a theocentric to an anthropocentric way of thinking about Islamic law, moving as one of the team members put it 'from eisegese to exegese'.[21] As such, it resonates with Wahyudi's criticism of the *fuqaha*'s tendency to adopt 'divine language'. The broader approach aims to safeguard human felicity, local wisdom and public reasoning as vouched for in the maqasid al-shari'a.

Perhaps not surprisingly, the counter legal draft was met with the MUI's rejection for introducing unlawful innovations (*bid'a*) and for alterations to the authenticity of Islamic law (*taghyir*), along with manipulative interpretations of the text of the Qur'an. The spokesman of the controversial Indonesian Mujahidin Council, Fauzan al-Anshari, insisted that the amendments challenged the core of Islamic doctrine and contradicted the conventional understanding of *maqasid al-shari'a*. Others used the funding provided to the working group by the Asia Foundation to warn against the dangers of *ghazwul fikri* (the invasion of ideas alien to Islam) and the involvement of western agents.

---

[20]   Wahid, 'Reformation of Islamic Family Law', pp. 87–88.
[21]   Wahid, 'Reformation of Islamic Family Law', p. 93. *Eisegese* is a form of *Hineininterpretierung* – that is, reading one's own thoughts or ideological convictions into a text – whereas *exegese* respects the balance between text and interpreter in terms of object and subject.

At the other end of the spectrum a range of advocacy groups for gender equality, human rights and pluralism expressed appreciation for the counter legal draft initiative. There was disagreement with the proposed ban on polygamy on the basis that the majority of the Muslim community would be uncomfortable with it. However, Masdar Mas'udi lauded the efforts of the working group, and the Muhammadiyah activist Moeslim Abdurrahman went against the grain of his organisation's conservative leadership in saying that, as a form of collective *ijtihad*, the alternative bill was a commendable exercise of fiqh's historical role of bringing about social change. Abshar-Abdalla felt that while the proposal was radical by any Muslim standards, the alternative bill could revolutionise Islamic law if it was accepted.

Under pressure from the MUI and others, the minister of religious affairs effectively banned the counter legal draft proposal in early 2005. One of the project's initiators, Marzuki Wahid, identified several reasons why it had failed to win over the government, parliament and the majority of Indonesia's Muslim community. Apart from having to operate under the divided bureaucracy of the Ministry of Religious Affairs, the working group had underestimated the influence of reactionary and conservative elements in organisations such as the MUI, and the sensitivities of the majority of Indonesia's Muslims regarding radical changes to personal law. The working group had failed to develop a flexible and efficient strategy for lobbying policy-makers and influencing public opinion. However, despite the final outcome, the counter legal draft proposal has become a valuable resource for deliberating about alternative ways to integrate progressive interpretations of Islamic principles into Indonesia's legal system.

Conclusion

Varying strands of understanding of the shari'a across the Muslim world today are also present in Indonesia. While there was a post-independence parallel with Turkey in the locus of public Islam, the regime change of 1999 altered that course (as indeed has Turkey itself today): certain regions within Indonesia have taken advantage of the new political openness to campaign for the implementation of Islamic law in both the private and the public spheres. What sets Indonesia apart from many other Muslim countries is that, despite the tensions among the diverse positions on this issue, the debates occur in the context of a democratisation process that has progressed for some two decades. In this respect, the Indonesian case offers both hopeful and sobering lessons. Evidently it is possible to engage creatively with 'Islamic law' where the political system provides a free and safe public space. However, democratisation and the concomitant processes of legal reform take time to mature.

Since the regime change in 1999, Indonesia has successfully been through four rounds of fair and free elections. From the beginning of this democratisation, Muslim activists have made full use of the opportunities offered by the new openness of the public sphere, which is unprecedented in Indonesia's own historical experience, but also in relation to developments elsewhere in the Muslim world. When Indonesia's democratisation moved from transition to consolidation, the real test as it pertains to the place of Islamic law came in 2005. With a series of fatwas by the MUI and a conservative turn in the top leadership echelons of the Muhammadiyah and NU that year, intellectual and political debates became increasingly antagonistic, while local initiatives by emboldened Islamists have come to pose a challenge to a uniform rule of law in Indonesia. As far as democratic governance is concerned, the post-Suharto governments compare favourably with many in the Muslim world, including neighbouring Malaysia and Brunei. Yet by failing to take an unambiguous position on the place of Islamic law in Indonesian society, not least with respect to minorities, they have been less successful in providing a clear sense of direction. Without guidance from the centre, intra-Muslim debates in this regard will remain a delicate issue.

Further Reading

Auda, Jasser. *Maqasid al-Shariah as Philosophy of Islamic Law: A Systems Approach*. Herndon, VA, 2008.

Bowen, John R. 'Justifying Islamic Pluralism: Examples from Indonesia and France', in *Diversity and Pluralism in Islam: Historical and Contemporary Discourses amongst Muslims*, Zulfikar Hirji, ed., pp. 163–183. London, 2010.

Daly, Patrick, R., Michael Feener and Anthony Reid, ed. *From the Ground Up: Perspectives on Post-Tsunami and Post-Conflict Aceh.* Singapore, 2012.

Feener, R. Michael. *Shari'a and Social Engineering: The Implementation of Islamic Law in Contemporary Aceh, Indonesia*. Oxford and New York, 2014.

Hallaq, Wael. *The Shari'a: Theory, Practice, Transformations*. Cambridge, 2009.

Hefner, Robert. *Shari'a Law and Modern Muslim Ethics*. Bloomington, IN, 2016.

Johns, Anthony and Abdullah Saeed. 'Nurcholish Madjid and the Interpretation of the Qur'an: Religious Pluralism and Tolerance', in *Modern Muslim Intellectuals and the Qur'an*, Taji-Farouki, Suha, ed. Oxford, 2004, pp. 67–96.

Kersten, Carool. *Islam in Indonesia: The Contest for Society, Ideas and Values*. London and New York, 2015.

Kersten, Carool. *A History of Islam in Indonesia: Unity in Diversity*. Edinburgh and New York, 2017.

The Shariʻa in the Western Landscape

Rex Ahdar and Nicholas Aroney

The place of the shariʻa within liberal democracies in the western world straddles law, politics, statecraft, history, culture and religion. It is certainly a sensitive topic in the corridors of power, as well as in the more commonplace cafés, cyberspace chatrooms and living rooms of society. Scarcely a week goes by without a controversy erupting over some aspect of Muslim ritual, symbolism, belief or practice.

Take the following whirlwind global sampling of examples from 2009. In the United Kingdom, the Home Office asked civil servants not to eat lunch in front of their Muslim colleagues during the month of Ramadan.[1] A Christian couple running a guest house in Liverpool appeared in court on a public order offence charge after telling a Muslim woman guest that Islamic dress was oppressive to women and put them into 'bondage'.[2] In Melbourne, Samir Abu Hamza, a Muslim cleric who instructed his male married followers to hit and force sex on their disobedient wives, drew a harsh rebuke from the prime minister, Kevin Rudd.[3] In New Zealand, the Department of Corrections revealed that all meat served to prisoners had undergone *halal* slaughter,[4] and a Muslim woman complained to the Human Rights Commission over her removal from the public gallery of a courtroom for refusing to take

---

[1] D. Gardham, 'Home Office Told: "Don't Eat in Front of Muslims during Ramadan"', *Daily Telegraph*, 20 September 2009.
[2] J. Bingham, 'Christian Couple Face Losing Hotel after Criminal Charges for Offending Muslim Woman', *Daily Telegraph*, 20 September 2009. The couple were later acquitted in the Liverpool Magistrates' Court; N. Britten, 'Hoteliers Cleared of Abusing Muslim Guest', *Daily Telegraph*, 9 December 2009.
[3] 'It's OK to Hit Your Wife, Says Melbourne Islamic Cleric Samir Abu Hamza', *The Australian*, 22 January 2009.
[4] 'Only Halal-Certified Meat Served to Prisoners', *Otago Daily Times*, 9 October 2009.

off her headscarf.[5] In the United States, when Major Nidal Malik Hasan shot 12 of his army colleagues at Fort Hood, Texas [and, according to witnesses, shouted 'Allahu Akbar' ('God is great') before he opened fire] the incident sparked renewed debate about the loyalty of Muslims in the US military to American values.[6] In France, President Nicolas Sarkozy called for a ban on the *burqa* on the basis that it perpetuated the subservience of women.[7] And, as the year ended, there was a stormy response to the verdict of the majority of the Swiss public, by way of a binding referendum, to ban minarets on mosques.[8]

Such controversies have only increased since then. The doleful roll-call of recent Islamic State and other jihadist-led atrocities is too readily recalled: *Charlie Hebdo* newspaper, San Bernadino, the Boston Marathon, the Bataclan heavy metal rock concert, Brussels airport bombing and so on. Less well known are more everyday struggles, such as the successful discrimination claim brought by two British Muslims after their employer, Tesco, kept the supermarket's prayer room locked,[9] and, on the other hand, the finding of an Australian tribunal that a Muslim group unlawfully discriminated against a female member of the audience by requiring her to sit in a women-only area.[10]

Calm and dispassionate reflection has not been a feature of most discussions in this regard. There has, as the saying goes, been more heat than light. Consider the experience in two western countries that have

---

[5] 'Muslim Woman Furious at Courtroom Ban', *New Zealand Herald*, 2 September 2009.

[6] J. Berger, 'Army Chief Concerned for Muslim Troops', *New York Times*, 8 November 2009: accessible at http://www.nytimes.com/2009/11/09/us/politics/09casey.html; 'Fort Hood Shootings: The Meaning of "Allahu Akbar"', *Daily Telegraph*, 6 November 2009: accessible at http://www.telegraph.co.uk/news/worldnews/northamerica/usa/6516570/Fort-Hood-shootings-the-meaning-of-Allahu-Akbar.html.

[7] 'Nicolas Sarkozy pushes for burqa ban in France', *Daily Telegraph*, 12 November 2009.

[8] A Williams, 'Switzerland Risks Muslim Backlash after Minarets Vote', *Daily Telegraph*, 29 November 2009.

[9] 'Muslim Supermarket Workers Win Discrimination Case Against Tesco after Bosses Locked Their Prayer Room and Made Them Sign In and Out', *Daily Mail*, 3 October 2013: accessible at http://www.dailymail.co.uk/news/article-2442448/Muslim-Tesco-workers-win-discrimination-case-bosses-locked-prayer-room.html.

[10] *Bevege v Hizb ut-Tahrir Australia* [2016] NSWCATAD 44, 4 March 2016, discussed in Neil Foster, 'Islam, Women's Seating and Discrimination', *Law and Religion Australia*, 8 March 2016: accessible at https://lawandreligionaustralia.wordpress.com/2016/03/08/islam-womens-seating-and-discrimination/.

The Shari'a in the Western Landscape   195

grappled with official recognition of the shari'a, Canada and the United Kingdom. The Ontario provincial government in 2005 firmly rejected the notion of shari'a tribunals adjudicating family and civil disputes, but only after an acrimonious debate that began immediately after a Muslim civil justice organisation floated the idea in late 2003. And the Archbishop of Canterbury's lecture on the shari'a and the law in 2008 elicited the fierce volley of criticism that inspired us to create a book that examined the question of the accommodation of the shari'a in western societies.[11]

As one informed commentator has pointed out, 'Intelligent discussion of Islamism, democracy, and Islam requires clear and accurate definitions. Without them, analysis will collapse into confusion and policymaking will suffer.'[12] The key concepts in any area require clarification, and this is especially true here. Accordingly, we shall commence this chapter with brief definitions of the principal matters under consideration before setting out what we take to be the key issues in the debate.

However, one final opening remark. The question of the public place of the shari'a is not one for specialists alone. If we operate from the premise that the shari'a makes claims to function in the public square, then everyone, Muslim and non-Muslim, has a stake in the task of what Abdullahi Ahmed An-Na'im calls 'negotiating the future of shari'a'.[13]

The Shari'a

References to the shari'a in western circles have, as Tariq Ramadan puts it, become something of a bugbear, evoking dark images of floggings, stonings, amputations, women peering meekly out of eye-slits in sombre full-length garments, wide-eyed bearded imams issuing death decrees against blasphemers and so on.[14] How, then, should we understand the shari'a? Ramadan explains that there is no single definition of the term, and he offers a bifurcated one:

1. *Al-shari'a*, on the basis of the root of the word, means 'the way' ('the path leading to the source') and outlines a global conception of creation, existence, death, and the way of

---

[11]   Rex Ahdar and Nicholas Aroney, ed., *Shari'a in the West* (Oxford, 2010).
[12]   B. Tibi, 'Islamist Parties: Why They Can't Be Democratic', *Journal of Democracy* 19 (2008), p. 43.
[13]   A.A. An-Na'im, *Islam and the Secular State: Negotiating the Future of Shari'a* (Cambridge, MA, 2008).
[14]   T. Ramadan, *Islam, the West and the Challenges of Modernity* (Leicester, 2001), p. 47.

196 *The Shari'a*

life it entails, stemming from a normative reading and an understanding of scriptural sources. It determines 'how to be a Muslim.'

2. *Al-shari'a*, for ... jurists, is the corpus of general principles of Islamic law extracted from its two fundamental sources (the Qur'an and the Sunnah).[15]

The term appears just once in the Qur'an.[16] The phrase 'Islamic law' is often used interchangeably with the shari'a. This usage has its critics, but others defend it. An important related concept is fiqh, which literally means comprehension or understanding. Fiqh is the body of reasoned reflection and opinion of Islamic scholars and jurists, as well as the science or method of deducing such opinions, concerning what they consider the shari'a to require of Muslims in the particular time and locality they find themselves. Fiqh, in other words, is the developing jurisprudence of the shari'a. Many scholars, including Ramadan, have been at pains to distinguish between the shari'a and fiqh. An-Na'im puts it thus:

It is clear that there is no uniform and settled understanding of Shari'a among Muslims that can be enforced by the state. This is true even within the same school of Sunni or Shi'a jurisprudence, let alone across different schools and sects. It should be emphasized at this level that since every understanding of Shari'a, even if universal among Muslims, is a human interpretation, none should be enforced as state law in the name of Shari'a or Islam as such. At another level, because Shari'a is always the product of human interpretation of divine sources, any interpretation of it will reflect the human limitations of those who are interpreting it, despite the divinity of the sources they are working with. From this perspective Shari'a will always remain open to reinterpretation and evolution, in response to the constantly changing needs of Islamic societies and communities in different times and places.[17]

Between Ramadan and An-Na'im there is a subtle difference, however. Ramadan characterises the shari'a as being derived from the

---

[15] T. Ramadan, *Radical Reform: Islamic Ethics and Liberation* (Oxford, 2009), pp. 359–360.

[16] Qur'an, 45:18: 'We have put you on the (true) Path [Shari'a] of religion; so follow that...', see F. Griffel, 'Introduction', in A. Amanat and F. Griffel, ed., *Shari'a: Islamic Law in the Contemporary Context* (Stanford, CA, 2007), pp. 1–2.

[17] An-Na'im, *Islam and the Secular State*, pp. 282–283.

The Shari'a in the Western Landscape   197

Qur'an and the Sunna.[18] An-Na'im characterises it as 'a historically-conditioned *human* interpretation' of divine sources.[19] This apparently marginal difference in phraseology reflects a wider and more sharply defined disagreement between those who might be characterised as orthodox or even fundamentalist, who would endorse certain historical understandings of the shari'a as divinely authoritative, and so-called reformers, secularists or liberals, who would seek to modernise Islamic societies by reference to human rights and other standards ostensibly external to Islamic faith and tradition.[20] Plainly, views about the nature of the shari'a are shaped by both religious and scholarly considerations. Religious commitment to the revealed standards of Islam calls for an affirmation of the divine and authoritative status of the Qur'an and the Sunna, including the shari'a at least in its core, revealed content. However, juristic scholarship draws attention to differences in interpretation of the shari'a, and Islamic scholars debate the many questions of interpretation and application that inevitably arise.

In this context, talk of the shari'a is misleading to the extent that it suggests a monolithic, fixed and uniform body of positive norms and rules. This is to take an 'essentialist' perspective.[21] The better view is to acknowledge that there are different concepts of the shari'a in different contexts. An attempt to distil the shari'a to its core features or basic objects may simply produce a sort of lowest-common-denominator version that is as artificial as it is general. One may assert, notes An-Na'im,

> that all that is required is to observe the basic objectives or purposes of Shari'a (*Maqasid al-Shari'a*), while *fiqh* principles are subject to change from one time or place to another. But

---

[18]   T. Ramadan in *Western Muslims and the Future of Islam* (Oxford, 2004) describes the shari'a as 'the corpus of reference in which Islamic universality is written down' (pp. 32–33). But he also recognises the unavoidable human element, characterising the shari'a as an 'expression' of the 'way to faithfulness' in his *Islam, the West and the Challenges of Modernity*, p. 34.

[19]   A.A. An-Na'im, 'Islamic Foundations of Religious Human Rights', in J. Witte and J. van der Vyver, ed., *Religious Human Rights in Global Perspective: Religious Perspectives* (The Hague, 1996), pp. 337, 353 (original emphasis).

[20]   These views are canvassed in N. Hosen, *Shari'a & Constitutional Reform in Indonesia* (Singapore, 2007), Chapter 2.

[21]   J.M. Otto, 'The Compatibility of *Shari'a* with the Rule of Law. Fundamentalist Conflict: Between Civilisations? Within Civilisations? Or between Scholars?', in A. Groen et al., ed., *Knowledge in Ferment: Dilemmas in Science, Scholarship and Society* (Leiden, 2007), Chapter 9, p. 141.

198   *The Shariʻa*

the problem with this view is that the so-called basic objectives
of Shariʻa are expressed at such a high level of abstraction that
they are neither distinctly Islamic nor sufficiently specific
for the purposes of public policy and legislation. As soon as
these principles are presented in more specific and concrete
terms, they will immediately be implicated in the familiar
controversies and limitations of *fiqh*.[22]

Controversies such as these are, of course, the standard fare of jurisprudence within any legal system, whether religious or philosophical.
Modern liberalism seeks to resolve such disputes by bracket-
ing the most intractable of them out of consideration – namely,
the religiophilosophical, which the American moral and political
philosopher John Rawls (1921–2002) called 'comprehensive
doctrines'. Indeed, as An-Naʼim observes, 'To Muslims, Shariʻa is the
"Whole Duty of Mankind", moral and pastoral theology and ethics,
high spiritual aspiration, and detailed ritualistic and formal
observance; it encompasses all aspects of public and private law,
hygiene, and even courtesy and good manners.'[23] Less reformist
Islamic scholars would put this point even more forcefully. Whether
the comprehensive character of Islamic doctrine implies that there
can be no distinction between religious law and secular law, or
between the private and the public, remains an open question.
But it is on the possibility of such distinctions that the argument
about the accommodation of the shariʻa in western democracies may
very largely turn.

The West

To identify the West is not a matter of reaching for an atlas. There is,
admittedly, an incontrovertible geographical dimension to the term,
and, as an initial approximation, one could posit the West as comprising
Western Europe and its colonial offspring in Canada, the United States,
Australia and New Zealand. The way one characterises a thing depends,
however, on the nature of the object of the characterisation as well as
the purpose for which it is being characterised. In this book we are
concerned with the structure and regulation of human societies, not
trade patterns or military alliances. It is befitting in a book of this

---

[22]   An-Naʼim, *Islam and the Secular State*, p. 35.
[23]   Ibid., p. 11.

The Shari'a in the Western Landscape   199

nature, therefore, to quote the words of the doyen of law and religion scholarship, Harold Berman (1918–2007), on this point:

> What is called 'the West' is a particular historical culture, or civilization … The West is a cultural term. It is not, however, simply an idea; it is a community. It implies both a historical structure and a structured history. For many centuries it could be identified very simply as the people of Western Christendom.[24]

The people of western Christendom adopted and over time transformed Germanic customs, Greek philosophy, Roman law and Hebrew religion into a unique synthesis. The Australian Cardinal George Pell (b. 1941) puts it this way:

> The West is the product of a dialogue between what [Pierre] Manet calls 'the party of nature' – that is, the classical inheritance of the Greco-Roman world – and the party of grace – by which he means the revelation of the Christian religion. The party of nature emphasizes pride, magnanimity and the cultivation of the virtues that are natural to man. The party of grace emphasizes humility, renunciation, and the cultivation of the soul.[25]

The original idea of the West, notes Berman, lies in the distinction between the western and eastern divisions of the Roman Empire and of the Christian Church, a division that became especially sharp following the separation of the Roman and Orthodox communions in 1054. This separation coincided with a movement in western Christianity not only to make the Bishop of Rome the sole head of the church but also to differentiate the church as a political and legal entity from secular institutions. Berman argues that the West has ever since been characterised by a commitment to ongoing reform, expressed by a succession of 'revolutions' that have both reshaped and revitalised its governing institutions. Each such revolution – the Papal Revolution of the 11th century, the Reformation of the 16th century, the American and French revolutions of the 18th century, and the Russian Revolution of the 20th century – contributed, directly or indirectly, to the

---

[24] H. Berman, *Law and Revolution: The Formation of the Western Legal Tradition* (Cambridge, MA, 1983), pp. 2–3.
[25] G. Pell, *God and Caesar: Selected Essays on Religion, Politics & Society*, M. Casey, ed. (Washington, DC, 2007), p. 43.

200   *The Shariʿa*

western legal tradition as we know it today. Despite these revolutions, however, Berman felt that the tradition retained certain fundamental characteristics, the principal ones being (a) a relatively sharp distinction between legal institutions and other types of institutions (religious, moral, political); (b) a set of legal institutions administered by a special class of legal professionals (lawyers), themselves trained in a body of legal doctrine which had been systematised into a particular legal science or jurisprudence; (c) a conception of the law as a body of doctrine that develops and evolves over the course of centuries, according to an inbuilt capacity for organic change shaped by both an inner logic and a felt need to adapt to new circumstances and expectations; and (d) a conception of the law as both constitutional and constitutive in nature, supreme over the various governing authorities (church, state and civil society), making both necessary and possible the existence of a plurality of coexisting jurisdictions (initially of an ecclesiastical, royal, feudal, manorial, urban and mercantile kind) which both compete and cooperate with each other within the context of an overarching legal order.

As a consequence, the separation of church and state has long been fundamental to the constitutional structure of the West. Jesus Christ taught his disciples to render unto Caesar the things that are Caesar's and to God the things that are God's.[26] Augustine drew his famous distinction between the heavenly and earthly cities, while Pope Gelasius I (r. 492–496) likewise distinguished between priestly authority and the royal power, and Martin Luther spoke of two kingdoms, temporal and spiritual. The English Reformed theologian Roger Williams (ca. 1603–1683) referred to a 'hedge or wall of Separation between the Garden of the Church and the Wilderness of the world', and the American Founding Father Thomas Jefferson invoked a 'wall of separation between church and state', a formula taken up by the United States Supreme Court.[27] While each of these authors, separated by time and context, meant something specifically different, the idea of two distinct powers remained fundamental and has continued to shape western conceptions of the relationship between church and state. What has changed is the prevailing relationship between religion and the state.

Most pre-Christian societies drew no sharp distinction between religious authority and the governing powers. During the early

---

[26]   Matthew 22:21; Mark 12:17. Likewise, John 18:36: 'My kingdom is not of this world'.

[27]   *Everson v Board of Education*, 330 US 1, 15–16 (1947).

The Shari'a in the Western Landscape 201

Christian era, numerous appeals for religious toleration were made by both biblical and patristic writers, philosophical nominalists such as William of Ockham (ca. 1287–1347), and Jean Gerson (1363–1429) developed theories of natural rights and religious freedom founded on the idea of 'evangelical liberty'. The Reformation idea of the priesthood of all believers led to a moderate and incomplete form of religious toleration in some Protestant lands. These ideas in turn laid the foundations for a more wide-reaching principle of tolerance, in which freedom of conscience was the fundamental value. Indeed, it was largely those who were descended from, or sympathetic to, the radical wing of the Reformation who first pursued and implemented policies of disestablishment and toleration. Toleration was also later urged by important figures of the Enlightenment, and under that influence the disestablishment of religion and an increasing secularisation has become a feature of most contemporary western states. As Charles Taylor explains in one account of this secularisation,

> whereas the political organization of all pre-modern societies was in some way connected to ... some faith in, or adherence to God, or some notion of ultimate reality ... the modern Western state is free from this connection. Churches are now separate from political structures ... Religion or its absence is largely a private matter. The political society is seen as that of believers (of all stripes) and non-believers alike.[28]

Secularisation in this sense is compatible, Taylor points out, with large numbers of people in a society continuing to hold religious beliefs, and indeed practising their religion vigorously, albeit in private. Institutional and structural secularisation is different, however, from a second, individual manifestation of secularisation, in which the vast preponderance of the country's citizens are no longer *personally* religious. Thus, as many have observed, the United States is a country where religion is constitutionally disestablished, yet religious belief and practice appear to be thriving; whereas in the countries of Western Europe (many of which retain established churches or provide direct state funding for the incumbent traditional religious bodies), religious practice has declined to near terminal levels, except of course in the case of migrant groups, and especially among the Islamic communities of Europe.

---

[28]   C. Taylor, *A Secular Age* (Cambridge MA, 2007), p. 1.

202   *The Shari'a*

But Talal Asad strikes a cautionary note in this regard:

> 'the secular' should not be thought of as the space in which real human life gradually emancipates itself from the controlling power of 'religion' and thus achieves the latter's relocation. It is this assumption that allows us to think of religion as 'infecting' the secular domain or as replicating within it the structure of theological concepts ... Secularism doesn't simply insist that religious practice and belief be confined to a space where they cannot threaten political stability or the liberties of 'free-thinking' citizens. Secularism builds on a particular conception of the world.[29]

The prevailing secularisation discourse makes the issue of the accommodation of the shari'a in western democracies especially controversial and problematic. For Berman, the progressive secularisation of the West has precipitated a far-reaching sense of crisis – encompassing its legal institutions, procedures, values, concepts, rules and ways of legal thought – in which the idea of the western legal tradition is challenged. In part, this is due to forces within the West itself, its ascendant political motifs of secularism, liberalism and individualism, but it is also in part a consequence of the West's confrontation with non-western civilisations, theologies and philosophies.

When considered in this context, the controversy over the Archbishop of Canterbury's proposal that the shari'a should be accommodated in the United Kingdom not only resulted because of disparate views about the nature and attractiveness of the shari'a but also exposed simmering unease about the identity of the West itself, especially given its mixed inheritance of humanistic, religious and postmodern elements.[30] In France, for example, it manifests itself in the Gallic doctrine of *laïcité*, whereas in Canada the debate about the shari'a pivots on the commitment to non-discrimination and gender equality. In both countries, however, as in other western democracies, there is a felt tension, not clearly resolved, between various secular principles (non-establishment of religion, governmental neutrality, equality standards and human rights) and the problem of accommodating the diverse religious beliefs and practices of the resident population, both established and newly arrived. Further, the accommodation

---

[29]   T. Asad, *Formations of the Secular: Christianity, Islam, Modernity* (Stanford, CA, 2003), p. 191.
[30]   Archbishop Rowan Williams, 'Civil and Religious Law in England: A Religious Perspective', Appendix I in Ahdar and Aroney, *Shari'a in the West*.

The Shari'a in the Western Landscape   203

exercise is rendered that much more fraught when those who seek
to be acknowledged are immigrants of a different race from that of
the domestic citizenry, for then policy-makers have to contend with
certain persistent xenophobic voices that seize their opportunity to
be heard.

Western liberalism is supposed to offer a way in which peoples
of different religious commitments and worldviews are able to
live together, at least through some pragmatic *modus vivendi* – if
not, as Rawls hoped for, on the basis of some more principled
and enduring 'overlapping consensus'. However, as the mixed and
ambiguous responses to the shari'a that have emerged so far suggest,
there is reason to ponder whether western secularist statecraft has
the resources to accommodate Islam without assimilating it into
irreducibly western and derivatively Christian thought-forms, just
as there is reason to wonder whether Muslims can find within their
religious tradition the resources to accommodate themselves to
western traditions and forms of life without continuing to interpret
'the West' in a confined binary fashion, as ultimately either the *dar
al-harb* (the domain of war) or the *dar al-Islam* (the domain of Islam).
The accommodation of the shari'a in the West would seem to be a
litmus test of whether anything more than a *modus vivendi* between
these two forms of life is possible.

A Slice of Demography

Islam's global adherents number some 1.6 billion and can be found on
every continent. Figure 11.1 illustrates the territorial spread. Within the
West, Islam is growing. Figures 11.2–11.4 depict the number of Muslims
in western nations and the present proportions of the total population
they represent.[31]

---

[31] The figures are taken from the CIA World Factbook, *An Analysis of the
World Muslim Population by Country/Region* (2009): accessible at http://www.
factbook.net/muslim_pop.php. For updated figures (based on 2010 estimates),
see the Pew Research Center, 'Muslim Population by Country', 27 January 2011:
accessible at http://www.pewforum.org/2011/01/27/table-muslim-population-
by-country/. According to the Pew research, the percentage of Muslims in, for
example, the United Kingdom is 4.8 per cent, in France it is 7.5 per cent, in the
Netherlands it is 6.0 per cent and in Germany it is 5.8 per cent.

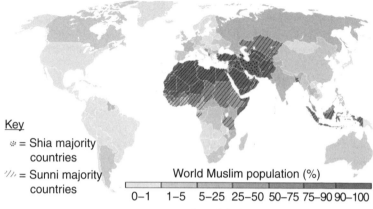

Figure 11.1 Islam globally.
Source: Pew Forum on Religion and Public Life (2009).

Figure 11.2: Muslims in Europe.
Source: Ahdar and Aroney.

Figure 11.3: Muslims in North America.
Source: Ahdar and Aroney.

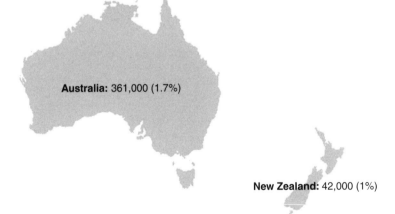

Figure 11.4: Muslims in Oceania.
Source: Ahdar and Aroney.

Islam, Islamism and Reform Islam

Islam and *Islamism* are not to be confused. Islam, as a religion, is distinct from Islamism and the various near-synonymous expressions, such as radical Islam, political Islam, puritanical Islam and Islamo-fascism. Islamism is a political philosophy and programme with varied means to achieve broadly the same ends. There are peaceful, institutional Islamists who seek to establish *nizam Islami* (an Islamic order) based on the shari'a through democratic and electoral means. And there are Islamists who wage jihad, in the sense of *qital* or 'violence', in order to bring about the same end. One of the more visible faces of Islam in Britain is Islam for the United Kingdom, a group that organised a march in London in October 2009 (later cancelled in the wake of strident counter-protests) calling for the full implementation of the shari'a.[32] While the objective of the organisation is 'to propagate the supreme Islamic ideology within the United Kingdom as a divine alternative to man-made law' – that is, *Izhaar ad Deen* (Domination of Islam worldwide)' – the group expressly disavows the violation of the life or property of UK residents, which locates it within the peaceful Islamist camp.

While these distinctions can be made, there can be no denying that Islamism is based on Islam. Islamism may or may not be authentic (in the sense of being a wholly sincere, coherent and accurate interpretation of Islam), but it is an interpretation of the faith and is rooted in it. 'Islam is a religion of peace', cry some, while others are equally vociferous in asserting the opposite.

---

[32] A. Jamieson, '"Muslims Want *Shari'a* Law in Britain" Claim', *Daily Telegraph*, 15 October 2009. See the *Islam for the UK* website, accessible at http://www. islam4uk.com/about-us. Groups opposing Islam for the United Kingdom, such as the Islamic Society of Britain, welcomed the cancellation: 'Democratic Muslims Pleased as *Shar'ia* Demo is Called Off', *Daily Religious.com*: accessible at http://www.dailyreligious.com/?p=23798.

A related theme concerns the so-called clash-of-civilisations thesis. The phrase is so firmly embedded that we forget its very recent coinage. Samuel Huntington's original 1993 article bore a question mark, which in our view remains apt.[33] To recap, Huntington's thesis posited emergent global fault lines as conflicts between civilisations instead of the political and ideological boundaries and flashpoints of the Cold War. He saw the principal clash as that between the West and a grand alliance of Islamic and Confucian civilisations. Events after 11 September 2001 have focused more on the Islamic half of the late Harvard professor's western nemesis. Criticism can of course be made that the real clash was something entirely different. For our purposes, the main attack has been that Huntington, along with Bernard-Henri Lévy, George Weigel and others, succumbed to an essentialist understanding of Islam. For broad-brush predictions of civilisational conflict to be postulated, Islam and Muslims must have a unity of mind and purpose, and a cohesive shared core. For critics, this sort of reductionism is inaccurate and fuels the very conflict it seeks to avert.[34]

Discussion of Islamism, clash of civilisations and so forth brings into focus the role of the ordinary, moderate Muslim. Like the vast majority of people of whatever faith, the predominant focus of the typical Muslim is not political. Rather, theirs is the perennial mundane task of earning a livelihood, paying bills, providing for the needs of their family and, quite simply, minding their own business. Moderate Muslims, by definition, do not subscribe to Islamism; arguably, they are its most frequent and numerous victims.

On both sides, if sides there must be, mutual understanding is required. Gross injustices have been perpetrated by (and against) Muslims, Christians and secularists alike, and those who have suffered most find it difficult to forget. But beyond the injustices and underlying the mutual suspicions are theological and philosophical differences that need to be understood, especially when we consider issues such as the possible accommodation of the shari'a within western legal systems.

---

[33] S. Huntington, 'The Clash of Civilizations?', *Foreign Affairs* (Summer 1993), p. 22. His book version, *The Clash of Civilizations and the Remaking of the World Order* (New York, 1996), omits the question mark.

[34] Huntington's *Clash of Civilizations* 'From an academic standpoint is a shoddy performance', castigates one critic: A. Ahmad, 'Islam, Islamisms and the West', *Socialist Register* 44(1) (2008), p. 20. His 1993 'clash' thesis is found wanting both empirically and theoretically according to another: R. Mottahedeh, 'The Clash of Civilizations: An Islamicist's Critique', *Harvard Middle Eastern and Islamic Review*, 2 (1995), p. 1.

208   *The Shari'a*

To begin with, it is important for liberal secularists in the West to appreciate that many more Muslims feel a continuing link with God. As Wael Hallaq points out,

> The idea of giving to Caesar what is Caesar's and to God what is God's does not wash in the Muslim world-view, for Caesar is only a man, and men, being equal, cannot command obedience to each other. Obedience therefore must be to a supreme entity, one that is eternal, omnipotent, and omniscient.[35]

For many committed Muslims, this link shapes attitudes to law and politics. Another important characteristic of Islamic and especially Sunni jurisprudence is that it has historically been administered by a body of jurists that is generally independent of state regulation. In contrast to Roman and European civil law, which is primarily legislative in character, and unlike English common law, which is essentially judicial in origin, Islamic law is a law of jurists and legal scholars. Moreover, Islamic jurisprudence offers a comprehensive framework for the whole of life: no area of human endeavour is untouched by the shari'a as a vision of the good life.

As in the medieval and modern West, there is a strong insistence within traditional Islam on the rule of law: according to classical and medieval Islamic thought, all political authorities are bound by the law and responsible to administer it. Although many Muslim jurists were customarily appointed to administrative and judicial positions, the body of law that they studied and expounded on operated very largely outside state influence and provided a kind of counter-balance to it. Yet there was less of the separation of life into different spheres governed by distinct jurisdictions that emerged in medieval Christendom; the pluralism in the Islamic tradition lay in the variety of schools of interpretation and the multiplicity of states in which the shari'a was applied. Western colonisation of the Islamic world during the 19th and early 20th centuries led to the creation of sovereign nation-states and the enactment of positive legal codes embodying secular legal values. These codes, on the model of 19th-century legal positivism, displaced the Islamic jurists and their shari'a.

In this context, in the last century or so, Muslim reformers have sought, through various techniques of Qur'anic interpretation and jurisprudential logic, to carve out a middle way between literalism

---

[35] Wael Hallaq, "'Muslim Rage" and Islamic Law', *Hastings Law Journal*, 54 (2003), pp. 1705–1719.

The Shari'a in the Western Landscape 209

and secularist modernism. It seems to us to be of great significance that these projects are not simply juristic or philosophical, but also theological in character. Reformists characteristically seek to identify the spirit, as distinct from the letter, of the law, thus avoiding the literalism of the traditional schools. But such reformism is premised on a rejection of the fundamental principle of Ash'arite theology, which asserted that human reason is independently incapable of distinguishing between right and wrong, and of discerning the *ratio legis* of the shari'a. On the contrary, the reformists follow the lead of pioneers such as Muhammad Abduh (1849–1905), who maintained that there is an inherent harmony between the deliverances of sound reason and the dictates of divine revelation: if there appears to be a contradiction, it is because one or the other has been misunderstood. Such a move is remarkably reminiscent of the synthesis of reason and revelation inaugurated in profoundly influential terms by Thomas Aquinas in 13th-century Europe.

Liberal Democracies and the Shari'a: The Broad Policy Options

Any comprehensive philosophy or ideology must deal with those who oppose its basic tenets. Liberalism is no exception. Like medieval Christianity, contemporary liberal democracy will defend itself when its fundamental premises or major institutions are directly challenged. Liberalism has, necessarily, an in-built antipathy to religions that oppose its teachings about truth, goodness and meaning.

A landmark case of direct relevance here is the unanimous 2003 decision of 17 judges of the European Court of Human Rights in *Refah Partisi (No 2) v Turkey*.[36] Refah Partisi (the Welfare Party) was the largest political party in Turkey's parliament, and in a coalition government, when in January 1998 it was dissolved and its assets confiscated. The Constitutional Court of Turkey at first justified this action on the grounds that the party was a 'centre of activities contrary to the principle of secularism'. This decision was in turn upheld by the European Court of Human Rights in Strasbourg on 31 July 2001, and reaffirmed by the Grand Chamber of that court on 13 February 2003. The Strasbourg court's grounds for upholding such drastic action were that the Welfare Party had been shown to advocate and intend the introduction of the shari'a, either for everyone or as part of a plural

---

[36]   (2003) 37 EHRR, 1.

210 *The Shariʿa*

system of laws for citizens of different faiths, and that its leaders' statements about jihad did not clearly rule out a resort to force to achieve its aims. Significantly, the court observed that even in the absence of threats of force, both the shariʿa and religiously based legal systems were in themselves inherently incompatible with the European Convention on Human Rights, and the conceptions of democracy and the rule of law that it enshrines. Indeed, the court invoked the principle of militant democracy in the face of 'political movements which sought to destroy it'.[37]

There are others, however, also working within the framework of liberal democratic politics, who do not share that strident response to the recognition of the shariʿa. In its fullest variant, the accommodationist stance sees a parallel system of justice operating alongside existing state law. More qualified accommodations (e.g. that advocated by Archbishop Rowan Williams) involve certain safeguards to the admission and enforcement of the shariʿa, including restrictions on its jurisdiction, maintenance of its entirely voluntary nature, and subordination of religious rules and judgments to human rights norms. Thus, for example, some suggest that the shariʿa should govern certain areas of law only, most commonly only civil law, family and financial affairs, and not criminal law. In addition, some insist that the shariʿa must not be imposed on people, especially the vulnerable or oppressed (including women). Underlying these specific policy responses to the shariʿa are different attitudes to the state's treatment of minorities, and their religious and cultural needs.

Within the framework of liberal-democratic political thought, the various views can be spread along a continuum. At one end is assimilation. In its pure form, assimilation allows no exceptions at all for minorities. The law is the law and, 'when in Rome, do as the Romans do'. Migrants and their offspring, as well as indigenous peoples, are to blend into the dominant culture. When believers of a particular religion find themselves in conflict with the general law, then it is they, and not the state, who must yield. And if they will not, or cannot, the believers will have to face the consequences – fines, arrest, imprisonment, deregistration and so on.

In the West, the long-standing policy of assimilation has been replaced by multiculturalism as the preferred governmental stance towards minorities and migrants. Multiculturalism has come under sustained critique of late, but this debate cannot be pursued in depth here. The point of the present concern is that self-consciously multicultural societies seek to make due allowance for difference. A liberal and tolerant state on this view

---

[37] *Refah Partisi (No 1) v Turkey* (2002) 35 EHRR, p. 3.

The Shari'a in the Western Landscape 211

recognises religious pluralism and the genuine call of conscience by making *reasonable* accommodation of cultural and religious minorities *within* the framework of a comprehensive system of law. But note the emphasised words. It is not accommodation at all costs but only an allowance for what is due and reasonable. What is reasonable is for the powers that be to determine, given all the usual exigencies and countervailing concerns such as public health, safety, order and the rights of others. Further, accommodation is located firmly within the existing legal framework of constitutional norms. It is seen as a concession conferred from the single overarching law for all citizens, and not an acknowledgment of a rival legal order for some citizens on the basis of their faith.

Yet accommodation is an elastic notion. It may take two broad forms: (a) exemptions from the general law; and (b) enforcement of transactions governed by religious norms.[38] Exemptions from the law of the land are familiar and usually uncontroversial: Sikh motorcycle riders are permitted not to wear crash helmets and devout doctors may be excused from having to perform or counsel abortions. Sometimes the exemptions are more contentious, however, and one thinks here of the sacramental use of narcotics, such as marijuana for Rastafarians, or peyote for Native American tribes.

What the former Archbishop of Canterbury meant in his lecture when he referred to 'supplementary jurisdictions' was the recognition and enforcement of transactions by religious tribunals according to religious norms, the second form of accommodation noted above. In simple terms, he envisioned tribunals with limited powers being able to resolve certain kinds of dispute according to their own religious law, and the state cooperating by enforcing those judgments. However, the existing UK arbitration law, the Arbitration Act 1996, already embraces religious tribunals within its framework. Hence the proposal was either a statement of the obvious or was about significantly more than just affirming the rights of individual believers to agree to submit their disputes to the arbitration of religious courts. Indeed, Williams referred explicitly to 'something like a delegation of certain legal functions to the religious courts of a community', which suggests a kind of permanent recognition of a system of religious courts with a form of presumptive jurisdiction over all those identified with that religion. But at the same time, he proposed this subject to the bedrock condition that any religious court process must have in-built safeguards, such as the right of appeal to the regular civil courts, and be subject to continual

---

[38] See J. Waldron, 'Questions About the Reasonable Accommodation of Minorities', in Ahdar and Aroney, *Shari'a in the West*, Chapter 7.

212   *The Shari'a*

monitoring by the state in order to ensure that the rights and liberties of vulnerable individuals are protected.

Such an arrangement, if secured on these grounds, does not quite amount to a comprehensive regime of devolution and autonomy, or what the Archbishop of Canterbury referred to (and expressly refused to support) as parallel jurisdictions. Still, it might over time come close. Notably, Williams considered the recognition of religious tribunals to be properly understood as a matter of communal rights and public legitimacy. He rejected the idea that the state be conceived as a sovereign order which confers on other, subordinate orders merely the right to exist. Rather, he suggested that the ultimate grounds of such accommodation ought to be a commitment to 'human dignity as such', no matter how any particular community might understand itself and its rights.

Conceiving the question of the accommodation of shari'a courts in this way, however, runs the serious risk of oversimplification and a failure to grapple with the much stronger claims that may be made. This involves a kind of autonomous self-government.[39] Autonomy of this kind is a third level of accommodation. Within this stronger model, religious courts are in no sense subordinate or subject to review by the ordinary civil courts. Under such a regime, a wider range of possibilities emerges, which could include the imposition of punishments for violations of distinctly religious norms and rules (e.g. fines, corporal and even capital punishment for blasphemy, apostasy and adultery); or punishments that are more severe than those in the general law for certain crimes (e.g. amputation for theft).

Conclusion

The existence of the shari'a within the West is, for many, a confronting issue – perhaps a litmus test of the capacity of western liberal-democratic states to accommodate religious difference. This is because the shari'a is much more than a matter of personal piety and private religious practice. It is, at its core, a vision of the good of life, expressed culturally and collectively, in private and in public. For many it regulates all manner of domains generally assumed in western societies to be differentiated and compartmentalised: marriage and family life, personal hygiene and etiquette, food and diet, trade and finance, taxation, crime

---

[39]   See J.-F. Gaudreault-Desbiens, 'Religious Courts' Recognition Claims: Two Qualitatively Distinct Narratives', in Ahdar and Aroney, *Shari'a in the West*, Chapter 4.

and war. The shari'a is a type of law, *but not the kind of law that most westerners are familiar with*. It is neither the positive law of the state, nor a kind of natural law that can be fully discerned by human reason. For many devout Muslims, it is a law that stands loftily paramount over the asserted authority of all other laws. Western democracies have learnt to accommodate peoples of many different religious and cultural backgrounds in their societies, but this has generally occurred in a manner that has preserved the supremacy of the state and its law. The question of the accommodation of the shari'a within western systems is controversial precisely because it proposes a religious accommodation of a deeper and more far-reaching kind.

Further Reading

Ahdar, Rex and Nicholas Aroney, ed. *Shari'a in the West*. Oxford, 2010.

Amanat, Abbas and Frank Griffel, ed. *Shari'a: Islamic Law in the Contemporary Context*. Stanford, CA, 2007.

An-Na'im, Abdullahi A., *Islam and the Secular State: Negotiating the Future of Shari'a*. Cambridge, MA, 2008.

Asad, Talal. *Formations of the Secular: Christianity, Islam, Modernity*. Stanford, CA, 2003.

Emon, Anver. 'Conceiving Islamic Law in a Pluralist Society: History, Politics and Multicultural Jurisprudence', *Singapore Journal of Legal Studies* (December 2006), p. 331.

Hallaq, Wael. '"Muslim Rage" and Islamic Law', *Hastings Law Journal*, 54 (2003), pp. 1705–1719.

Hallaq, Wael. *The Origins and Evolution of Islamic Law*. Cambridge, 2005.

Ikuenobe, P. 'Diverse Religious Practices and the Limits of Liberal Tolerance', in *Democracy and Religion: Free Exercise and Diverse Visions* D. Odell-Scott, ed., p. 309. Kent, OH, 2004.

March, Andrew. *Islam and Liberal Citizenship: The Search for an Overlapping Consensus*. Oxford, 2009.

Ramadan, Tariq. *Radical Reform: Islamic Ethics and Liberation*. Oxford, 2009.

Roy, Olivier. *Secularism Confronts Islam*, trans. G. Holoch. New York, 2007.

12

Secularism and the Shari'a:
Lessons from an Ontario Debate

Jennifer A. Selby

'There will be no sharia law in Ontario. There will be no religious arbitration in Ontario.

There will be one law for all Ontarians.'
Statement by the Premier of Ontario (11 September 2005)[1]

On 8 September 2005, three days before this announcement, several hundred people gathered at the usually quiet Canadian embassy in Paris, motivated by concern that the Canadian provincial government of Ontario endorsed the use of so-called 'Shari'a law' in private family law arbitration. The boisterous group on avenue Montaigne included more than 20 pro-secular and feminist groups who had prepared hundreds of letters and petitions for the Canadian ambassador. In the midst of their cheers, one of the speakers reminded the crowd that 'Sharia in Canada is not only a Canadian affair!'[2] These anti-faith-based arbitration (FBA) positions in Paris shed light on secular norms galvanised by the

---

[1] C. Freeze and K. Howlett, 'Mcguinty Government Rules out Use of Sharia Law,' *The Globe and Mail*, 12 September 2005: accessible at http://www.theglobeandmail.com/news/national/mcguinty-government-rules-out-use-of-sharia-law/article18247682/.

[2] Writer and atheist activist Jocelyn Bézecourt also traced a possibility for FBA in France, through what he calls the 'Sarkozy [then-prime minister], UOIF [Union of Islamic Organisations of France] and European Fatwa Council-stream'. This statement is the sole instance I have located where FBA is considered feasible in France by a public figure. Transcripts of speeches given at the embassy are available online (ReSPUBLICA, 'Refuser l'Offensive Islamiste,' *Le journal de la gauche républicaine, laïque, écologique et sociale* 392 (2005): accessible at https://fr.groups.yahoo.com/neo/groups/respublica/conversations/topics/403).

216   *The Shari'a*

Ontario debate. From a 2003 proclamation by the Islamic Institute of Civil Justice (IICJ) that it would open 'shari'a courts' in the province, to the supposed banning of FBA in 2006, the propriety of binding religiously based family law arbitration was of interest to many outside Ontario, especially in Europe where 'shari'a' is increasingly heard in often Islamophobic discussions about the public presence of Islam. On 11 September 2005, after a number of similar international protests, in an effort to quell anxiety and restore so-called normality, the Premier of Ontario announced that FBA in alternative dispute resolution (ADR) would be outlawed in favour of 'one law for all Ontarians'. The statement referred to substituting existing law that allowed for binding FBA with a supposedly secular-only model.[3] This chapter considers the 'normality' constructed in contrast to 'shari'a law'. I examine the role played by shari'a law as a foil for the secular.

In particular, in order to undertake this analysis I draw on two contexts: first, the secular and feminist organisations' anti-FBA protest in Paris in 2005, many of whom were present at the embassy; and, second, a subsequent Ontario controversy on the funding of religious schools. The first case is useful in comparing the logic that drives the delineations of the 'secular'. The latter, in 2007, exemplifies the continued parameters and privileges accorded by this normality in Ontario. These moments underpin three arguments about secularism in Ontario: first, its non-neutral Christian biases; second, despite assumptions of their clear separation, the utility of blurred distinctions between private and public spheres, typically referenced in considering the 'secular'; and third, a privileging of an 'anti-visible religion' feminist politics. In sum, this examination calls into question the assurance of neutrality in 'one law for all' with the end of FBA.

Secularism's Partiality

Ontario's so-called shari'a debate brought to light variances in the marking out of secularism. Does it protect a freedom *for*, *of* or *from* religion in the public sphere? Scholars have argued that secularism is

---

[3]   An amendment in February 2006 (the Family Statute Law Amendment Act) legally ended FBA in Ontario. However, informal mediation by imams has always been more common in Ontario. Further, religion can continue to inform an arbitrator's rulings so long as the texts of final rulings use the language of Canadian law.

Secularism and the Shariʿa 217

often presumed to separate, situate and regulate 'the religious' or the private spaces of morality from domains considered public or political.[4] It should be clear that, in theory and practice, secularism is always tethered to religion. Despite studies that convincingly argue that its meaning and application are far from uniform, significant historical factors have conditioned how secularism is expressed in relation to mainstream Christianity.[5] For the philosopher Marcel Gauchet, the secular can also refer to an official state political position of neutrality vis-à-vis religious beliefs and practices, or to an 'exit from religion', which keeps religion as referent while situating it outside the shared political sphere. Clearly, deeming one person and/or space as secular and another as religious is not neutral assignation. Talal Asad reminds us of a common assumption, including among theorists of secularism, that there is an *unconscious* motive in religious acts.[6] Again, in these variations, the secular consistently defines and manages religion.

Historically, Ontario has had a majority-Christian population, but today its urban population is among the world's most religiously and ethnically diverse. Jewish- and Orthodox-Christian-based legally binding FBA existed under the radar in Ontario for 12 years without any fanfare. In contrast, the public-relations-poor announcement in late 2003 by the IICJ that it would set up arbitration services (as was its legal right) to conduct similar ADR caused international outcry. Again, the Jewish Beit Din and the cross-Canada Ismaili Conciliation and Arbitration board had used faith-based dispute resolution without public controversy, whereas the IICJ's announcement initiated vociferous debate. A six-month-long commission conducted a formal review of the use of arbitration and accepted submissions from individuals and organisations. Its author, the former attorney general, Marion Boyd, concluded in her 191-page report that binding religious arbitration of family law issues based on 'Islamic legal principles'

---

[4] See Michael Walzer, 'Liberalism and the Art of Separation,' *Political Theory* 12 (1984), pp. 315–330; José Casanova, *Public Religions in the Modern World* (Chicago, IL, 1994); Jeff Weintraub, 'The Theory and Politics of the Public/ Private Distinction,' in J. Weintraub and K. Kumar, ed., *Public and Private in Thought and Practice: Perspectives on a Grand Dichotomy* (Chicago, IL, 1997), pp. 1–42.

[5] See Rajeev Bhargava, 'What is Secularism For?' in R. Bhargava, ed., *Secularism and Its Critics* (Delhi, 1998), pp. 486–542; G. Levy and T. Modood, ed., *Secularism, Religion and Multicultural Citizenship* (Cambridge, 2009).

[6] Talal Asad, *Formations of the Secular: Christianity, Islam, and Modernity* (Stanford, CA, 2003), p. 11.

was permissible, a conclusion later set aside following international attention, as illustrated in Paris.[7]

The perceived continued problem with the IICJ's directive that 'good Muslims' use its FBA made evident a 'Christo-secular' bias, a term I introduce that parallels the French historian Jean Baubérot's characterisation of *laïcité* (French secularism) in contemporary France as *catholaïcité* (or 'catho-secularism').[8] Baubérot's coinage suggests that the separation of church and state is modelled on Christian theological notions of religion and, in the case of France, works best for French Catholics. Indeed, the category of secular remains imbued with Christian references, beginning etymologically, with the categorisation of this-worldly time and other-worldly sacred moments sanctioned by a Christian God.[9] At the time of writing, 66 per cent of Ontarians are Christian, which might further contribute to a privileging of Christian versions of religion in the public sphere.

Let us turn to a concrete example from the same Canadian province. One might have the impression that the 'one law for all' outcome of the shari'a debate ensured a newfound separation of religion and politics in its public policy. A 2007 controversy known as the 'One School' debate that followed the shari'a debate demonstrates the provincial government's continued lack of uniformity with regard to religious neutrality. At issue in this later case was the public funding of Catholic schools in Ontario. To be clear, other private religious denominational schools do not receive public money. The province discussed this question in October 2007 during provincial elections. Public funding for private Catholic schools in Ontario was defended by the ruling provincial Liberal Party with reference to the Constitutional Act of 1867, in which Section 93 enshrined Catholic schools' rights before Confederation as both historic and exceptional. Separate Roman Catholic publicly funded schools have thus existed since the 19th century. The then Conservative Party of Ontario leader John Tory focused his election platform on the public funding of private religious schools, suggesting that the province should extend its financial support of private Catholic schools to all other religious denominations, including Muslims, Jews and Hindus.

---

[7]   M. Boyd, 'Dispute Resolution in Family Law: Protecting Choice, Promoting Inclusion', *Ministry of the Attorney General* (2004), p. 133: accessible at www. attorneygeneral.jus.gov.on.ca/english/about/pubs/boyd/fullreport.pdf.

[8]   Jean Baubérot, 'Editorial', *Libération* 15 (December 2003), p. 39.

[9]   See, for example, Charles Taylor, 'Modes of Secularism', in Rajeev Bhargava, ed., *Secularism and Its Critics* (Delhi, 1998), pp. 119–136.

Secularism and the Shari'a 219

The opposition leader was not alone in his critique. This continued privileging of Catholic schools in the province has been ruled as contrary to international legal standards. In 1999 and 2005, the United Nations Human Rights Committee officially censured Ontario for violating equality rights by virtue of religious discrimination in the province's school system. Some critics have shown that the current system may contravene the federal Charter of Rights and Freedoms.[10] However, unlike the debate on religiously based family law arbitration two years earlier, discussions about extending funding to non-Christian schools did not garner interest in the international press. No one appeared outside the Canadian embassy in Paris to protest that non-Christian children were not accorded the same rights as their Catholic counterparts, or to demand that their funding be retracted.

The Ontario premier at the time, Dalton McGuinty, and his majority Liberal Party, which was against the proposed change to fund publicly all religious schools, noted that the publicly funded education system 'invite[s] children of all backgrounds and faiths, economic circumstances to … learn together'.[11] Indeed, McGuinty argued that funding Muslim, Sikh or Hindu schools might counter agreed democratic ideals and disintegrate 'secular' society. And it would be costly to extend public funding to all. Perhaps for this reason, the issue did not resonate with many Ontario voters, who mostly felt that the question of school funding was best left alone.[12] There was no discussion of the possible savings of moving to a public-only system, or that such a change would necessitate a constitutional amendment. John Tory ultimately lost his seat, and subsequently the leadership of the party. Many suggest that these losses were the result of this particular issue.

The Ontario government has thus continued with the status quo and funds only public Catholic schools. Despite the aforementioned international condemnation by the United Nations, opinion polls suggest that there was not sustained popular public concern about

---

[10] L. Weinrib, 'Ontario Tories Tout Direct Funding for Faith-Based Schools', *Law Times*, 27 August 2007: accessible at http://www.lawtimesnews.com/200708272829/headline-news/ontario-tories-tout-direct-funding-for-faith-based-schools.

[11] L. Greenberg, 'Faith-Based Schools Idea Backward – McGuinty; Tory's Pledge Seized as an Election Issue', *National Post*, 23 August 2007.

[12] In a conversation about the 2007 debate, one of McGuinty's advisers conceded that while the premier privately acknowledged that the current system was unfair, he knew he would not have won the election with such a contested issue. The adviser explained: 'McGuinty knew he couldn't touch that whole issue. It's like political suicide' (telephone interview with the author, 6 July 2008).

the inequality of the current funding model. The continuing Christo-secular bias evident in the status quo funding structure can be explained in part by the majority-Christian population, but also by the theological underpinnings of the secular itself. The 'One School' debate exemplifies how the preservation of religious neutrality or equality within public policy in Ontario is selective, calling into question the status quo's impartiality. A 'one law' approach introduced to conclude the 'shari'a debate' could have proposed to abolish funding Catholic schools – politically disadvantageous for the Liberals, and perhaps difficult given that it would require consensus to amend the constitution – or, like John Tory's proposal, might have extended support to all religious schools. Neither emerged as a viable option. Unlike the conclusion of the debate where McGuinty announced that 'one law' ensured 'our common ground', dismantling Christian privilege in the current system was not on the political agenda.

Shifting Private–Public Distinctions

Neutrality was not the only secularist norm articulated during the Ontario shari'a debate. The controversy also underscored the blurred separation of the 'private' spaces of morality and belief from 'public' political spaces. Public and private spaces reflect a common organisation in western societies, following the forcible withdrawal of religion from modern states and economies. Within these two spheres, citizens can be religious in the private sphere so long as they respect publicly established forms, ceremonies and laws; religion is putatively extricated from the shared public domain. This arrangement has been critiqued, including by some feminists, in consideration of how the privatisation of domestic sphere happenings problematically 'shield[s domestic] abuse and domination from political scrutiny and legal redress'.[13] Here again, determinations of what is private and what is public are not neutral. Their indeterminacy is what grants power to those who establish their contours.

The public/private binary is thus based on the supposition that the political sphere works best when a certain formulation of religion is kept outside. In this debate, fears of undesired private religiosity invading the public realm centred on concerns for women's rights in Islam and in Islamic law (understood in the public debate as the shari'a when fiqh would be more accurate). Most of the provincial and international

---

[13] Weintraub, 'Theory and Politics,' p. 29.

Secularism and the Shariʿa   221

public debate, as we saw in Paris in September 2005, centred on accommodating ethnic and religiocultural diversity in the context of a commitment to women's equality. In Ontario, critics of the IICJ, such as the Canadian Council of Muslim Women, expressed concern for the agency of newly settled Muslim women and their disempowerment within religiously based alternative dispute-resolution agreements. In this section I suggest that part of the unease with regard to religious law-based arbitration and women's rights is related to this pivoting of public and private realms, which is intrinsic to common articulations of the secular. Public commentators also conflated the legal rights of women and the family (often understood as interests within the public sphere) with the legitimacy of religious practice and belief (focused on the private sphere).

From 1991 to 2005, appointed representatives of religious organisations could tangibly interpret law in legally binding rulings, so that the debate generated a conundrum. On the one hand, granting legal status to decisions about the family by religious leaders within traditions, which have often rationalised a secondary status for women, could doubly marginalise religiously practising women, in a system that replicates existing social inequities. On the other hand, religiously practising women were positioned simplistically as disenfranchised members within civil society and within their religious traditions. No matter which side stepped up to the microphone, because of the sharp relegation of religion to this private sphere, religiously practising women were assumed to be disenfranchised and in need of intervention by the public. Their private Muslimness (especially when rendered publicly visible with a headscarf) was cast as precluding the protection of their rights. Islam was thus positioned as unquestioningly patriarchal and undesired, even in the private sphere. The private/public binary was mobilised to uphold this presumption. The debate reveals the continued relevance of religion in Canadian public life, but with specificities: certain elements of religious law (read: Muslim) were deemed 'too religious' (and thus archaic or anti-woman), while others remained untouched. In short, the secular renders visible, and problematises, certain expressions of religiosity more than others.

Considering the centrality of this positioning of the religious invites us to flip this coin momentarily, to consider a possibility born from this blurring. When 'religious' concerns enter public debate they can also signal a transformative move that pulls apart the public/private binary. Put differently, the always already blurred distinction of private/public in this particular debate makes clear that their boundaries are not so discrete, nor is the public sphere ever devoid of so-called religious sensibilities. José Casanova's claim for the continued evidence of the 'de-privatization' of religious traditions in western contexts affirms this point.[14] Casanova argues that while secularisation in the West has entailed three elements – differentiation of tasks historically taken on by the church (now taken up by the state and non-governmental organisations), the decline of religious beliefs and practices, and the marginalisation and privatisation of religion – it nevertheless can also be described by what he calls 'de-privatization'. This refers to religion's return from the private sphere to the public arena. For Casanova, this move can take place through demands for the recognition of religion, as in the case of FBA and public funding for religious education, and through religiously informed political lobbying. In other words, when the slippage between boundaries is accepted as part of the nature of the secular, religiously based claims can be considered as legitimate topics for discussion in the public political sphere. In re-emerging in the public sphere, religiously based lobbying arguably allows for a differing perspective, creating a more dynamic and more versatile public debate, in this case in shedding light on secular norms.

Potential benefits become evident when we look to how the 'de-privatization' of religion played out in the Ontario debate. For Wahida Valiente, then-vice president of the Canadian Islamic Congress, there was a missed opportunity to recast 'shari'a', tellingly never adequately defined, in the Canadian sphere and to create better general knowledge of Islam and Islamic law. Moreover, according to the half-dozen imams and Muslim community leaders I interviewed in the Greater Toronto Area (GTA) between January and July 2008, many Muslims in the GTA became politically mobilised in the 'One School' debate on the public funding of Catholic schools. There was a sense of urgency in this lobby that had not emerged initially in the Shari'a debate that signals how mosques are public gathering places where these political questions are increasingly discussed and debated.

The wake of the debate can thus be considered the beginning of a period of deprivatisation, as Muslims in the GTA began engaging in provincial public policy debates emphasising their religiousness. One member of the Islamic Institute of Toronto mosque in Scarborough, Mounir, a Canadian of Pakistani origin working in the provincial

---

[14] José Casanova, *Public Religions in the Modern World* (Chicago, 1994). Jürgen Habermas similarly argues that religious groups, in particular churches and religious organisations, are 'increasingly assuming the role of "communities of interpretation" in the public arena of secular societies': 'Notes on a Post-Secular Society', *signandsight.com*, 18 June 2008: accessible at http://signandsight.com/features/1714.html.

Secularism and the Shari'a   223

legislature, was inspired by the 2007 discussions in the mosque to begin teaching public policy and government courses one evening a week. His aim was to help members, first-generation Canadian Muslims in particular, to navigate the provincial political system to teach them advocacy skills.[15] One of the two-hour courses I attended in May 2008 described the breakdown of municipal politics, and offered useful insider-perspective advice about when were the best moments to affect policy change. Mounir stressed to the six male students in the evening class that advocating change at town hall meetings was too late. An informed citizen must lobby his or her council member prior to the conception of a bill. This political emphasis on Muslim-informed citizenship is significant because it implies a qualified rejection of the modern idea of secularism, which tends to regard religion and religiously informed lobbying outside language used in public, political debates. In the religiously diverse GTA, choosing to frame one's civic engagement in a public political lobby reflects the blurring of public and private identities. Gender dynamics are central to these notions, a point to which I now turn.

Privileging a Specific Feminist Politics

Thus far I have focused on the privileging of Christian perspectives and the private/public category complications highlighted by the shari'a debate, but much of the family law arbitration debate in Ontario was centred on the perceived harm done to women within the Islamic legal system. In September 2005 I was undertaking doctoral ethnographic research on immigration and gender politics among Muslim women of North African origin in a suburb of Paris.[16] At that time I was also

---

[15] A number of studies show that mosque attendance is a predictor of civic engagement. See Amaney Jamal, 'The Political Participation and Engagement of Muslim Americans: Mosque Involvement and Group Consciousness', *American Politics Research* 33(4) (2005), pp. 521–544; Fenella Fleischmann, Borja Martinovic and Magdelena Böhm, 'Mobilising Mosques? The Role of Service Attendance for Political Participation of Turkish and Moroccan Minorities in the Netherlands', *Ethnic and Racial Studies* 39(5) (2015), pp. 746–763.

[16] None of the Muslims with whom I spoke in 2004–2005 in this Paris suburb expressed knowledge of, or concern about, the tensions related to FBA in Ontario. In his comparison of Muslim institutions in France and the United Kingdom relating to so-called shari'a councils, John Bowen shows how there is little possibility of such councils in France because of governmental intolerance of difference on religious grounds, and the relative doctrinal homogeneity of its largely Maghrebi Muslim population: *On British Islam: Religion, Law, and Everyday Practice in Shari'a Councils* (Princeton, NJ, 2016), pp. 6, 230.

conducting research with a French feminist organisation, Femmes Solidaires (Women in Solidarity), which was active in promoting French secularism (*laïcité*) in that neighbourhood and in the French public sphere. Reflecting a primary value in contemporary French public culture, members of this organisation defend secularism as being integral to the feminist movement and to assuring women's rights. In their publicly available documentation and literature, the organisation locates visibly headscarf-wearing Muslim women outside the accepted boundaries of women's rights. They were active in 2005 in demonstrations against the shari'a tribunals in Ontario. In a petition by the group's national president, Sabine Salmon, circulated by members at the aforementioned anti-religiously based family-law arbitration protest at the Canadian embassy, the threat of Islam to secularism and women's rights was made clear. The petition stressed:

> Our experience as an association has shown us the importance of secularism for the respect of women, their rights, and their citizenship ... The Canadian Sharia court must [therefore] be outlawed. (My translation of the document, dated 7 September 2005)

Over the course of this demonstration at the embassy, several speakers referenced the work of Homa Arjomand of the International Campaign against Shar'iah Court in Canada and the No Religious Arbitration coalition, with 80 groups and organisations under its umbrella. Beyond the important legal differences in how religion is governed in France and Canada, for Femmes Solidaires and other French commentators, the possibility of this allowance of religion in the public sphere in Ontario also promotes multiculturalism. This is deemed undesirable in normative French discourse because of its implied promotion of communitarianism (*communautarisme*), wherein the state loses its pre-eminence and the individual is subordinated to an ethnic or religious community.

In the Ontario context, discourses positioning secularism as a guarantor of women's rights gave little space for practising Muslim women in support of religiously based family law arbitration. Katherine Bullock describes how visible Muslim women like herself, who voiced their support for arbitration, were largely absent from the mediatised debate and not granted nuance in the coverage. That a Muslim woman could be both conservative and a feminist was not part of the picture. Analysis of media coverage of different positions in the debates

Secularism and the Shari'a   225

demonstrates an imbalance.[17] Similarly, a comparison of the positions and experiences of two women among the 30 whom I interviewed concerning their engagement in the debate further reflects this point: Homa Arjomand, who regards herself a 'secular Muslim', and 'Amina', a first-generation Somali female university student, who is a 'practising Muslim'. I interviewed Arjomand at a busy food court in Markham, and Amina with a group of six young Somali women following *jumu'ah* (congregational) prayer on a Friday evening at a mosque in Scarborough. Markham and Scarborough are both suburbs in the GTA. Let us turn to how they describe encountering this secular women's rights equation in the debate.

Arjomand, an Iranian-born women's rights activist who migrated to her Toronto suburb in the 1990s, is an outspoken advocate of secularism in Canada. On her website, in media interviews and in our interactions, she asserts that she seeks to preserve democracy by demonstrating that all religiously based law is inappropriate because of the damage it can cause to women. As one of the most vocal critics of the IICJ's proposal, she advocates a human rights culture. Echoing a position made famous by Susan Okin about the perils of multicultural politics for women, Arjomand says she fears that multiculturalist perspectives and ethnocultural group rights give too much power to cultural difference in the public domain. In an interview in January 2008, she remained pleased with the outcome of the debate. Yet she was fearful about the safety of Muslim women under non-legally binding religious mediation, and about the advancement of political Islam in Canada. With regard to her experiences in Iran, she feels that all versions of Islam in the public sphere are dangerous:

> To me they [women who supported FBA] are trying to save political Islam. They don't know the damage they are causing in their own country, with their own people … I'm seeing Canada as the most vulnerable country. Because of this multiculturalism.

---

[17] See Natasha Bakht, 'Family Arbitration Using Shariah Law: Examining Ontario's Arbitration Act and Its Impact on Women', *Muslim World Journal of Human Rights* 1(1) (2004), pp. 1–24, and Katherine Bullock, '"The Muslims Have Ruined Our Party:" A Case Study of Ontario Media Portrayals of Supporters of Faith-Based Arbitration', in A.C. Korteweg and J.A. Selby, ed., *Debating Sharia: Islam, Gender Politics and Family Law Arbitration* (Toronto, 2012), pp. 257–276; A.C. Korteweg, 'The Sharia Debate in Ontario: Gender, Islam, and Representations of Muslim Women's Agency', *Gender & Society*, 22 (2008), pp. 434–454.

226   *The Shariʿa*

This policy of multiculturalism and government help everyone ignore [the dangers of] what's happening around them.[18]

Arjomand garnered much attention as *the* voice for Muslim women in the debate. She was quoted in the anti-FBA protest in Paris. However, she did have less visible critics. A group of young Somali women who arrived in Scarborough as child refugees in the 1990s were upset by the attention given to Arjomand as *the* Muslim woman, when she had said elsewhere that she is an atheist. In a round-table interview with them in the women's section of their mosque, one of these first-generation women, Amina, 23 years old, observed:

> When the whole debate erupted we had never heard of it [binding arbitration] before and then suddenly people were wondering what we thought about the whole thing. When we saw her [Arjomand] on TV saying things about how Muslim women are repressed by their husbands and don't have their own perspectives, it was really insulting [other young women nod in agreement]. Ok, maybe that's true in Iran, but she can't just take her personal experience and say it's true for all of us. I'm a first-generation immigrant too, and it's an insult. Ok yeah, get rid of religious law because Canada is secular, but don't say it's to protect me from myself.[19]

Amina and her friends do not disagree with the outcome of the debate but they find Arjomand's rationale paternalistic and her vision of the extraction of Islam as a guarantor of gender equality inappropriate. Their experience of Islam and gender differs for many reasons, including their different socioreligious experiences. These young women are well aware of how their hijabs render them visibly religious, but they see the secular as protecting their right of expression, not as precluding it. The agency of covered women is increasingly debated in Ontario, in schools, citizenship ceremonies and courtrooms.[20]

---

[18] Interview, 22 January 2008.

[19] Interview, 18 January 2008.

[20] In 2008 an Ontario woman sought to testify in a preliminary inquiry in a childhood sexual assault case in a courtroom wearing a niqab. The accused claimed that their right to cross-examine her would be unfairly restricted if her face were partially covered. The Supreme Court of Canada ultimately settled the 'N.S.' case (so called to protect the niqab-wearing woman's anonymity) in 2012. A split decision held that courts should make determinations on the niqab on a case-by-case basis, considering the sincerity of the religious belief, trial fairness and whether alternative accommodations are available (R. v N.S., 2012 SCC 72).

Secularism and the Shari'a 227

In 2015, as his popularity waned before a federal election, Canada's then-prime minister, Stephen Harper, asked: 'Why would Canadians, contrary to our own values, embrace a practice [the niqab] that is not transparent, that is not open and frankly is rooted in a culture that is anti-women?'[21] Although Harper lost the election, pollsters noted the popularity of this rhetorical move towards barring niqabs in citizenship ceremonies. However, it was, found to be unconstitutional a few months later.

So what were the positions of pro-FBA, practising Muslim women in the Ontario debate? While they are surely multiple, they share a reluctance to embrace the idea that equality requires secularism. In addition, similar to Bullock's characterisation, several women in the GTA noted to me in interviews, and in a discussion group at a Mississauga mosque, that they felt that the debate unfolded too quickly. This left them with no real opportunity to participate. A sense of frustration characterised the experience of most of the Sunni women of Pakistani origin at this mosque.

For others, the assumption that they should be involved in a debate about private arbitration was problematic: as non-specialists in the shari'a, they felt unqualified to respond to questions in the media.[22] Yet others felt that their responsibilities in raising children and caring for their families left little time for political engagement. These practical concerns were likely compounded by the demographic reality of the diversity in Ontario's Muslim community. While reduced to a single category, 'the Muslims', by the way in which the debate was articulated in the press and by political leaders, Canadian Muslimness reflects a complex reality. There are more than 60 ethno-cultural groups and Islamic organisations, with more in the making; they vary from groups self-defined as secular Muslims through to more conservative religious groups. Since Muslim organisations were split on the question of FBA, there was no single representative body. This diversity was also

---

The ruling positions courts to make ad hoc decisions, in contrast to the 2011 French ban on full-face veils in the public sphere. The N.S. case is similar to the One School debate in that the contours of secularity (here in a court of law) are shaped by debates about non-Christian signs and practices.

[21] Steven Chase, 'Niqabs "Rooted in a Culture that is Anti-women", Harper says', *The Globe and Mail*, 10 March 2015: accessible at http://www.theglobeandmail.com/try-it-now/?articleId=23395242.

[22] See M.L. Fernando, 'The Unpredictable Imagination of Muslim French: Citizenship, Public Religiosity and Political Possibility in France', in A. Masquelier and B.F. Soares, ed., *Muslim Youth and the 9/11 Generation* (Albuquerque, NM, 2016), pp. 123–150.

228   *The Shariʿa*

made clear regarding *where* activism took place. While many Muslim advocates for the public funding of private Muslim schools met in local mosques in the GTA, others pointedly did not.

Given their centrality because of the secular emphasis on their agency, some women were privileged in how the media typically covered the debate. If secular mores are underpinned by certain feminist positions and understandings of agency, these norms must be made more evident, so as to address the concerns of visibly religious women in the domestic and private sphere who felt they were ignored throughout the debate. What do standard secular appellations imply for women? Policing Muslim women in the name of gender equality is not a new phenomenon, and it has a centuries-long colonial history.[23] Ultimately, however, the equation of the secular with women's rights has meant that certain women, here those against FBA who did not wear visible religious signs, gained a favoured space in the debate.

Conclusion

I have considered formulations of the secular in contemporary Ontario through the lens of the 2003–2006 shariʿa debate and its aftermath. I have sought to shed light on the varied and shifting understandings of secularism and religion in the public sphere: How does Christianity maintain a privileged position in the current neutral system? In what ways might deprivatisation be evident following the Ontario debate, and what might be the impact of this shift? Why are the agency and welfare of some Muslim women so scrutinised? Responses to the IICJ's 2003 proclamation made clear the partiality of a Christo-secularism and anti-Islam biases. At the same time, as evidenced in the One-School debate about publicly funding private Catholic schools in 2007, even if not dismantling biases, non-Christian religiously based lobbying has gained ground in the public sphere. Mounir's courses on public policy at the IIT in Scarborough attest to this. I have also suggested that while secular lobby groups might legitimately call to protect the separation of religion and the

---

[23]   L. Ahmed, *Women and Gender in Islam: Historical Roots of a Modern Debate* (New Haven, CT, 1992); L. Abu-Lughod, 'Do Muslim Women Really Need Saving? Anthropological Reflections on Cultural Relativism and Its Others,' *American Anthropologist* 104 (September 2002), pp. 783–790; C. Hirschkind and S. Mahmood, 'Feminism, the Taliban, and the Politics of Counter-Insurgency,' *Anthropological Quarterly*, 75(2) (2002), pp. 337–354.

state as a measure to protect women's rights, this positioning may unintentionally silence the political participation of some religiously practising Muslim women. I assume that non-patriarchal space does not exist, and I question the assumption that secular norms necessarily protect women better.[24]

In part, this Canadian province's changing demography makes the non-neutrality of the promise of 'one law' more evident. Especially since 1967, non-Christian religious traditions have increased in Canada's urban centres. In 2011, Muslims made up 7.7 per cent of the GTA's population. Indeed, the 2007 provincial election following the debate captures a significant shift in the way in which Muslims are politically perceived in the province: the Muslim vote did not especially interest politicians in the 2003 election, but it was part of an imagined suburban vote for victory in 2007, evidencing the political importance of Muslim communities. The growing number of visits to mosques by Canadian representatives of different institutions further reflects the recent solicitation of Muslims for political and nationally related issues.[25]

We can look at the political lobbying inside and outside mosques during the 2007 Ontario provincial elections, and to the heated and extended Ontario shari'a debate, to see how Canadian secular norms may be questioned in a broader sense. Situating the secular within this so-called shari'a debate, manifest in protests in Ontario, Paris and elsewhere, is also an occasion to take stock of the order of things, the power implications within the status quo, and the regulation of religion, including but not only Islam.

Further Reading

Asad, Talal. *Formations of the Secular: Christianity, Islam, and Modernity.* Palo Alto, CA, 2003.

Bakht, Natasha. 'Family Arbitration Using Shariah Law: Examining Ontario's Arbitration Act and its Impact on Women', *Muslim World Journal of Human Rights*, 1(1) (2004), pp. 1–24.

---

[24] Lori Beaman argues that the question of women's equality protected by religion or secularism distracts from a broader recognition of patriarchy: '"Everything is Water": On Being Baptized in Secularism', in J. Berlinerblau, S. Fainberg, and A. Nou, ed., *Secularism on the Edge: Rethinking Church-State Relations in the United States, France, and Israel* (New York, 2014), pp. 237–246, 239.

[25] For example, see J.A. Selby, 'Promoting the Everyday: Pro-Sharia Advocacy and Public Relations in Ontario, Canada's 'Sharia-Debate', *Religions* 4 (2013), p. 435.

Bhargava, Rajeev. 'What is Secularism For?', in *Secularism and Its Critics*, Rajeev Bhargava, ed., pp. 486–542. Delhi, 1998.

Bowen, John R. *On British Islam: Religion, Law, and Everyday Practice in Shari'a Councils*. Princeton, NJ, 2016.

Casanova, José. *Public Religions in the Modern World*. Chicago, IL, 1994.

Gauchet, Marcel. *La religion dans la démocratie: parcours de la laïcité*. Paris, 1998.

Hurd, Elizabeth Shakman. 'International Politics after Secularism', *Review of International Studies* 38(5) (2012), pp. 943–961.

Khan, Sheema. 'The Ontario Sharia Debate: Transformational Accommodation, Multiculturalism and Muslim Identity', in *Belonging?: Diversity, Recognition and Shared Citizenship in Canada*, Keith Banting, Thomas J. Courchene and F. Leslie Seidle, ed., pp. 475–485. Montreal, 2007.

Levy, Geoffrey Brahm and Tariq Modood, ed. *Secularism, Religion and Multicultural Citizenship*. Cambridge, 2009.

Walzer, Michael. 'Liberalism and the Art of Separation', *Political Theory* 12 (1984), pp. 315–330.

Weintraub, Jeff. 'The Theory and Politics of the Public/Private Distinction', in *Public and Private in Thought and Practice: Perspectives on a Grand Dichotomy*, Jeff Weintraub and Krishan Kumar, ed. Chicago, 1997, pp. 1–42.

Zine, Jasmin. 'Sharia in Canada? Mapping Discourses of Race, Gender, and Religious Difference', in *Debating Sharia: Islam, Gender Politics and Family Law Arbitration*, A. Korteweg and J. Selby, ed. Toronto, 2012, pp. 279–306.

Index

Page numbers in *italics* indicate figures; 'n' indicates the footnote number.

Abduh, Muhammad, 67, 70–1, 115, 144, 175, 209
Abdulla, Raficq, 12, 119–34
Abdurrahman, Moeslim, 189
Abshar-Abdalla, Ulil, 182, 189
Abu al-Atahiya, 42
Abu Hanifa, 130
Abu Zayd, Nasr Hamid, 103, 115
accommodation, 8
  as elastic notion, 211
  religious accommodation, 16, 213
  shari'a courts, accommodation of, 211–12
  shari'a within the West, 15–16, 195, 198, 202–3, 207–8, 210, 211–12, 213
adab (proper conduct), 142
Adam, 91, 92, 97
adat (customary law), 175
adjudication, 119, 161
ADR (alternative dispute resolution), 12, 129, 132, 216, 217
  see also arbitration; dispute resolution; FBA; Ontario, secularism and shari'a
adultery, 49, 50, 212
al-Afghani, Jamal al-Din, 70–1

Afghanistan, 4, 28, 70, 148, 149
Aga Berber, Mustafa, 167, 168
Aga Khan IV (Shah Karim al-Husseini), 74, 75
  see also AKDN
Aga Khans, 74, 165
Ahdar, Rex, 15–16, 193–213
ahkam (rules), 6, 36, 47, 102, 103
  ahkam al-zawaj/laws of matrimony, 106
Ahl-i Hadith (scripturalist school, India), 49, 50–1, 52
Ahmadiyya, 177, 180, 183
AKDN (Aga Khan Development Network), 10, 74–6, 78
  Aga Khan Foundation, 74
  Aga Khan Fund for Economic Development, 74
  Aga Khan Trust for Culture, 74
  Institute for the Study of Islam, Aga Khan University, 75–6
Aleppo, 157, 164, 166, 169
Ali ibn Ali Talib, first Shi'i Imam and fourth caliph, 6, 42, 60, 74
  shrine at Najaf, 153
al-Alwani, Taha Jabir, 120, 121
al-Amili, Zayn al-Din, 156
analogy (*qiyas*), 62, 184
Andalusia/al-Andalus, 64, 141

animal slaughter, 149, 193
An-Na'im, Abdullahi, 2, 61, 195, 196–8
Ansar al-Shari'a, 7
apostasy, 72, 82, 161, 212
Appiah, Kwame, 149
Aquinas, Thomas, St. 209
Arab Spring (2010–11), 3, 7, 8, 14, 71
arbitration, 7, 123
    1996 Arbitration Act, UK, 211
    communal arbitration, 28
    Conciliation and Arbitration Boards, 132, 217
    see also ADR; dispute resolution; FBA
Archbishop of Canterbury, see Williams, Rowan
Arendt, Hannah, 56
Aristotle, 136, 141, 150
    virtue ethics, 12, 135, 140, 150
Arjomand, Homa, 224, 225–6
Arkoun, Mohamed, 115, 184
Aroney, Nicholas, 15–16, 193–213
Asad, Talal, 202, 217
Ash Shiddieqy, Hasbi, 174–5
Ash'ari school, 54, 102, 184, 209
al-Ashmawy, Muhammad, 2n3
Ataturk, Kemal 14, 70
'Attar, Farid al-Din: *Memorial of the Saints/Tadhkhirat al-Awliya*, 89
Attia, Gamal Eddin, 121
Auda, Jasser, 185
Auda, Othman, 121
Augustine, St., 200
Australia, 193, 194
authoritarianism, 8, 173, 177
autonomy, 12–13
    autonomy of choice, 9, 34
    autonomy of conscience, 27
    bioethics, 135, 137–8, 147, 150
    maslaha and, 137

moral responsibility and, 41
awqaf (endowments), 28, 62
'*awra* (private parts), 96–7, 107
al-Azhar University, 82, 125, 146, 148

Badawi, Mohamed Zaki, 125–6, 127, 130
balance, *see mizan*
Barlas, Asma, 11, 84
Baso, Ahmad, 184
Batiniyya, 155
Baubérot, Jean, 218
Bayezid II, Ottoman Sultan, 157
bearing witness for the divine, 30, 31, 33
Beauchamp, Thomas, 138–9, 140
beauty, 23, 25, 44, 53, 56, 99
    God's beauty, 20, 92
    husn, 21–2, 25
    jamal, 92
Ben Ali, Zine El Abidine, 71
Bencheikh, Sohaib (former Grand Mufti of Marseilles), 82
Berman, Harold, 199–200, 202
Bézecourt, Jocelyn, 215n2
bid'a:
    heresy, 44
    unlawful innovations, 188
bioethics, 12–13
    autonomy and, 135, 137–8, 147, 150
    beneficence, 135, 138
    fatwa, 136, 144, 145–6, 148
    feminism and, 141
    justice, 135, 138
    Kantian deontology, 140, 150
    legitimacy and, 137, 147
    maslaha and, 136, 146, 147–50
    maslaha mursala, 136, 137, 144, 147–8
    modern legacy and prospect, 144–50

non-maleficence, 135, 138
post-mortems, 144, 146
principlism and, 135, 136,
   137–41, 145
principlist/narrative ethics
   hybrid, 136–7, 147, 150
reproductive issues, 135, 137
Universal Declaration on
   Bioethics and Human Rights,
   137
utilitarianism, 13, 140, 147, 150
virtue ethics, 12, 136, 140–1,
   150
see also euthanasia; medicine;
   organ donation; principlism;
   reproduction; stem cell
   therapy
blasphemy, 50, 180, 212
Boko Haram, 7
Bowen, John, 223n16
Boyd, Marion, 217–18
Buddhism, 1
Bullock, Katherine, 224, 227

Cairo, 142, 143
Canada:
   GTA/Greater Toronto Area,
      222, 223, 225, 227, 229
   National Canadian Council of
      Muslims, 74
   shari'a in, 195, 202
   see also Ontario, 'One School'
      debate; Ontario, secularism
      and shari'a
Canadian Islamic Congress, 222
Casanova, José, 221–2
CCMW (Canadian Council of
   Muslim Women), 10, 74, 78,
   221
CEDAW (Convention on the
   Elimination of All Forms
   of Discrimination Against
   Women), 101–2, 114, 188

Central Asia, 3, 4, 70, 111
Centre for Effective Dispute
   Resolution, 129
charity, 5, 10, 47, 62, 94
   sadaqa, 68
   zakat, 183, 184–5
child, 105, 188
child abduction, 12, 119, 122–4,
   133
   CCP/Central Contact Point,
      124
   maqasid, 124, 133
   mediation, 122, 123, 124
Childress, James, 138–9, 140
Christendom, 199, 200–1, 208
   1054 Roman/Orthodox
      separation, 199
   Reformation, 199, 201
   religious toleration, 201
Christians, 14, 63, 70, 193, 218
citizenship, 14, 224
   equal citizenship, 7, 16
   Muslim-informed citizenship,
      223
civil society, 10, 65, 124
   pluralist civil society, 17
   quality of life and, 59, 73–7, 78
'clash of civilizations', 55, 207
colonialism, 28, 64, 70, 126, 208
   colonial laws, 28, 137, 144,
      175
   encounter with colonial
      modernity, 11, 107, 110, 111
   gender and, 16, 110, 228
   Indonesia, 15, 175
common law, 27, 28
   English common law, 208
community, *see umma*
Companions of the Prophet, 10,
   43, 68
compassion (*tarahum*), 22, 35,
   68, 92
Confucius, 141, 207

conscience:
autonomy of conscience, 27
freedom of conscience, 72, 201
public good and, 66
shari'a and, 18
social conscience, 10, 68, 74–5
consensus, 108, 126, 220
community elders as
consensus-builders, 28
ijma/legal consensus 62, 102,
105
'overlapping consensus', 8, 203
context (historical context), 26–7,
36, 46, 62, 84, 173
historically embedded nature of
all interpretive endeavours,
85
corruption, 8, 33, 46, 61, 68, 161
power and 31
Council for American-Islamic
Relations, 74
Crosbie, William, 124
culture, 10, 16–17, 28, 36, 52
engagement with different
cultures, 69–70
importance of, 62
custom, 64, 65, 186
adat/customary law, 175
custom-based law, 24
urf, 62

Daesh, 7
see also Islamic State
al-Dakhwar, 143
Damascus, 143, 163
Darul 'Uloom Deoband (India),
48
darura (necessity), 119, 129, 130
Das, Veena, 52
democracy, 8, 11, 28
democratic governance, 23
Indonesian democratisation,
173, 177, 189–90

liberal democracies and the
shari'a, 15, 209–12
liberal democracy, 15, 193–4
demography, 203, 206, 229
Indonesia, world's largest
Muslim society, 14–15, 173
Muslims in Europe, *204*
Muslims in North America, *205*
Muslims in Oceania, *205*
World Muslim population, *203*
Deobandis, 48, 50, 51, 52
development, 67, 78
a secular concept, 68
shari'a and, 67–71, 77
see also AKDN
devotion, *see 'ibadat*
diaspora, 6, 76, 122
western diaspora, 5, 8, 12, 15,
131, 133, 147
dignity, 24, 52
norms of dignity/*al-sunan
al-karamiyya*, 47
see also human dignity
dihliz (threshold space), 53
din (religion, faith, spirit), 39, 60
din/*dunya* symbiotic
relationship, 60, 63, 68, 75, 78
mysticism and, 40
as normative order, 40
participation in the public
sphere towards the common
good, 40
see also religion
disapproved act, *see makruh*
dispute resolution:
child abduction, 122
community elders and, 28
mediation, 122, 123, 129, 131
sulh/negotiated settlement, 123,
130
see also ADR; arbitration; FBA
Divine Attributes, 91–2
absolute sovereignty, 89, 90

beauty, 20, 92
  jalali attributes, 92, 93, 94
  jamali attributes, 92–3, 94
  mercy, 26, 34, 45, 92
  see also Divine Names; God
divine guidance, 3, 4, 17, 29, 31,
  32, 98
divine law, 20
  shari'a as framework of divine
    law, 3–5
Divine Names, 91–2
  the beautiful names/*al-asma
    al-husna*, 91
  names of beauty/*jamal*, 92
  names of majesty/*jalal*, 92
  see also Divine Attributes; God
divine will, 19, 20–1, 22, 23, 30,
  32, 83
divorce, 12, 129–31
  divorce by mutual consent/
    khul', 105
  men's right to unilateral
    divorce, 106, 108
  patriarchy, 11, 104, 112–13
  repudiation of wife/*talaq*, 106,
    130
  women's equal rights to divorce
    112–13
  see also gender issues; marriage;
    women
doubt (*shubha*), 6–7
Down's syndrome, 139
Dubai, 129
dunya (world, life, matter), 60,
  68, 75
  see also din

Ebussu'ud, 13, 159, 160, 161,
  165–6, 170
eclecticism, *see talfiq*
Edhi Foundation, Pakistan, 10,
  73–4, 78
egalitarianism, 63, 101

egoism, 34, 88n6, 89
Egypt, 14, 67, 72
El-Fadl, Khaled Abou, 9, 19–37,
  115
end-of-life issues, 135, 137
  see also bioethics; euthanasia
endowments, *see awqaf*
Enlightenment, 55, 69, 201
Ennahda (Renaissance Party,
  Tunisia), 55–6, 71, 72n20
environment, 17, 147
esoterism, 6, 10–11
essential objectives, *see
  maqasid*
ethics (*khuluq/akhlaq*), 40
  as aesthetic space, 53
  ethical change, 43
  fiqh and, 54, 145
  gender ethics, 84, 87
  Islamic law and, 47
  retrieval of ethical reasoning,
    144–5
  see also morality; right and
    wrong; shari'a, ethical
    approach to
EU (European Union), 122
  Euromed Justice Project,
    124
eudaimonia (exemplary living,
  happiness), 140
Euromed Justice Project, 124
European Court of Human
  Rights, 209–10
euthanasia, 12, 135, 141
  see also bioethics; end-of-life
    issues
Eve, 97
evil, 157, 161
  'banality of evil', 56
  enjoining good and resist evil,
    32, 33
  soul and, 88, 89
extremism, 15, 64, 72

family law, 11, 108, 116
  fiqh and, 111–12, 116
  human rights and, 119
  hybrid family law, 112
  Indonesia: Family Law Counter
    Draft, 187–9
  justice and gender, 103
  mediation and, 122, 123, 129
  UK, 110, 119, 130
  see also child abduction;
    Ontario, secularism and
    shari'a
family life, 16, 63, 131
faqih/fuqaha', see jurist
al-Farabi, 141
fard al-'ayn (everyone's
  obligation), 66
fasting, 5, 47, 106, 181, 193
Fatima, daughter of the Prophet
  Muhammad, 74
Fatimids, 163
fatwa (juridical opinion), 13, 131,
  182
  bioethics, 136, 144, 145–6, 148
  Deoband fatwa, 48, 51
  Indonesia, 176, 177, 182, 183,
    190
  Ottoman Empire, 157, 158,
    169
FBA (faith-based arbitration),
  129, 228
  France, 215–16, 223n16, 226
  Ontario, 215–16, 217–18, 221,
    222, 227
  see also ADR; arbitration;
    dispute resolution; Ontario,
    secularism and shari'a
feminism, 84, 103, 107–8
  bioethics and, 141
  feminist fiqh discourses, 87
  Islamic feminism, 11, 114–15
  Ontario, 'anti-visible religion'
    feminist politics, 216, 223–8

Femmes Solidaires (Women in
  Solidarity), 224
FGM (female genital mutilation),
  137, 148
financial products, see Islamic
  banking; Islamic finance
fiqh (juristic tradition/
  jurisprudence), 2, 6, 7, 23, 28,
  39, 63, 81, 83, 102, 208
  definition 196
  discernment and, 10, 53, 54
  epistemic dissonance
    between jurisprudence and
    contemporary science, 146
  epistemological framework of,
    29
  ethics and, 54, 145
  family law and, 111–12, 116
  gender equality and, 86–7, 94,
    95, 110
  gender inequality and, 104–7
  gender issues and, 98, 110, 116
  governance and, 10
  Indonesian fiqh/Fikih
    Indonesia, 173, 175
  methodology, 145, 183, 196
  shari'a/fiqh distinction, 20, 63,
    85, 102, 144, 196
  shari'a/fiqh relationship, 19, 87,
    196, 197–8
fitra (human nature), 113
forbidden, see haram
France, 16, 215–16, 226
  catholaïcité, 218
  laïcité, 202, 218, 224
  shari'a councils in, 223n16
Free Aceh Movement (Gerakan
  Aceh Merdeka), 178
freedoms, 8n19
  freedom of conscience,
    72, 201
  freedom of religion, 8
fundamentalism, 197

Galen, 136, 142, 143
gambling (*maysir*), 125, 128, 129, 181
Gauchet, Marcel, 217
Gelasius I, Pope, 200
gender equality, 11, 84, 101
    female legal testimony, 96
    fiqh and, 86–7, 94, 95, 110
    Ibn al-'Arabi, Muhyi al-Din, 82, 90–9
    legal equality, 102, 111
    ontological equality of every human being, 82, 84, 94
    policing Muslim women in the name of gender equality, 16, 228
    Qur'an and, 84, 85, 94, 108
    Reformism/Feminism and, 111, 114–15
    sainthood, 94–5
    secularism and, 224–7
    social realities and, 93
    Sufism and, 84, 87, 98–9
    Tunisia, 111
    women's equal sociolegal capacity, 95–6
    see also ritual leadership of Muslim women; women
gender inequality:
    basis of inequality in the 'legal shari'a', 101
    egotism and male superiority, 89–90
    fiqh and, 104–7
    gender discrimination, 85, 87, 194
    gender hierarchy, 84, 85, 90
    gender segregation, 107, 114, 144
    Neo-Traditionalism: gender balance or inequality redefined, 111–14
gender issues, 11, 101, 147

colonialism and, 16, 110, 228
ethics/gender/Islamic law relationship, 81
fiqh and, 98, 110, 116
gender ethics, 84, 87
gender and honour, 149
jamal/jalal integrated balance, 95
modernity and, 110–14
religion and human rights, 16
rethinking authority in the shari'a, 84–7
Sufism and, 83, 87–90
see also gender equality; patriarchy; women
Gerson, Jean, 201
Ghannouchi, Rachid, 55–6, 71
al-Ghazali, Abu Hamid, 21, 43–4, 54, 84, 89, 141, 147
    on marriage, 104, 112
    on *maslaha*, 120–1
    The Revivification of the Sciences of Religion/Ihya 'ulum al-din, 54, 104
    shari'a in, 25, 44
al-Ghazali, Muhammad, 121
God, 53
    God–human relationship, 81, 83, 84, 86, 99
    remembrance of God, 88
    tawhid, 91
    see also Divine Attributes; Divine Names
godliness, 20, 30
    fadila/achieving godliness, 25
    imperative of godliness, 30–1
    quest for, 34–5
    shari'a and, 25, 30
good/the good, 5
    shari'a as path to goodness, 19, 33, 34, 77, 102
    striving for the good/*al-nafs al-lawamma*, 11

governance, 5, 8, 10
  democratic governance, 23
  governance of the self, 54
  hakama/hukm, 65
  integration of shari'a
    and secular systems of
    governance, 6, 13, 17
  public good and, 65–7
  revelation and, 46
  shari'a and, 64, 65
  shari'a governance, 44, 45
  siyasa, 46
  societal governance and shari'a,
    59–61
Gülen, Fethullah, 76–7
  ash-shari'a al-Fitriya, 77

Habermas, Jürgen, 222n14
hadd, see hudud
Hadith, 1, 20, 63
  'God created Adam in God's
    own form', 91
  'My mercy precedes my wrath',
    92
  self-knowledge in, 34
  'The heavens and earth contain
    me not...', 89
Hague Conference on Private
  International Law, 124
Hague Convention on Civil
  Aspects of International Child
  Abduction, 122, 123, 124
Hajar, mother of Ismail, 95
hakama/hukm, see governance
al-Halabi, Ibrahim: *The
  Confluence of the Seas/Multaqā
  al-abḥur*, 161
halal (permissible), 64, 128, 186,
  193
Hallaq, Wael, 3, 208
  Impossible State, 17
Hamdy, Sherine, 146
Hanafi, Hassan, 121, 185

Hanafi school of law, 64, 48–9,
  129, 130
  Imrana case, 10, 48–9, 50, 52
  Ottoman Empire, 13–14, 154,
    158, 159, 161, 170
Hanbali school of law, 25–6, 41,
  45, 64, 120, 157
haqiqa, see truth
haram (forbidden), 3–4, 64,
  186
harm:
  darar, 130
  fasad, 46
Harper, Stephen, 227
Hasan al-Basri, 61
Hasan-i Sabbah, 163
Haynes, John, 129
Hazairin, 174, 175
heart (*qalb*), 88, 89
heresy, 44, 166
hijab, 97, 107, 193–4, 226
  burqa, 107, 194
  fiqh and, 107
  niqab, 226n20, 227
  Ontario, 226–7
  as seclusion/confinement, 101,
    107
  women's rights and, 194, 221,
    224, 226
  see also women
al-Hilli, al-Muhaqqiq, 104–5
Hindu tradition, 1, 113, 148, 219
Hippocrates, 142
Hizmet (Gülen Movement,
  Turkey), 10, 76–7, 78
homosexuality, 147
honour killing, 137, 148, 149
  patriarchal honour, 149
hospital, 62, 73, 76, 136, 138,
  142
HTI (Hizbut Tahrir Indonesia),
  176, 182
hudud (fixed criminal

punishments), 22, 26–7, 64, 114
    meaning of, 26n9
    see also punishment
human dignity, 10, 31, 35, 39, 57,
    68, 121, 212
    see also dignity
human rights, 11, 119, 138, 147,
    197
    European Convention on
        Human Rights, 210
    gender, religion and, 16
Huntington, Samuel, 207
Husaini, Adian, 181–2
Husayn b. Ali, 153
husn, see beauty

IAIN al-Raniry (Islamic State
    Institute), 178, 179, 180
'ibadat (ritual and devotion), 5,
    47, 54, 63, 103, 183
    marriage contract and, 105
    rulings on covering, 107
    see also ritual
Ibn Aqil, Abul Wafa, 26, 45–6
Ibn al-'Arabi, Muhyi al-Din, 42,
    90n10
    autobiography, 95
    gender equality in, 82, 90–9
    human archetype/al-insan
        al-kamil, 11, 91, 92, 94
Ibn Ashur, 120, 121
Ibn Hanbal, Ahmad, 25
Ibn Hazm, 184
Ibn al-Jawzi, 46
Ibn Khaldun, 43
Ibn Khalil, Ishaq, 105
Ibn al-Khatib, 142–3, 144
Ibn Miskawayh, 141
    The Refinement of Character/
        Tahdhib al-Akhlaq, 12
Ibn al-Nafis, 143, 144
Ibn Qayyim al-Jawziyya, 24–5,
    26, 41

I'lam, 45
Paths of Governance/al-Turuq
    al-hukmiyya, 44–5
Ibn Rushd, Abu al-Walid
    (Averroes), 25, 98n30, 144,
    184
    The Jurist's Primer, 47
Ibn Sina: Canon of Medicine/
    Qanun al-Tibb, 142, 143
Ibn Taymiyya, 157, 166, 170
    Epistle on the Transgressions of
        the Nusayris, 157
ICMI (Indonesian Association
    of Muslim Intellectuals/Ikatan
    Cendekiawan Muslim se-
    Indonesia), 177, 178
identity, 5, 7, 13
    identity politics, 3, 15
    Muslim identity, 11, 107, 125,
        173
idolatry, 34, 50, 186
IICJ (Islamic Institute of Civil
    Justice), 216, 217, 218, 221, 225,
    228
    see also Ontario, secularism
        and shari'a
ijma, see consensus
ijtihad (individual reasoning),
    20n2, 55–6, 62, 103, 159
    as duty, 21
    ijtihad jama'i, 175, 189
    Indonesia, 71, 175, 184, 189
    limitations imposed on, 59,
        66–7, 69
    restoration of, 59, 70–1
Imamate, 159
    imamate of women, 82, 97–8
imitative reading/practice, see
    taqlid
Imrana case, 9–10, 48–52, 53, 57
    Ahl-i Hadith, 49, 50–1, 52
    Deobandis/Deoband fatwa, 48,
        50, 51, 52

Hanafi school of law, 10, 48–9, 50, 52
   rape, 10, 48, 49–52
India, 52, 70, 165
   see also Imrana case
Indonesia, 15
   2004 tsunami, 179
   Aceh, 15, 178, 179, 180, 181
   conservative turn, 15, 173–4, 190
   'Declaration of Indonesianess'/ *Maklumat Keindonesiaan*, 182
   democratisation, 173, 177, 189–90
   Dewan Dakwah Islam Indonesia, 176
   Family Law Counter Draft, 187–9
   fatwa, 176, 177, 182, 183, 190
   ijtihad, 71, 184
   ijtihad jama'i, 175, 189
   Indonesian fiqh/*Fikih Indonesia*, 173, 175
   Islamic law in, 173, 174–6, 177, 189–90
   Islamisation of, 15, 173, 177, 181, 187
   Jakarta, 15, 178–9, 181
   'Jakarta Charter', 174, 177, 181
   maqasid al-shari'a, 182, 183, 184, 185–6, 187, 188
   mazhab nasional/national school of Islamic law, 175
   NAD Act, 178, 180
   New Order, 176, 177
   Pancasila/Five Principles, 15, 174, 181, 182
   perda syariat, 15, 178, 179
   perda syariat and material law, 180–1
   perda syariat, debate on, 181–2
   post-Suharto governments, 177, 190

   secularism, 176, 177, 182, 183
   shari'a in, 173, 178–9, 188, 189
   Shari'a Office, 179
   usul al-fiqh, 182–5, 186, 187
   Wilayatul Hisbah, religious police, 179
   world's largest Muslim society, 14–15, 173
innovation, 39, 43–4,
   Islamic finance, Malaysia, 128
   Muhammad's reforms, 63, 108
al-insan al-kamil (human archetype), 11, 91, 92, 94
Iqbal, Muhammad, 71, 115
Iran, 7, 70, 113, 114, 136, 225, 226
   ijtihad, 71
   see also Safavids
Iraq, 46, 60n2, 136
islah (social reform), 143–4
Islam, 6, 206
   Islam/Islamism distinction, 206
   Muslimness, 221, 227
   reformism, 71, 174, 175, 208–9
Islam for the United Kingdom, 206
Islamic banking, 12n28
   see also Islamic finance
Islamic Defenders Front (*Front Pembela Islam*, Indonesia), 176
Islamic finance, 12, 65
   bai al-dayn/sale of debt, 125, 127
   bai al-inah, 125, 127
   credit card, 127
   gharar/uncertainty, 128
   Malaysia, 119, 125–9, 133
   maqasid and, 128–9, 133
   maslaha and, 125, 127, 128–9
   riba/usury, 12, 127
   shari'a finance, 125–6, 128–9, 133

sukuk/fixed income
    instruments, 127–8
tawarruq, 125, 127
see also gambling
Islamic jurisprudence, *see* fiqh
Islamic law, 46–7, 64, 81
    al-ahkam al-shari'a, 19
    ethics and, 47
    female legal testimony, 96
    five parities of, 186
    gendered assumptions of, 82–3
    incorporating Islamic laws into
        Western legal systems, 70
    Islamic law/shari'a distinction,
        19, 59, 144
    Islamic legal system, 24, 27–8,
        223
    legal guilds, 9, 27, 28, 35
    mukhatti'a/*musawwiba* schools,
        20
    norm-making today, 47
    as purposive in nature, 120, 126
    reform of, 126
    shari'a as Islamic law, 196
    see also Indonesia; shari'a, legal
        approach to
Islamic Modernism, 112
Islamic State, 113, 194
Islamic theology, 54, 61, 83,
    102–3, 184, 198, 209
Islamisation, 15, 128, 173, 177,
    181, 187
Islamism, 23, 195, 207
    definition, 206
    Islam/Islamism distinction, 206
Islamophobia, 74, 216
Ismail I, Shah, 158
Ismailis, 155, 157, 163–6, 169, 171
    1816–1818 Ismaili revolt, 166–8
    persecution of, 14, 166
    Suwaydani/Hajjawi factions,
        164–5
    see also Ottoman Empire

istislah (unprecedented judgement
    motivated by public interest),
    62
istishsan (exceptional deviation
    from a rule), 62

al-Jabri, Muhammad Abed, 121,
    185
Jafari school of law, 64
Jami: *Haft Awrang*, 17
Jefferson, Thomas, 200
Jews/Judaism, 14, 63, 147
jihad, 3, 161, 206, 210
    jihadist, 194
Jillani, Tasadukh Hussain, 124
Jordan, 124, 148
judge (*qadi*), 13, 28, 96, 153, 154,
    156, 162
judiciary, 27, 28, 156, 170
    institutionalisation of, 13
juridical opinion, *see fatwa*
jurist (*faqih*/*fuqaha'*), 13, 31, 46,
    47, 54, 103, 188
    crisis of epistemology and, 110
    'the fatigue' of shari'a, 29
    independence from state
        influence, 208
    mujtahid, 20, 21
justice, 12, 33, 64, 93, 94, 101
    bioethics and, 135, 138
    peace and, 35
    revealed texts and, 102–3
    shari'a and, 24, 26, 44–5, 47
    social justice, 68, 73, 74, 99
al-Juwayni, 21, 120

Kadızadeli movement, 158,
    166
al-Kahf (Syria), 155, 163–4,
    166–7, 168
Kahn, Paul, 8
Kamali, Mohammad Hashim,
    121, 125–6, 127

Kant, Immanuel, 139
 Kantian deontology, 140, 150
Karim, Karim H., 10, 59–79
Kersten, Carool, 15, 173–91
Keshavjee, Mohamed M., 12,
 119–34
Khansari, Mehdi, 17
khilafat Allah (vicegerency), 32,
 34, 185
khuluq/akhlaq, see ethics
al-Kindi, 25, 141

Lapidus, Ira M., 60n2
law,
 colonial laws, 28, 137, 144,
 175
 custom-based law, 24
 hybrid legal system, 70, 112
 law of the state, 23–4, 28, 213
 legal pluralism, 14, 28
 legal tradition is dynamic, 85
 myth: shari'a as framework of
 divine law, 3–5
 public law, 14, 15, 19
 secularisation of law and legal
 systems, 116, 202
 spiritual legal discourse, 98
 western legal tradition, 200,
 202, 208
 see also common law; divine
 law; family law; Islamic law;
 rule of law
law of the land, 23, 133, 154, 211
 shari'a as, 4, 71
leader/ruler:
 community elders, 27–8
 community elders and dispute
 resolution, 28
 Islamic law and, 24
 shari'a and political authority's
 legitimacy, 10, 13, 24, 48,
 154, 170–1
legalism, 115, 135, 136, 144

legitimacy:
 bioethics and, 137, 147
 citizenry as source of, 28–9
 law of the state, legitimacy of,
 23
 Ottoman Empire, legitimacy
 of, 13, 153, 154, 155–6, 158,
 168, 170
 political authority, legitimacy
 of, 45–6
 shari'a and political authority's
 legitimacy, 10, 13, 24, 48,
 154, 170–1
Lévy, Bernard-Henri, 207
liberalism, 16, 198, 209
 liberal democracies and the
 shari'a, 15, 209–12
 liberal democracy, 15,
 193–4
 liberal pluralist ideology, 16
 liberal secularism, 8–9
 Western liberalism, 203
litigation, 28, 123
lobbying, 189, 222, 223, 228, 229
Luther, Martin, 200

madhahib, see schools of law
Madjid, Nurcholish, 121, 176
Mahfouz, Naguib, 39
Mahfudh, Sahal, 182–3, 185
 Nuances of Social Fiqh, 183
Mahmood, Saba, 17
Mahmud II, Sultan, 167
makruh (disapproved act), 3, 186
Malaysia, 4–5
 Islamic finance, 119, 125–9,
 133
Maliki school of law, 64, 105, 121,
 183
Mamluk rule, 155, 157, 159, 166
al-Ma'mun, Abbasid caliph, 42
mandub (recommended), 3, 186
Manu, 141

maqasid (essential objectives), 119, 121–2
child abduction and, 124, 133
five/six traditional *maqasid*, 4, 33, 35–6, 44, 121, 185
Islamic finance and, 128–9, 133
maslaha/*maqasid* relationship, 128–9
maqasid al-shari'a, 120, 121, 132, 197–8
maqasid al-shari'a, Indonesia, 182, 183, 184, 185–6, 187, 188
maqasid al-shari'a as Islamic philosophy of law, 121, 185–6
restricted approach to, 120
shari'a councils, UK, 131, 133
usul al-fiqh and, 121, 185, 186
al-Maqrizi, 142
ma'rifa (gnosis, wisdom), 6, 61
marriage, 47
contract of coitus/*'aqd al-nikah*, 104
contracting, consummating a marriage/*nakaha*, 49
disobedience/*nushuz*, 106
Family Law Counter Draft, Indonesia, 187
fiqh: from contract to control, 104–6, 108–10, 113
Hanafi school of law, 48–9
laws of matrimony/*ahkam al-zawaj*, 106
'limping marriage', 130
maintenance/*nafaqa*, 106
'marriage of dominion', 108–9
obedience/*tamkin*, 105
patriarchy and, 11, 104, 108, 109, 112
Qur'an and, 49
rape and nullification of marriage, 48–50, 51
repugnant marriages/*ziwaj al-maqt*, 49

rights and obligations, 105
shari'a within the West, 16
see also divorce; gender issues; women
maslaha (public good/welfare), 2, 10, 12, 13, 19, 66, 121–2
autonomy and, 137
bioethics, 136, 146, 147–50
Islamic finance and, 125, 127, 128–9
istislah, 66
maslaha/*maqasid* relationship, 128–9
maslaha mursala, 136, 137, 144, 147–8
methodology, 66
shari'a and, 66, 69, 119
shari'a councils, UK, 131
Tunisia, 71
usul al-fiqh and, 120–1
see also public good
Masud, Khalid, 185
Mas'udi, Masdar, 182, 183–4, 189
Religion of Justice, 183, 184–5
Masyaf (Syria), 163, 164, 169
Masyumi (Islamic political party, Indonesia), 174, 176, 177, 182
Maududi, Abul Ala, 112–14
Purdah and the Status of Women in Islam, 113
al-Mawardi, Abu al-Hasan, 39–40, 41–2, 46
Ethics of the World and Religion/*Adab al-dunya wa al-din*, 40
May, Theresa, 131
maysir, see gambling
McGuinty, Dalton, 219, 220
Mecca, 3, 159
medicine, 10, 45, 136, 140, 141–3
Black Death, 142–3
healthcare and human responsibility, 142

medieval Islamic medicine, 138, 142–3
  see also bioethics; hospital
Medina, 3, 159
  Constitution of Medina, 63
Mehmed I, Sultan, 156, 159
Mehmed, Ustuvani, 158
Merali, Amaan, 13–14, 153–71
mercy, 24, 39, 44–5, 63, 92–3, 94
  God's mercy, 26, 34, 45, 92
Merdeka Centre, 4
methodology, 62, 59, 184
  fiqh, 145, 183, 196
  maqasid al-shari'a, 185, 186
  maslaha, 66
  al-Mawardi, Abu al-Hasan, 41–2
  shari'a as, 62, 66
  shari'a as 'problem-solving methodology', 65, 69, 75
  see also ijtihad
Middle East, 3, 4, 14, 141
MiKK (Internationales Mediationszentrum für Familienkonflikte und Kindesentführung), 122, 123
Mir-Hosseini, Ziba, 11, 101–17
mizan (balance, proportionality), 35
modernisation, 67, 71, 176, 197
modernity, 2, 17
  'alternative modernities'/ 'multiple modernities', 68
  encounter with colonial modernity, 11, 107, 110, 111
  gender issues, 110–14
  modernity/non-western society's traditions contradiction, 67
  myth: shari'a as incompatible with modernity, 7–9
  see also secularism

modesty, 94, 96–7
  haya, 109
Moosa, Ebrahim, 9–10, 39–57, 146
morality, 22, 63
  Muhammad, the Prophet, 41
  religion and, 39, 40–1
  religion as the completion of morality, 41
  tradition in moral contexts, 53–5
Morocco, 71, 124
Morsi, Mohamed, 72
mosque, 44, 153, 222, 227, 229
  gender-inclusive mosque spaces, 98
  Swiss minaret-ban, 194
mu'amalat (social acts/relations), 5, 54, 63, 103, 183
  marriage contract and, 105
  rulings on covering, 107
  social context of, 103
  see also society/social relations
mubah (neutral, permissible act), 4, 186
Mughal Empire, 69, 70
Muhammad, the Prophet, 3, 6, 68
  biography/*sira*, 63
  morality and, 41
  Prophet's life as model for Islamic society, 75
  reforms introduced by, 63, 108
  shari'a and, 25, 45, 61
  see also Hadith; Sunna
Muhammad-Shahi Nizari, 165
Muhammadiyah (Indonesia), 15, 174, 176, 177, 184, 189, 190
al-Muhasibi, 88n6
MUI (Indonesian Ulama Council/ *Majelis Ulama Indonesia*), 176–7, 178, 179, 182, 183, 188, 189, 190
multiculturalism, 210–11, 224, 225

Murata, Sachiko, 93n18
Muslim Brotherhood, 14, 72, 148, 177
Muslim civilisation, 62, 66, 69–70
Muslim ethics, 53, 137, 141, 150, 185
  maslaha mursala in, 144
Muslim Law (Sharia) Council (UK), 129–32
Mutahhari, Morteza: *System of Women's Rights in Islam*, 113–14
Mu'tazili school, 21, 102–3, 184
mysticism, 40

nafs, see soul/self
nationalism, 14, 70, 76, 175
Natsir, Mohammad, 176
necessity, *see darura*
Neo-Traditionalism, 111–14
neutral act, *see mubah*
New Zealand, 193
NGO (non-governmental organisation), 146, 180, 187, 222
Nigeria, 8, 28, 126
Noer, Deliar, 182
non-Muslims, 128, 188
  poll tax for non-Muslims/*jizya*, 166
  shari'a and, 2, 3, 4, 5, 65–6
NU (Nahdlatul Ulama, Indonesia), 15, 176, 177, 182, 183, 184, 187, 190
Nursi, Bediuzzaman Said, 1
Nusayris, 14, 157, 164, 165, 166, 167–8, 169

Oakeshott, Michael, 41
Obama, Barack, 5
Okin, Susan, 225
Onal, Ayse, 148

Ontario, 'One School' debate, 218, 220, 222, 226n20, 228
  funding of religious schools, 16, 216, 218–19, 222, 227
  United Nations Human Rights Committee, 219
  see also Ontario, secularism and shari'a
Ontario, secularism and shari'a, 16, 216, 228–9
  'anti-visible religion' feminist politics, 216, 223–8
  FBA, 215–16, 217–18, 221, 222, 227
  media coverage of debates, 224–5, 226, 227, 228
  non-neutral Christian biases, 216, 218, 220, 226n20, 229
  'one law for all', 215, 216, 218, 229
  private/public spheres blurred distinctions, 216, 220–3
  'shari'a debate', 195, 215–16, 224–8
  shari'a law as foil for the secular, 216, 221
  shari'a tribunals in family and civil disputes, 195, 215, 216, 217–18
  women's rights, 221, 223, 224–7
  see also Ontario, 'One School' debate
organ donation, 12, 135, 145, 146
  Coalition for Organ-Failure Solutions, 146
orthodoxy, 48, 50, 55, 144, 197
  Ottoman orthodoxy, 13, 14, 153–4, 155, 159, 162, 163, 167, 170
  Sunni orthodoxy, 13, 180, 184
Ottoman Empire, 13, 69, 70, 153, 155
  civil code/*Mecelle*, 7, 154

fatwa, 157, 158, 169
Hanafi school of law, 13–14,
    154, 158, 159, 161, 170
imperial legal system, 153,
    156–7, 158, 170
imprisonment, torture,
    execution, 153, 156, 167, 168
integration of shari'a and
    secular laws, 13, 28, 156–7,
    158–9, 167–8, 170
Ismailis, 155, 157, 163–8, 169,
    171
Kızılbaş revolts, 158–9
learned hierarchy, 156, 161–2
legitimacy of, 13, 153, 155–6,
    158, 170
millet, 162
Nusayris, 14, 157, 164, 165, 166,
    167–8, 169
Ottoman orthodoxy, 13, 14,
    153–4, 155, 159, 162, 163,
    167, 170
religious legitimacy/imperial
    authority confluence, 154,
    155–6, 168, 170
rivalry with Shi'i Safavids, 13,
    155, 158–9, 165, 170
shari'a and, 156–9, 166, 167,
    168, 170
Shi'a, persecution of, 14, 153,
    157, 162–3, 166, 169–70
Sunni Islam, 155, 158, 170
Tanzimat, 70, 154
taxation, 156, 157, 164, 165–9
see also Ismailis

Pakistan, 28, 50, 114, 146, 148,
    149
Pashazade, Kemal, 13
    Treatise on Exposing the
        Heresies of the Infidels,
        159–60
paternalism, 137–9, 226

path, 77–8
    pathways, 17, 81
    Qur'an, 36
    Qur'an 45:18: 'We have set you
        on a clear religious path…',
        1–2, 59–60, 196n16
    shari'a as path, 1–2, 19, 33, 34,
        77, 85–6, 102, 195–6
    sirat, 36, 77–8
    straight path/*al-sirat al-*
        mustaqim, 25, 36, 77–8
    see also tariqa
patriarchy, 11, 84, 101, 116, 147,
    221
    critique of patriarchal power
        relations, 89, 90, 93
    divorce and, 11, 104, 112–13
    gender in classical fiqh: the
        sanctification of patriarchy,
        104–7
    Islamic feminist critiques of
        shari'a-centred patriarchy,
        11, 114–15
    lack of spiritual discernment
        and, 90
    male body as signifier of social
        and ontological superiority,
        87
    marriage and, 11, 104, 108, 109,
        112
    patriarchal context of
        revelation, 84, 101
    patriarchal honour, 149
    Sufism and, 84
    traditionalism, 149
    women's covering and
        seclusion, 11, 104
PBB (Crescent and Star Party/
    Partai Bulan Bintang), 177, 178,
    179, 182
peace, 34, 93
    salam, 35
Pell, George, 199

Persatuan Islam (Persis, Indonesia), 174, 176
Pew Centre, 4
Philips, Melanie, 132
philosophy of law, 184
    maqasid al-shari'a as Islamic philosophy of law, 121, 185–6
pilgrimage, 5, 153
    hajj, 95, 156
PKS (Justice and Prosperity Party/ *Partai Keadilan Sejahtera*), 177, 178, 179
Plotinus, 141
pluralism, 9, 64
    legal pluralism, 14, 28
    liberal pluralist ideology, 16
    pluralist civil society, 17
    Qur'an, pluralistic message of, 2, 6
    religious pluralism, 64, 211
    shari'a: pluralism/diverse interpretations, 4, 6, 62, 196–7
political Islam, 114, 116, 176, 206
    Canada, 225
    Ennahda, 56, 72n20
    'political religion', 3
    'return to shari'a', 114
    shari'a as ideology, 102
politics,
    identity politics, 3, 15
    religious leaders and, 8
polygamy, 106, 108, 109, 187, 189
populism, 5, 9
power, 13, 31
    patriarchal power relations, 89, 90, 93
prayer, 5, 77, 180, 194
    gender-inclusive mosque spaces, 98
    ritual prayers/*salat*, 82, 97–8, 107

principlism, 13
    corporate/industry influence, 139–40
    criticism of, 138–40, 141, 147, 150
    principlism, shari'a and *maslaha*, 141–4, 147–9
    reasoning and 135;
    reflective equilibrium, 138
    see also bioethics
private parts, *see* '*awra*
Proclus, 141
proper conduct, *see* *adab*
prophethood, 89, 97
public good, 66
    governance and, 65–7
    Sunna and, 69
    see also *maslaha*
public sphere, 17
    al-din and, 40
    shari'a and, 30, 195
punishment, 212
    capital punishment, 147, 212
    criminal punishment, 6n14, 22, 26–7, 65, 114, 212
    shari'a and, 6n14, 59, 64, 69, 78
    see also *hudud*

qadi, *see* judge
Qadmus (Syria), 155, 163–4, 167, 168
al-Qaeda, 7
qalb, *see* heart
al-Qaradawi, Yusuf, 120, 121
Qasim-Shahi Nizari, 165
al-Qasimi, Jamal al-Din, 44
qiyas, *see* analogy
quality of life:
    civil society and, 59, 73–7, 78
    deterioration of, 69
    governance and public good, 65–7
    Muhammad's reforms, 63

shari'a and material and
spiritual enhancement,
59–65, 77
societal governance and shari'a,
59–61
Sunna and, 62–3, 78
Tunisia, 73
Qur'an, 1, 3, 9, 32
45:18: 'We have set you on a
clear religious path…', 1–2,
59–60, 196n16
enjoining good and resist evil,
32, 33
gender equality and, 84, 85, 94,
108
God 'taught Adam all of the
names', 91
historical context of, 26–7
hudud, 26–7
imperative of godliness, 30
interpretation of, 22
legal imperatives in, 2, 4
marriage, 49
pluralistic message of, 2, 6
salary for teaching the Qur'an,
44
'the soul that incites to evil', 88
Surat al-Fatiha, 77–8
umma, 5
see also revelation

Rabb, Intisar, 6–7
Rabia al-Adawiyya, 11, 89–90
al-Raghib al-Isfahani, 44
Rahardjo, M. Dawam, 182
Rahman, Fazlur, 102, 115, 145,
185
Ramadan, 106, 160, 193
Ramadan, Tariq, 145, 195–7,
197n18
rape, 10, 48, 49–52
as adultery by coercion, 49, 50
see also Imrana case

rationality, 8–9, 32, 33–4, 102, 115
'moral rationality', 139
Rawls, John, 138, 198, 203
al-Razi (Rhazes), 141
al-Razi, Fakhr al-Din, 21
reason, 33–4, 126
synthesis of reason and
revelation, 209
reasoning, 12–13
ethical reasoning, 144–5
limitation on the use of reason,
66–7
moral reasoning, 56
'reasoning with God', 9, 19, 33,
34, 36
thinking, 56–7
traditionalist reasoning, 146–7
see also ijtihad
recommended, *see mandub*
Red Heads (Kızılbaş), 158
Refah Partisi (Welfare Party,
Turkey), 209–10
religion:
morality and, 39, 40–1
nationalism and, 14
religious pluralism, 64, 211
see also din
religious anthropology, 11, 82–3,
84, 91, 94, 95
reproduction (human
reproduction), 135, 137
abortion, 12, 135, 141, 147
pre-natal genetic diagnosis, 149
reproductive technologies, 12,
137
see also bioethics
required act, *see wajib*
revelation, 32, 47, 108
governance and, 46
'ibadat and mu'amalat, 5
justice and, 102–3
patriarchal context of, 84, 101
shari'a and, 25, 35

synthesis of reason and
revelation, 209
see also Qur'an
Reza Shah, 70
Rida, Rashid, 71, 120, 121, 144
right and wrong, 19, 57, 126
right/wrong distinction, 48, 56,
209
ritual, 2
myth: shari'a as ritual and
social regulation, 5–7
sa'i rites, 95
see also 'ibadat
ritual leadership of Muslim
women, 81–2
Ibn al-'Arabi, Muhyi al-Din, 82,
97–8
imamate of women, 82, 97–8
mixed congregations and, 82,
97
spiritual and ontological
equality between men and
women, 82
ungendered and equal access to
ritual leadership, 82, 98
see also gender equality;
women
ritual/spiritual devotion,
see 'ibadat
ruh, see spirit
rule of law, 8, 74, 190, 208, 210
ruler, *see* leader/ruler
rules, *see* ahkam

Sachedina, Abdulaziz, 110
sadaqa, see charity
Safavids, 28, 69, 158
Ottoman rivalry with, 13, 155,
158–9, 165, 170
sainthood, 95
axial saint/*qutb*, 95
Sajoo, Amyn B., 1–18, 135–51
salafism, 49

Salah al-Din, Ayyubid Sultan, 163
salam, see peace
Saleh, Soad, 82
Sander, Frank, 129
al-Sanhuri, Abd al-Razzaq, 7
Sardar, Ziauddin, 62
Sarkozy, Nicolas, 194, 215n2
Satan, 92
Saudi Arabia, 7, 28, 70, 111, 126,
127
schools of law (*madhahib*), 7, 20,
25, 63–4
patriarchy and, 11
tradition and, 54
see also Hanafi school of law;
Hanbali school of law; Jafari
school of law; Maliki school
of law; Shafi'i school of law;
Zahiri school of law
secularisation, 64, 70, 71, 110,
176, 201–2, 222
individual secularisation, 201
secularisation of law and legal
systems, 116, 202
the West, 202
secularism, 5, 197, 202, 217
'de-privatization' of religious
traditions, 222
'development' as secular
concept, 68
faith/identity relationship, 7
France: *catholaïcité*, 218
France: *laïcité*, 202, 218, 224
gender equality and, 224–7
Indonesia, 176, 177, 182, 183
liberal secularism, 8–9
secular globalisation, 13
'statism', 17
see also modernity; Ontario,
secularism and shari'a
Selby, Jennifer A., 16, 215–30
Selim I, Ottoman Sultan, 157,
158–9, 163

separation of state and church, 23, 31, 200–1, 218

al-Shabab, 7

Shabestari, Mohammad Mojtahed, 115

al-Shafiʻi, Muhammad b. Idris, 46

Shafiʻi school of law, 40, 52, 64, 127, 182–3, 184

Shahrur, Mohammed, 145

Shaikh, Saʻdiyya, 10–11, 81–99

Shaltut, Mahmud, Shaykh al-Azhar, 175

Shaʻrawi, Muhammad, 146

shariʻa, 15, 36
  definition of, 62, 85, 195–6, 198, 212–13
  'essentialist' perspective, 197
  etymology, 19, 78
  'the fatigue' of, 29–30
  founding age of, 1, 3, 61–2
  guiding role of, 10, 11, 17, 23, 69, 78, 85
  pluralism/diverse interpretations, 4, 6, 62, 196–7
  purposes of, 66, 86
  scope of, 5, 66, 77
  sources for, 62–63, 196–7
  as 'Whole Duty of Mankind', 198
  see also path

shariʻa, ethical approach to, 1–2, 9–10, 18, 59, 119
  shariʻa as ethical norms, 46, 55
  shariʻa as ethical paradigm, 39
  shariʻa as ethical truth, 44–6
  shariʻa as a matter of *voluntary* choice, 61
  shariʻa as value system of natural virtues, goodness and beauty, 23, 36

shariʻa, historical approach to, 2, 4, 9

shariʻa, legal approach to, 2, 3–5, 21–2, 46
  campaigns against 'shariʻa law', 5
  Islamic law/shariʻa distinction, 19, 59, 144
  shariʻa/fiqh distinction, 20, 63, 85, 102, 144, 196
  shariʻa/fiqh relationship, 87, 196, 197–8
  shariʻa as Islamic law, 196
  shariʻa as rigid set of prohibitions and punishments, 59
  shariʻa as a set of laws, 31–2, 36, 47, 48, 60, 64, 77, 197

shariʻa, mythology on, 3–9
  shariʻa is a framework of divine law, 3–5, 25
  shariʻa is incompatible with modernity, 7–9
  shariʻa is ritual and social regulation, 5–7

shariʻa court, 178–9, 211–12, 216

shariʻa in the West, 193–5, 212–13
  accommodation, 15–16, 195, 198, 202–3, 207–8, 210, 211–12, 213
  assimilation, 210
  Canada, 202
  controversies, 193–5, 213
  defining 'shariʻa', 195–8, 212–13
  defining 'the West', 198–203
  France, 202
  Islam, Islamism and Reform Islam, 206–9
  liberal democracies and the shariʻa, 15, 209–12
  multiculturalism, 210–11
  secularisation discourse, 202
  western legal tradition, 200, 202, 208

Sharpe, Virginia, 139–40

Index 251

al-Shatibi, Abu Ishaq, 66, 120,
121, 183, 184
Shi'i Islam, 6, 10, 64
as deviant/heresy, 153, 157, 160,
162–3, 167, 168, 169, 180
persecution by Ottomans, 14,
153, 157, 162–3, 166, 169–70
shubha, see doubt
social reform, *see islah*
society/social relations:
jamali attributes for human
beings and, 93
shari'a and, 5, 33, 35
shari'a-oriented society, 36
social conscience, 10, 68, 74–5
social construction of shari'a
practices, 46
social justice, 68, 73, 74, 99
social mobility, 63
virtuous society, 33, 35, 36, 141
see also mu'amalat
Soroush, Abdolkarim, 101, 103,
115, 145
soul/self (*nafs*), 88
'blaming soul'/*al-nafs
al-lawamma*, 11, 89
'commanding soul'/*nafs
al-ammara*, 11, 88, 89, 90, 93
governance of the self, 54
jalali qualities, 92, 93
self-knowledge, 34, 91
'the soul at peace'/*al-nafs
al-mutma'inna*, 11, 89
South Africa, 81
South/Southeast Asia, 4, 70, 113
sovereignty, 24, 28, 89, 90, 154
spirit (*ruh*), 88
spirituality, 1, 10–11
shari'a and, 61
see also Sufism
Stanhope, Hester Lucy, 167
state:
Constitutions, 14, 71–3

divine will and, 22–3
ethics of virtue and, 23
imperative of godliness and,
30–1
Islam and, 173
modern state, 5, 14, 17, 23, 27,
29, 30, 31, 32
nation-state, 27, 29, 67, 111,
112, 208
power and control, 27, 31
state as custodian and guardian
of the law, 29
state law, 23–4, 28, 196, 210,
213
'statism', 17
see also separation of state and
church
state and shari'a, 23, 31, 196
'the fatigue' of shari'a, 29–30
modern state as custodian and
enforcer of the shari'a, 9, 23,
150
shari'a/secular state
comparison, 6n14
state-centric discourse, 7, 17
stem cell therapy, 12, 137, 149
subjectivity, 19–20, 32, 43, 81,
135, 140
human subjectivity in Sufism,
88
Sudan, 67
Sufism, 10–11, 61, 83, 86, 184
gender equality and, 84, 87,
98–9
gender issues, 83, 87–90
human/spiritual refinement
and, 83, 88, 90, 91
human subjectivity in, 88
legal tradition and, 83–4
patriarchy and, 84
purification, 88, 89, 91
shari'a and, 87
shari'a/*tariqa* relationship, 86–7

spiritual practices, 88–9
Sufi psychology, human nature
   and gender, 87–90
Suharto, 173, 176, 177
Suleyman I, Ottoman Sultan, 157,
   159
Suleyman Pasha, 167–8
sulh, see dispute resolution
Sunna (teachings and conduct of
   the Prophet), 4, 75
   public good and, 69
   quality of life and, 62–3, 78
   shari'a and, 62–3
   Shari'at Muhammad, 19
Sunni Islam, 6, 10, 14
   Ottoman Empire and, 155, 158,
      170
   Sunni jurisprudence, 208
   Sunni orthodoxy, 13, 180,
      184
survey (public opinion), 4–5
al-Suyuti, Jalal al-Din, 21
Syria, 14
   Greater Syria, 155, 157–8, 159,
      163, 165, 166, 170

al-Tabari, Abu Ja'far, 98
talfiq (eclecticism), 175
the Taliban, 7
taqlid (imitative reading/practice),
   54, 55, 126
tarahum, see compassion
tariqa (the way), 61, 78, 86–7
   see also Sufism
taxation:
   Ottoman Empire and, 156, 157,
      164, 165–9
   poll tax for non-Muslims/*jizya*,
      166
Taylor, Charles, 201
terrorism, 5, 194
Tory, John, 218, 219, 220
tradition, 1, 2

canonical tradition, 43, 53
change and, 43, 54
power of, 52
renarration of, 54, 55
schools of law and, 54
tradition in moral contexts,
   53–5
traditionalism, 13, 43
   Islamic post-traditionalism,
      184
   patriarchy and, 149
   traditionalist reasoning, 146–7
Treaty of Najran, 63
truth, 9, 30
   haqiqa, 6, 61, 66
   legal truth, 21
   tawhid, 53
   truth-seeking, 53
al-Tufi, Najm al-Din, 26, 120, 184
Tunisia, 14, 111
   Constitution, 59, 71–3, 78
Turkey, 14, 70, 76–7, 189
al-Tusi, Nasir al-Din, 141

UK (United Kingdom), 126, 193
   1996 Arbitration Act, 211
   ADR institutions in, 132
   family law, 110, 119, 130
   official recognition of the
      shari'a, 195
   shari'a councils in, 131–2, 133
   see also Muslim Law (Sharia)
      Council
ulama (moral authorities/
   scholars), 49, 50, 52, 53, 54
umma (community), 5, 33, 121,
   141, 143
urf, see custom
US (United States), 5, 194
usul al-fiqh (principles of
   jurisprudence), 103, 120–1
   Indonesia, 182–5, 186, 187
utilitarianism, 13, 140, 147, 150

Valiente, Wahida, 222
values, 86, 141, 186, 188
  communal values, 66
  ethical values, 10, 11, 47, 132
  Islamic values, 68, 73, 74, 125, 47
  liberal values, 3
  religious values, 102, 178
  shari'a values, 17, 23–4, 30, 33
  see also maqasid
vicegerency, *see khilafat Allah*
violence, 15, 72, 93, 170
  domestic violence, 188
  qital, 206
virtue, 1, 47
  moral virtues, 53
  shari'a and, 24–5, 34, 35–6, 45, 47
  spiritual virtues as gender inclusive, 94
  virtuous society, 33, 35, 36, 141
virtue ethics, 136, 141
  Aristotle and, 12, 135, 140, 150
  bioethics, 12, 136, 140–1, 150
  eudaimonia, 140
  state and, 23

Wadud, Amina, 11, 81–2, 84
Wahhabis, 166, 170
Wahid, Marzuki, 189
Wahyudi, Yudian, 185–6, 188
wajib (required act), 3
water, 17
  as core metaphor of the shari'a, 17, 59–60, 78
Weigel, George, 207
the West, 55, 56
  reforms/revolutions in, 199–200
  separation of state and church, 200

western diaspora, 5, 8, 12, 15, 131, 133, 147
  see also shari'a in the West
West Africa, 3, 4
westernisation, 64, 67, 70
William of Ockham, 201
Williams, Bernard, 51, 52, 53
Williams, Roger, 200
Williams, Rowan (former Archbishop of Canterbury), 195
  shari'a accommodation in UK, 202, 210, 211–12
Winkel, Eric, 90n10, 98
wisdom, 42
  hikma, 25
  shari'a and, 44–5
  see also ma'rifa
women 11;
  covering, 11, 96–7, 104, 107, 112, 114
  modesty, 94, 96–7
  property ownership 11, 110
  seclusion, 11, 101, 104, 113
  sexuality, 82, 105, 107, 109, 113
  subjugation of, 108–10
  'women in Islam', 110–11, 112–13, 115
  women's rights, 87, 110, 112, 115, 121, 188, 220, 221, 223, 224–7, 228
  see also divorce; gender equality; gender inequality; gender issues; hijab; marriage; ritual leadership of Muslim women
world, life, matter, *see dunya*

Yusanto, Ismail, 182
Yusril Ihza Mahendra, 182

Zahiri school of law, 64